The Farnam Method of Defensive Handgunning

Second Edition

John S. Farnam

Farnam Method of Defensive Handgunning
Second Edition
by John S. Farnam

© 2000, 2005 by DTI Publications, Inc
All rights reserved.
First edition published 2000, Second edition 2005

Printed in the United States of America. No part of this book may be used or reproduced in any form or by any means, or stored in a database or retrieval system, without prior written permission of the publisher, except in the case of brief quotations embodied in critical articles and reviews. Making copies of any part of this book for any purpose other than your own personal use is a violation of United States copyright laws.

For information, address:
DTI Publications, Inc.
3571 Far West Blvd
PMB #94
Austin TX 78731

ISBN-13: 978 -0-9659422-4-9
ISBN-10: 0-9659422-4-4

Warning and Disclaimer
This book is sold as is, without warranty of any kind, either expressed or implied. While every precaution has been taken in the preparation of this book, the author and DTI Publications, Inc. assume no responsibility for errors or omissions. Neither the author nor DTI Publications, Inc. shall have any liability to any person or entity with respect to any loss or damage caused or alleged to be caused directly or indirectly by the instructions contained in this book. It is further stated that neither the author nor DTI Publications, Inc. assumes any responsibility for the use or misuse of the information or instructions contained herein.

To Vicki

About the Author

John S. Farnam, president of Defense Training International, Inc. has been teaching defensive firearms courses for over 30 years. He is a combat veteran of the Vietnam War, a major (Retired) in the U.S. Army Reserve and a police officer with many years of practical experience. Mr. Farnam is an acclaimed and prominent author, lecturer, expert witness and consultant. Through Defense Training International, Inc., he teaches the latest defensive firearms techniques to police departments, federal and state agencies as well as foreign governments.

In 1996, John Farnam was awarded the prestigious "Tactical Advocate of the Year" title by the American Tactical Shooting Association in recognition of his commitment to presenting dependable tactical information to those attending his training programs. His years of experience in the military as well as law enforcement have allowed him to gain first hand knowledge of what works most reliably in lethal force confrontations.

Acknowledgments

I dedicate this book to my instructors. My cadre of instructors come to me willing to evangelize and endure all the frustrations and disappointments inherent to sharing the True Way with an often ignorant and close-minded world. They do it out of an incurable love for The Art and an enduring enthusiasm for the advancement of The Art. All of them are eminently successful in their own right. They are extremely busy, and yet they somehow find the time to join Vicki and me at our classes. The joy of watching students lifted from a state of unconscious incompetence to a state of enlightened awareness and launched on a lifetime journey of advancing and refining their warrior skills and their personal magnificence is something for which my instructors are willing to repeatedly sacrifice their valuable time.

The easiest thing in this life anyone can do is stay where they are, particularly if where they are is a comfortable place. Enduring the risks, pain and drudgery of continuous self improvement is something we all know we should be doing, but few of us ever really get around to it. We do!

To each and every one of us, your dedication has not gone unnoticed. Good show!

Dan Abbott
Debra Adkins
Colby Adler
John Adler
Will Andrews
Nick Anton
Ralph W Ball Jr
Anthony M Barrera
Rick Benson
Edward S Bierce
Shawn Bjerke
Fred Blish
Joseph M Bobovsky
Alan J Booth
Rossouw Botha
Mike Bradford

Jack L Branson
Keith E Brown
Thomas A Burris
John Butterfield
Steven Camp
Scott Camp
Rick Campbell
James Colborn
Keith Conroy
Gordon J Cook
SuAnn Cook
Jennifer Coy
Kevin R Crisp
Jeff Curless
Mark Dahlsten
Mike Daniels

Joe DaSilva
William S DeWeese
Jeffrey A Donnell
Phillip Duclose
Chuck Dunfee
Bert Duvernay
Andrew J Evans
Vicki L Farnam
Will Flagg
Ron Frier
Gregg Garrett
Jim Garthwaite
Tom Givens
Richard D Green
Mark Guzy
Mark Hallada

The Farnam Method of Defensive Handgunning

Jim Hart	Joseph L Meyers	James Rossman
Stanly B Heckbrodt	Michael L Mixon	Mike Shovel
Chuck Hinson	William S Modzelewski	Robert Sikora
Steven L Hoch	Robert M Morgan	Robert Skar
William R Hollar	Steve Moses	Daryl A Smith
Jerry Hollombe	David Nelson Jr	Joseph G Smolarz
Kevin Houlihan	Diane Nicholl	Vickie Southard
Shawn C Jacobs	John-Michael Nickerson	Danny Steele
Don Johnson		Steve Sutliff
Emanuel Kapelsohn	Elbert W Northrup	Richard A Thompson
Matthew Kartozian	Anthony Pagni	W Dennis Tobin
Andy Kemp	Gregory Pate	Dennis Tueller
Dave L Lamprecht	Ann M Person	Jeff Tueller
Andy LouDerBack	Peter R Pi	Stephen R Van Mol
R David Manning	Coenraad F Potgieter	Marcus Ward
Dave Marra	Paul A Puglia	Kirk Webb
James R Mason	Frank Pytko	Wayne Welsher
Neil L Matthews	Michael J Quaintance	Peter S Williamson
Allan W McBee	Marion S Ratliff	Lee Winter
James M Mccormick	Jack Richard	Richard O Wright
Bill McLennon	Marc Richard	Warren Lee Youmans

Contents

1. Mental Toughness — 1
2. Personal Tactics — 11
3. Defensive Weapons — 29
4. The Stealth Existence — 45
5. Self-Defense — 51
6. Use of Force — 57
7. When Confronting Criminals — 59
8. First Aid for Gunshot Victims — 65
9. Interacting with Law Enforcement Officers — 67
10. Arrest and Searches — 73
11. Firearm Safety — 85
12. Accidental and Unintentional Discharge — 95
13. Modes — 99
14. Defensive Handgun Operator Systems — 103
15. Cycle of Operation and Parts — 111
16. Defensive Handgun Mechanical Systems — 131
17. Safe Gun Handling — 137
18. Tactical Handgun Operation: Stance — 167
19. Tactical Handgun Operation: Draw — 173
20. Tactical Handgun Operation: Sight Alignment — 191
21. Tactical Handgun Operation: Trigger Control — 195

22. Tactical Handgun Operation: Follow Through and Decocking	203
23. Tactical Handgun Operation: Reloading	209
24. Tactical Handgun Operation: Stoppages	221
25. Ammunition Recommendations	227
26. Dry Fire and Maintenance	241
27. Epilogue	245
DTI Defensive Handgun Proficiency Test	247
Resources	251
Index	253

Introduction

Most defensive firearms training that I've witnessed consists of exposing students to a series of psycho-motor subroutines and then drilling the skills until students can pass some kind of practical test. Basically, we have been teaching people how to skillfully operate a machine under a number of different sets of circumstances.

However, that is only part of the necessary preparation. Simply learning how to operate a machine means very little without exposure to the philosophical overlay without which none of it makes much sense.

Every civilization has its Warrior Class. I'm not talking here merely about standing armies. Most "soldiers" in standing armies today are not warriors at heart. A famous fighting general during The Great War pointed out that of every hundred men sent to him at the front, twenty never even arrived, being counted among the sick, lame and lazy. Sixty arrived, at least in body, but were little more than "animated targets," mostly fearful, self consumed and paralyzed, unable to carry the war effort forward in any significant way. Men of straw. They were known as "users, boozers and losers." The remaining twenty were actually functional soldiers who could be counted upon to at least be where they were supposed to be and do what they were supposed to do, but when they fired their weapons, they fired just to make them go off, just so they could convince themselves that they were doing "something." Their shots were never aimed. Most went up in the air. However, out of that twenty, five were enthusiastic warriors.

Those five didn't just talk about being a warrior. They lived it! They would, on their own, train and hone their fighting skills constantly. Their weapons were always with them and were always ready, whether it was considered "proper" or not. They didn't wait around to be issued necessary gear. They didn't worry about "permission." They got what they needed, any way they could. Those five actually understood the importance of the war effort and their contribution to it. They were top-flight marksmen and looked for opportunities to make contact with the enemy. They aimed their shots, and they hit! They always thought in terms of victory and were cool and composed under fire. Those five provided the inspiration for everyone else. They rarely received medals because the people who granted medals were curiously absent when real fighting took place. The five didn't care about medals. A bird doesn't sing because it has a song. A bird sings, because, if it didn't, it would burst! The five went valiantly forward in battle, always leading the way, not because they were ordered to but because they could not stay back.

This book is written for, and in honor of, The Five. That being the case, it will probably never be a best seller, just as men of honor, dignity and purpose are never a majority.

So, fellow warriors, we must constantly refine our fighting skills and continually teach them to the worthy among us, so that they will be carried through the generations and not be lost and have to be relearned, at great cost, by our sons who will have to fight future conflicts. Mostly, we must inspire our fellow warriors and awaken the warrior spirit in the hearts of all our students.

Merely learning and teaching fighting skills is just the frosting. The heart of the warrior is at the center. A famous proverb says, "A wise man never tries to warm himself in front of a picture of a fire." Even so, we must be genuine, fearless and relentless followers of The True Way, the Way of the Warrior.

Victory is the only reality in the universe!

John S Farnam
February 2005
Ft Collins, CO

Chapter 1

Mental Toughness

Most people in our age are what we call "grass eaters." They have failed to claim their own magnificence. They have failed to acknowledge and appreciate their own warrior heritage and often fail to respect the value of their own lives. When danger threatens, they shrink away. They are weak, delusional and in constant denial of reality. They venture too little, hesitate too long, repent too soon. They live frightened, insecure, unworthy lives. Grass eaters are easily identified by criminals and are consistently selected for victimization.

On the other side of the ledger, we meat eaters have fearlessly claimed our own magnificence. We proudly claim the title of warrior. To us, life is either a daring adventure or it is nothing. We are righteously indignant when our safety is threatened by criminals. Our self-confidence is evident to all. When necessary, we are unapologetic fighters.

A fighter will make a good accounting of himself in any fight. He will seek out and exploit to the maximum every weakness of his opponent. He will not win every fight, but he will earn the undying respect of every opponent. He is dangerous with any weapon, even no weapon at all. He has skill, intelligence and, yes, good equipment (sometimes); but mostly, a good fighter has heart.

Here is where the difference between the terms "martial artist" and "fighter" often become muddled. There are many martial artists who may have studied at length several oriental fighting styles, yet would have their ass handed to them right readily by even a fledgling fighter of a far lower skill level.

Brains, skill, success and even superior equipment, by themselves, do not a good fighter make. The world is full of educated derelicts, gifted losers and affluent washouts. There was never a good fighter who did not have heart. Without heart, the rest is of scant consequence, for, as Plato said, "It never troubles a wolf, how many the sheep be."

A fighter does not submerge himself in denial and does not make excuses. Specifically, he does not lament endlessly about the limitations and imperfections of his equipment and circumstances. He does not use the convenient pretext of equipment deficiency to excuse his own incompetence. He simply uses what is available to his best possible advantage and does not waste valuable time complaining or feeling sorry for himself. As the saying goes, *"Show me a good loser, and I'll show you a loser!"* A fighter does not spend valuable time looking for an excuse to lose. He spends his time finding a way to win!

If you want to be a fighter, you must start with your own attitude. You must decide what (if anything) in your life is worth fighting for. You must decide whether or not you have the heart of a fighter. If you do, then you must make the life-long commitment in time and resources to acquire and continuously update the critical skills and equipment. The journey from fledgling to master fighter is long and challenging but, at the same time, rewarding and fulfilling.

Nearly any object can be, and probably has been, used effectively as a personal defensive weapon and the resourceful fighter will make good use of whatever is at hand. However, many martial arts students spend far too much time training with obsolete and outmoded instrumentalities that are better suited to a museum display than to the street. Swords, long staffs, and sickles are all interesting and may have had an illustrious history, but they are impractical and sadly ill adapted to today's needs. Today, the handgun, knife and short stick are the three weapons that the fighter should learn and master first. The handgun is particularly germane to the modern environment. Skill with the handgun is indispensable. However, no good fighter becomes overly attached and partial to a particular weapon or weapon type. Victory dwells in the fighter's heart, not in his tools. A gun, any gun, is just a machine.

Modern defensive techniques with the handgun constitute a legitimate and germane martial art. Many schools of and students of the other martial arts are now realizing that skill with a handgun is just as important as the unarmed skills and is an essential component of every fighter's repertoire. There is an old poker players' proverb, "The best player is not the one who is dealt the good hand. It is the one who plays the poor hand well."

In our civilization, there are people who "prey upon" other people. That is, some people will, in obvious and contemptuous defiance of the law, physically attack other people in such a way that serious bodily injury or death is the likely result. Like auto accidents, such attacks are not a daily occurrence for most of us, but they do happen and when they do, the results are often appalling and always irrevocable.

Perhaps one person in one thousand will, under certain circumstances, initiate a precipitous and unjustified, violent attack upon another for reasons which, at

Chapter 1: Mental Toughness

the time, are apparently sufficient for him. The chances of anyone being attacked at any particular moment are usually remote; however to the person actually being attacked, the probability is real enough! When the question is naively asked, "How often are people really killed around here?," the correct answer is, "Only once!" Perhaps an even better answer is, "How often do they have to be killed, before they take reasonable precautions to protect themselves?"

To the true fighter, the art of fighting and winning is not just one of life's trifling distractions, nor is it pursued solely for its recreational or amusement value. Fighting, to the true fighter, is a lifelong exploration, a striving toward perfection. The true fighter is a perpetual and relentless student of the genuine (not the sanitized) fighting arts. He is interested in all the arts, not superficially or just for the glamour or the novelty but rather for the pure practical and honorable utility. Good fighters are intelligent, original, capable, unpredictable, aggressive, brave and dangerous. Most have a dark side. Popularization and over participation degrades fighting arts just as their parent, overpopulation, degrades, cheapens and probably dooms our species. In the end, we're all dead anyway. Meanwhile, it is good to *be willing to fight and able to win*. A fortunate fighter fights seldom if ever, but he is always a dangerous man. I intend to be one until I die.

Keys to Survival

The possibility of physical assault exists to some degree in every place and at every moment. Furthermore, we cannot rely upon police, whose basic function is one of reaction as opposed to pro-action, to protect us. Personal mental preparation, therefore, is an indispensable discipline for any warrior. You must think in advance about situations where you may be compelled to use force in order to save your life. You must be well acquainted with all your options and must have mentally and physically rehearsed the viable ones.

The keys to survival are:

- **Be always alert.** Avoidance is almost always possible if you see trouble far enough in advance.

- **Trust your senses** when they tell you that something is not right. Don't go into denial.

- **Have a plan.** Acquire in advance the knowledge, skills and equipment necessary to assure the winning advantage in any lethal altercation. *To fail* *to plan is to plan to fail.*

- **Act at the critical moment.** Be decisive. Have the courage to do what you have to do when it needs to be done. Remember, "Small deeds done are better than great deeds planned."

In defensive shooting, just as in defensive driving, if you see trouble in the making far enough in advance, you will usually be able to avoid it, or prepare for it, if it cannot be avoided. On the other hand, if, through lack of alertness, you allow a dangerous situation to creep up on you; by the time you are finally awake to what is happening, your skills, even though you bring them into play quickly and expertly, may be taxed to the limit and, even then, may not suffice to keep you alive.

If one courageously confronts a formidable opponent and is ultimately overpowered, it is unfortunate, but certainly understandable. It is far less understandable and certainly less forgivable when one loses a fight he should have won, simply because he carelessly allowed himself to be taken by surprise. All your knowledge, training, skill and equipment will be of little use if you are in deadly danger and don't know it. If someone is to be surprised, let it be your opponent. The best kind of fight (from the winner's perspective) is the one that is over before the loser knows there has been one!

A Superior Gunman is best defined as a person who can be depended upon to use his superior judgment to keep him out of situations that would require the use of his superior skills.

Tachy-Psyche Effect

Recent studies have established that profound and unavoidable changes take place in the human body and brain when a person is under severe stress, such as he would be during a lethal confrontation. The term that is used to describe these changes is "The Tachy-Psyche Effect." To be effective, defensive training must obviously address and be reconciled to these changes. We are satisfied that this effect will take place in nearly everyone, regardless of how he has prepared himself beforehand. Good training can minimize certain aspects of it, but the effect will be present regardless. Listed below are the components of this effect and the training accommodations necessary to integrate them:

Spontaneous urination or defecation. Many people are embarrassed over this common phenomenon, but you have no control over it and it is nothing

Chapter 1: Mental Toughness

to be ashamed of. It is a normal function of the body when it is fearful and is preparing to flee or fight.

Shivering or shaking. Likewise many people find the fact that they are shivering or shaking embarrassing and disturbing. Actually, it is perfectly normal. When threatened, the human body will withdraw blood from the extremities and concentrate it in the major muscles. The outward effect is that you will feel cold and start shivering.

Loss of color perception. In lethal encounters, most participants report seeing everything in black and white only.

Coordination. Eye-hand coordination is severely and negatively affected by alarm. Fine movements of the fingers and hands are degraded most of all. Under stress, you will not have nearly the physical coordination you do under more normal circumstances, particularly in your fingers. In training we therefore substitute large body movements for fine finger movements whenever possible. Any time a defensive technique requires finely coordinated movements with your fingers, such as locating and operating small buttons and levers, that procedure will stand a good chance of breaking down under stress and thus may be unusable as a defensive procedure. Many otherwise flashy and glamorous martial arts techniques suffer from this same drawback.

I believe certain pistols were designed by people who never had to try to make small parts work in concert (in a hurry) when they were cold, dirty, smelly, sick, hungry, thirsty, exhausted, confused, surprised, lost, terrified and alone, all in a muddy ditch at night in the rain! Under such circumstances, it is difficult enough just to keep the muzzle and the trigger organized.

The ability to make critical decisions. Not only is physical coordination degraded, but also mental coordination suffers as well, probably to a greater degree. Under severe alarm, normal intellectual processes become impossible and the mind automatically defaults to its most primitive and basic responses. If your fighting techniques, for example, present you with many options and require you to make decisions requiring high-level intellectual gymnastics, they will probably become muddled and thus be unusable during an actual lethal encounter. In training therefore, we, to the greatest extent possible, present the student with the least possible number of electives. Options, variations and decisions are reduced to the absolute minimum. This, in turn, reduces vacillation, hesitation and panic. *When it comes to fighting, think less. Act more.*

Mental track. Under stress your eidetic memory will be degraded and you will lose your ability to manage your memory of rapidly occurring events. A classic example is trying to remember how many rounds you have fired so that you can arrange to reload your firearm at exactly the right moment. Your memory will fail completely. In general, you will have fired two to three times as many shots as you can remember firing. Relying on your memory in such situations is foolish. In training we therefore no longer ask you to try to keep track of things. If you do, you will probably be grossly inaccurate anyway. Instead, we build into your routine all the things you need to do to keep firing (including reloading), so that you will do them automatically, without having to consciously remind yourself.

Tunnel vision. Under stress, your attention will be focused on the source of danger to the exclusion of everything else. You will not be aware of danger to the sides and the rear. Even sources of danger directly adjacent to your focus of attention may well escape your notice. People who have been there describe the phenomenon as akin to looking through a tunnel. They are often able to describe, in intricate and elaborate detail, the gun that was pointed at them, yet they cannot recall if the person holding the gun was a man or a woman! You must be trained therefore to turn your head at the first safe opportunity. Physically twisting the head from side to side is the only effective way to break up tunnel vision. Simply shifting the eyes does not suffice.

Auditory exclusion. Peripheral sounds, as well as sights, tend to be blocked out when a person is under stress. So intense will be your concentration on the source of danger that you will not be aware of instructions shouted at you by an adjacent companion, nor will you hear his shots. Physically twisting the head from side to side, in addition to attenuating tunnel vision, also helps to restore normal auditory acuity.

Muscle tightening. Epinephrine (adrenaline) and other hormones automatically released into the blood during periods of extreme stress will cause all muscles to tighten. Your shooting position may be misconfigured if your stance and draw routine have not been sufficiently practiced. This is also one reason for training students of defensive handgun technique to keep their fingers out of the trigger guard and off the trigger until the handgun has cleared the holster, is in both hands, is aimed at the target and the decision to shoot has been made. Such a procedural routine is necessary in order to prevent tight muscles from causing a student to miscalculate the amount of pressure the finger is applying to the trigger while the muzzle is pointed at their own leg, some other body

Chapter 1: Mental Toughness

part, at a suspect or at an innocent person. The muzzle should not point at any body part at any time during the draw anyway, but I still insist that the finger go on the trigger only after the weapon is in both hands and well clear of the body. Having one's weapon discharge into the ground directly adjacent to his right foot is distracting, even when there is no personal injury. This is also why students are cautioned to stay away from handguns with triggers lighter than 2 kg (4.4 pounds). The degree of precision necessary to successfully operate such a light trigger will be diminished by muscle tightness.

Time-space distortion. Stress will distort your perception of time and space. Generally, events will appear to happen more slowly and perceived sources of danger will appear closer than is actually the case. Your recollection of distances and times may differ greatly from that of other witnesses, even when there is no attempt on anyone's part to be untruthful. This is one reason information provided by "eye-witnesses" is often fallacious. This is also why you are counseled to refrain from making either verbal or written statements about a lethal confrontation in which you were involved until you have had an opportunity to talk to your attorney.

Everyone who survives a violent event is affected emotionally and psychologically to one degree or another and the effects persist, to one degree or another, for the rest of their lives. Violent events are not something most of us experience every day. In fact, if you are involved in a fatal shooting or other violent event, you will likely find few individuals among your friends who will be able to relate to your experience on a personal level.

Physically, legally and financially surviving a fatal shooting can be difficult enough, but surviving the emotional, psychological and societal aftermath can be just as challenging and the consequences of losing just as catastrophic. Forewarned is forearmed, so here are the psychological and societal events shooting survivors experience:

There are generally three distinct stages to Post-Violence Trauma Syndrome. These are:

- **The shock/disruption phase**
- **The impact phase**
- **The coping phase**

The shock/disruption phase begins immediately in the aftermath of the event and lasts from several hours to several days. This phase is characterized by the brain's automatic defense system spontaneously reacting to a mind-searing experience. Normal emotional reactions are overridden. Indeed, one may be on what amounts to "automatic pilot" for a time, feeling detached and numb with occasional outbreaks of anxiety. It is thus important that the survivor be quickly taken from the scene and into protective seclusion so that he can have time, without distractions, to compose himself. He should not expect to return to a normal routine for several days or even weeks or longer.

Common symptoms are:

Adrenaline (epinephrine) "high" and subsequent "hangover." An adrenaline rush leaves a person over-stimulated, tense, anxious and irritable. As it wears off, this heightened state is followed by a condition of nausea and sometimes oblivious lethargy.

Denial. Disbelief and denial are among the common reflexive psychological buffers that the brain uses to shield itself from the full impact of the event. This is perfectly normal and, in the short term, should not necessarily be interpreted as symptomatic of a psychosis or an attempt at a cover-up.

Euphoria. Immediately after the event, euphoria may be experienced. This is not some perverted, ghoulish indulgence. It is simply an expression of the joy we all experience when we realize how great it is to be alive. That realization is stimulated when one confronts the fact that his life was nearly snuffed out.

As the shock wears off and the brain's protective shielding slowly deteriorates, the full impact of the event will finally arrive. This is the beginning of the "impact phase." It may last as little as a day or two or as long as a year. One will commonly experience:

Insomnia and nightmares. It is common to suffer periods of sleeplessness. However, sleep will finally come and nightmares should be expected. Nearly everybody gets them after a shooting, even if they have never had them before. The most common theme is a replay of the event itself. Sometimes the characters are reversed. Sometimes, in the dream, you will shoot the attacker, with no results. There are many variations, and they may go on for several months.

Flashbacks. Even daydreams are affected. The event will be replayed over and over. Flashbacks can be stimulated by a return to the scene or an encounter with an object that serves as a "reminder." Getting away from "reminders," to the extent that it can be done, is usually a good plan.

Risk avoidance. Having come so close to death, you now know, on a personal

Chapter 1: Mental Toughness

level, that it can happen to anyone, anytime. No longer do you nonchalantly walk about, oblivious to danger. In fact, you may suddenly become super-cautious and make excuses for not going out.

Appetite disturbance. It is not uncommon to lose interest in eating. It is another symptom of the preoccupation with reliving the incident.

Psychosomatic illnesses. These include headaches, stomach and digestive problems, difficulty concentrating, irritability and nervousness.

Sexual dysfunction. A significant percentage of shooting survivors of both sexes experience a period of sexual impotence. This is not abnormal, but for someone who has never experienced it before, it can be devastating, particularly when combined with everything else.

Depression. It is not difficult to understand, with all these symptoms, how one might become depressed and it is easy to give in to depression when your entire world seems to be crashing down around your shoulders. Depression is aggravated by the combination of legal, financial, security and emotional burdens that fall on the individual all at once.

Family stress. Other family members may or may not try to help, but there will be considerable tension within the family until you are able to wind down and regain control of your emotions.

Social withdrawal. You don't want to get together with anyone, because there is no one who can relate to your experience. Your friends and family want to help, but they are afraid of saying something that will upset you, so they say nothing. You, in turn, think they are rejecting you because they think you did something terrible and the cycle of isolation goes on and on. It can be broken, however, by caring friends and family who extend a hand, even at the risk of rejection for saying something stupid or "doing the wrong thing." That is what friends are for. The worst possible thing either side can do is to do nothing.

"Mark of Cain" syndrome. In this society, we refer to a man or woman as being divorced, as if "divorced" were a title, like "Doctor" or "Sir." The person has probably done many important and significant things with his life since being divorced but all we remember about him is the fact that he is "divorced." It is not fair, but that is the way things are. Likewise, the fact that you killed someone will be remembered by the people with whom you associate long after the details of the event have faded from everyone's memory (except yours). The title of "killer" will stick for a long time.

Coping. The final phase is coping, and it necessarily involves acceptance and resolution. It lasts for the rest of the person's life, but the important work of coping must begin as soon as practicable. It may require the assistance of a health-care professional. One should not hesitate to get help if he feels he is "stuck" in the impact phase or on a particular symptom. Depression particularly must be fought and conquered. It is important that you not allow depression to deteriorate into despondency, because despondency, if it is not reversed, will lead to alcoholism, permanent mental illness, even suicide.

The good news is that no matter how bad it seems at times, none of the symptoms will last. The symptoms are mostly temporary, and they can be outlasted. You must resolve that you are not going to let this temporary difficulty get the best of you. You must get on with your life and let all these things slowly fade away, as they surely will.

Chapter 2

Personal Tactics

If you carry a handgun regularly or keep one in your home for defensive purposes, you must reconcile yourself to the reality that there may come a time when, despite your best efforts, you will find yourself in a situation where your use of deadly force is immediately necessary in order to preserve your life or the lives of family members. In a typical domestic defensive scenario, the fight comes quickly and will likely be over in a few seconds, although it will be perceived as taking much longer.

Lethal encounters are come-as-you-are affairs. Once the fight is on, it is not over until hostilities cease and the parties separate. I will readily concede that the outcome of domestic lethal fights is usually decided before the battle is ever joined. Who the winner ultimately will be is determined by who was most alert, who was better prepared, who had the best training and equipment, who had the best position, who used the best tactics, who was most tenacious and, yes, who was luckiest. Questions of training and equipment are settled in advance, but tactics are something that comes into play during the fight itself. *Sound tactics can salvage even a desperate situation, can compensate for an initial lack of alertness and can literally snatch victory from the jaws of defeat.*

Tactics is the "art of advantage." The proficient tactician is the one who knows how to wait for the opportunity to act, recognizes opportunity and takes action at the critical moment. Tactics is not just a matter of minimizing risk. Some risk exposure will always be necessary. The object is to seek every advantage and maximize the opportunity it affords, identify openings, act decisively and neutralize the threat as quickly as possible. Floundering in indecision will almost certainly prove fatal.

When your safety is threatened, here are the things you should do in the order they should be done.

Wake up! If you are asleep or preoccupied, you must snap out of it quickly and devote your full attention to the developing tactical situation. *Don't allow yourself to wallow in denial.* Acknowledge the threat and face it squarely.

Get your gun. When your life is threatened, you want the option of a lethal response as quickly as possible. If more than five seconds elapse between when you need the gun and when it is in your hand and ready to fire, it is probably not in a high enough state of readiness to justify having it around at all.

If there is time, **get yourself in a strong position** relative to the likely direction of the incoming attack. Put as many obstacles in the path of the potential attacker as possible. Present him with a difficult and ensconced target.

When the application of lethal force is called for, **fire without delay and fire continuously, repeatedly striking the attacker's body midline** between the navel and the neck, until the attacker no longer poses a threat. If the attacker is wearing soft body armor or some other kind of protective apparel, you probably won't know it immediately and his reaction to being struck by your bullets will probably be the same if he is wearing none! That is, he will probably run away in either event. If he stands there while being struck, after firing a number of rounds it may be prudent to shift the point of aim to the groin or the head.

Scan. After the main threat has been repulsed, immediately look all around to see if there are additional threats of which you were not initially aware. Repel all additional threats without delay. *Don't assume the fight is over just because you don't see any threats at the moment.*

Reload. Reload if you can remember firing at all, regardless of how many rounds you believe you have fired. *Reload when you want to, not when you have to.*

Stay in your strong position or **get further away if possible.** If the suspect is down or has run away, he may still be a serious threat even though he has been mortally wounded. If a suspect is wounded but running and he appears to be running out of the house and away, let him go. Don't chase him unless he is heading in the direction of family members. *Never leave your strong position and approach a wounded suspect in an effort to provide him with first aid.* It is too dangerous. Leave him where he is and don't go near him for any reason.

Seek cover. If you are not already in a strong position, get into one as quickly as possible.

Check yourself over. Starting with the top of your head, run your weak hand over your body in an effort to discover if you've been shot, stabbed or otherwise seriously injured. If you've been shot, there is a good possibility that you won't know it. If you have sustained a life-threatening injury, you need to attend to it quickly in order to prevent further loss of blood.

Chapter 2: Personal Tactics

Once you're satisfied that you are uninjured, **account for the well being of every other innocent person of whom you are aware.** This may involve yelling to others in your home or leaving your position to physically check on them. If an innocent person has been hurt, you should try to discover it and get aid to them as quickly as possible.

Gather your family together, get them into your car and get away from the house. The safest place in your house is your car. Get your family into it as soon as possible and close the doors, surrounding them with metal. Then get away from your house. When police arrive with guns drawn looking for armed criminals, it is best that you and your family be a safe distance away. If there has been an armed confrontation in your home, I recommend that you get out of the house and a safe distance away **before** calling police.

Call the police. When they answer, say, "There has been a shooting." That will prioritize your call. Then be prepared to be frustrated and perplexed when talking with 911 operators. They are trained to ask a number of questions that will seem incredibly stupid and illogical at the time. Don't panic or become verbally abusive. Just speak slowly and clearly and answer their questions as best you can. If you don't know the answer to a question, *don't guess and don't speculate.* Just say, "I don't know" and leave it at that. Remember, emergency calls to police are always recorded. Under the circumstances, you will probably be out of breath and your voice will be squeaky and raspy, so you're going to sound a little crazy. In any event, don't make it any worse than it already is, because plaintiff's attorneys will have access to the tape.

Stay away from the scene. When the police arrive at your house, they will have guns out and you don't want to approach them. It is usually best to let them come to you. Talk them over to your location with your cell phone. Family pets are expendable. Don't risk your life trying to rescue them.

When police officers approach you, **put your open hands in front of you** with your open palms facing outward. Be sure you're not holding a gun, have a gun visibly stuffed in your waistband or have a gun anywhere where it can be seen. Greet them by saying, "Officers, I'm the one who called." Follow that with, "A man broke into our house and tried to kill us." Finally, "Officers, I'll be happy to answer all your questions as soon as my lawyer is here." Understand that, regardless of the circumstances, when you shoot someone, you are a criminal suspect in the eyes of the police as are the other members of your family. The police will attempt to interrogate you as they would any other criminal suspect and you may be arrested. It is always in your best interest to decline to answer substantive questions until you've had a chance to talk with your attorney. Politely but firmly insist on your right to remain silent.

Cover

When under deadly attack, if you can clearly see your attacker, you should immediately move laterally as you draw your weapon and engage him without delay. On the other hand, if you were perceptive enough to see the problem coming, take advantage of the few precious seconds the Almighty has seen fit to grant you and seek a strong position.

The goal when using cover is to use the object to mask as much of the vital areas of your body as possible while not compromising your ability to deliver effective fire to the target. In domestic defense, the time to think about cover is when you sense danger but before the bullets start flying. Diving for cover upon being surprised by a lethal threat is a desperate move and much less desirable. If possible, your strong position should be concealed also. The less sure an attacker is of your exact location, the less likely he is to press his aggression.

When shooting from behind cover, keep your weapon in a position to fire, "roll out," fire (if necessary), then roll back. Expose no more of yourself than necessary and stay exposed for only a few seconds at a time. When using the roll-out cover technique:

- Stay far enough back from the article of cover to enable you to engage threats coming from any direction.

- Keep the gun from protruding forward of your cover where it could be snatched away from you.

- Expose the minimum amount of your vitals to hostile fire; yet deliver effective aimed fire to the target. Don't expose elbows, knees or feet unnecessarily.

- Keep them guessing. Fire from different locations.

Don't "drape" yourself over the top of the object of cover. When shooting around the side, don't stick your gun out beyond the edge. Both of these methods expose more of your body than necessary and may get you disarmed if your attacker is closer or better trained than you thought. Instead, get well back from the edge and shoot past the cover. It is extremely important that you don't allow your weapon or your hands to protrude beyond the cover and into an area over which you have no control. A weapon poking into this area can easily be taken away by an adversary lurking there. This is especially important

Chapter 2: Personal Tactics

in the interior of buildings where there are a lot of vertical outside corners and many blind spaces.

Keep rolling out, but in a different place each time. Keep them guessing. Make it impossible for them to predict where you will next appear. If you continue to appear in the same spot, your adversary will know exactly where to have his gun aimed. Moreover, whenever you see your adversary, it is natural to convulsively withdraw behind cover and then slowly peek out again, usually from the same exact spot. The adversary will see you long before you can shoot. He will thus be waiting for you when you finally emerge.

Your strong-side elbow can also unintentionally telegraph your intentions when it protrudes shortly before your pistol does. You must keep your elbow (also feet and knees) tucked in.

Roll out, keeping as much of your body behind cover as possible.

Shooting from over the top of your cover will enable you to see more of the downrange area but will expose your head from the mouth up. Shooting from around the side will expose much less of your head, but also severely restricts what you can see. A good general rule is to look over the top of the cover first to get a look at the danger area. Locate the danger, then withdraw behind the cover and then actually engage targets from the sides. For low cover, such as a trashcan, the best shooting position is often kneeling with both knees on the ground. It is possible to lean and roll out to either side without having to change leg position.

If you are a right-handed person, shooting past the right side of cover is easy. You can shoot while exposing little of yourself, so long as you keep your elbow tucked in. However, when you try to maintain your stance and shoot around the left side of the object, you discover that you expose half of your body before the gun clears the edge. You can remedy this predicament in one of two ways. You can change gun hands or you can maintain your stance but rotate the gun ninety degrees counter-clockwise, thus causing the gun to clear the left edge of the cover before the rest of your body does. For most people, the latter technique makes the best solution. That way the gun stays in the familiar hand.

You should not allow your pistol or any part of your body to actually touch the cover as you are shooting. "Bracing" the pistol or the body by resting on the cover causes the gun to wrench violently every time it is fired, making recovery difficult. Bracing can work well with rifles, but it does not work well with handguns, unless you need to make a difficult shot.

A common error when shooting from behind cover is to imitate what you've seen on television and allow your arms to collapse as you get too close to the object being used for cover. The muzzle will usually point up into the air or down at your feet. Any time the arms thus withdraw from the normal shooting stance, an attacker lurking in the blind space on the opposite side of the cover can spring forth and overwhelm you before you will be able to get your gun pointed at him.

Another common error when shooting from behind cover is to flip the gun out, hastily fire a shot or two, then promptly disappear. This is referred to as the "Jack-in-the-box" technique, and it is discouraged. The user of this technique will routinely expose too much of himself and deliver inaccurate fire. Shots launched via this technique are invariably too fast and effective hits are infrequent and usually accidental.

Some exposure will be necessary if your shots are to be accurate and thus effective. There is always some risk, but the only alternatives are not to fire at all and thus give the adversary the opportunity to maneuver unopposed or to fire carelessly, which will not be fruitful and will only serve to quickly run down your very limited ammunition supply and needlessly jeopardize innocent people. You must use the sights and employ a careful trigger press on the handgun when firing from behind cover, just as you must when shooting in any other situation. The typical naive retort to that statement is, "But that takes too long!" The reply is, "If you don't think you have time to hit, when will you find the time to miss?" Or, as put by noted shooter Ross Seyfried, "You can't miss fast enough to catch up!" Words to live by. What you must learn to do is acquire your firing position before you ever expose yourself, so that your arms are in position and your front sight is within your lower peripheral vision. When you roll out, you must scan the downrange area as quickly as possible, but it does take some time.

The often-taught "quick peek" technique usually gets you a quick glimpse of nothing. Here, the tactician looks around a corner quickly, then immediately withdraws no matter what is there. The technique is quick all right, but often too quick to enable you really to see anything, which typically leads to a second

Chapter 2: Personal Tactics

quick peek from, you guessed it, the exact same spot.

Before leaving this subject, let us not forget the importance of concealment. Sometimes it is best to stay in a covered position for the duration of the fight, but this tactic is not always possible or prudent. Although it does not provide direct protection from bullets, concealment can keep your adversary confused and make it impossible for him to launch a concerted or effective attack. In reduced light, stay in the shadows. Stay behind any object that will break up your outline and confuse the enemy as to your exact location. Look from around the side, rather than over the top. Don't stay in any one place too long.

I had a conversation recently with an officer with a large agency. Some time ago, he shot and killed a certified desperado during an explosive gun battle in which he and his attacker were separated by only eight meters. Both the officer and the felon were armed only with handguns, and both were using their vehicles for cover. In fact, the officer's vehicle had rammed the rear of the felon's vehicle, and both vehicles had become disabled in the ensuing crash.

The felon opened the driver's door and started shooting immediately employing the jack-in-the-box technique using the partially open left rear door for cover. The officer opened his driver's door and commenced to return fire using the same technique. Both men were shooting much faster than they could hit and a dozen or so bullets were launched without effect.

The officer realized that he would soon run out of ammunition (he was using a Colt Government Model in 45ACP and had only one spare magazine) and that he had to connect with one of his rounds soon. He said he had to muster all his will in order to force himself to acquire a position and keep it and wait for the felon to reappear. The felon continued to bob and fire, without effect, but he appeared in the same place once too often.

As the felon came up to shoot (for what turned out to be the last time), the officer again had to concentrate and marshal all his emotional energy in order to force himself not to fire too fast but instead to watch his front sight and press the trigger carefully. After what seemed like several long seconds, his gun at last discharged. The bullet found its mark on the hapless and unwise felon. He was struck in the middle of his left eye. He abruptly lurched backwards and fell to the ground, kicking and convulsing. Death followed within seconds.

Yes, luck played a part, as it always does, but the officer had the presence of mind to fight off panic, keep control of himself and do exactly what he had been trained to do: look death right in the face and shoot straight and true. You must do likewise.

Movement

Movement by itself is a valuable ally. When threatened, if you do nothing but move, your attacker's hit-probability will be reduced by seventy-five percent. When you're in a strong position, you are probably best advised to stay there. When in the open, however, you should be moving constantly but unpredictably. You must stop to shoot but the rest of the time you should be moving.

Movement is also helpful as an individual tactic in getting you from a poor position to a better position. The utility of a particular position is usually measured in terms of the amount of usable cover and concealment it provides. It makes little sense to move from a good position to a poor one, unless you are compelled for some other reason to do so. It can become necessary if you find yourself becoming outflanked and your once-strong position is quickly becoming untenable.

When moving from cover to cover, make sure you know exactly where you are going, where your next position is and how you are going to occupy it once you get there. As a general rule, you should reload before you move, not while you're moving. Get a running start if your position permits it and move across the open space as quickly as possible. Once you have occupied your new position, reacquire your shooting position quickly and be prepared to shoot at once. Lingering in the open or moving slowly in the open is an invitation to a catastrophe. When you move, you must present your adversary with an elusive and transitory target. Otherwise, you will be an easy mark. When in the open, confine yourself to four shots from any one position. Move quickly. Stop and fire your four shots. Then, move again. Don't stand in one spot and shoot and shoot. Move while reloading. Move while reducing stoppages (see Chapter 24: Stoppage Reduction).

Don't try to move and shoot at the same time. You will miss the target and throw bullets all over the landscape. When you shoot, shoot carefully and from a stationary position, behind cover if possible. Only hits count. Precious seconds and ammunition are wasted when handgun bullets are impetuously fired. Don't depend on impulsive and capricious "firepower" to do anything but quickly run you out of ammunition. But, that may not be the worst of it. Misses count against you. A shot that is fired carelessly, without proper aiming, may well injure an innocent party. It will almost certainly do some property damage. Indisputable accusations of negligence on your part and the resultant civil liability are virtually inescapable under such circumstances. Missing is both tactically disastrous and socially irresponsible. In some close situations, moving and shooting simultaneously may be prudent. Most of the time, it is not.

Tactical engineering

Have a plan. In any tactical situation, quickly size up the situation and develop a plan. Know what you want to do. Don't vacillate. Don't hesitate. Carry your plan through enthusiastically and forcefully, but be flexible enough to take advantage of unexpected opportunities when they present themselves. Remember, even a poor plan executed decisively and on time is far better than a brilliant one executed hesitantly or too late.

Inflict fatal wounds quickly. A gun battle is actually a timed event. You have a finite amount of time to stop your opponent. If you take too long, he will have extra time to hit you, but, if you shoot too quickly and miss, you will have to take even more time to recover and hit him with your next round. The sure mark of a proficient gunman is a consistent first-round hit, regardless of the circumstances. It is the amateur who cannot control himself sufficiently to hit consistently. You must learn to shoot as fast as you can hit, but no faster.

The "Four D's of Defensive Shooting"

Deflect his focus. Move prior to drawing. Move as you draw. Use verbal challenges when possible. You must deconcentrate his focus by overloading his senses. The pivotal moment is when the "victim" immediately reverses the situation and attacks back into the assault, deflecting the attacker's focus and disrupting his plan. If you fail to do so without delay, your prospects for a long sleep are excellent.

Disrupt his plan. Use movement, cover, counterattack, and verbal commands to force him to alter his original plan. Every time his has to change his plan, his focus is defused, and the plan becomes delayed and disjointed. This gives you an opportunity to act while he dithers.

Disable his body. Shoot with sufficient volume and accuracy to cripple his body and make it impossible for him to continue. I suggest the "zipper" technique.

Our target is the body midline, between the navel and the neck. First round always goes into the navel. Subsequent three rounds go up the body midline as high as the neck. After four rounds, move and repeat as necessary. *Don't get your front sight too high too fast.* If you attempt to shoot him in the chest with your first round, he may duck and sidestep before you can shoot. If your first shot is into the navel, he cannot move in such a way that you will lose him.

Destroy his will to fight. Incapacitate him to the point where pain and disablement are overwhelming, where his spirit is broken, and he loses all interest in fighting.

Cars

If you come under attack while in a car, even an unarmored one, *remain in the vehicle.* Get down, look through the steering wheel and drive away. Don't exit the vehicle and try to shoot it out. If you are being shot at by a pedestrian, your car will have you out of the effective range of his weapon within seconds. All the time you and your passengers will have the protection of the vehicle itself. Most handgun bullets will not reliably penetrate to the interior of a typical passenger vehicle.

If your attackers are in another vehicle and chasing you and you cannot escape by out-driving them, drive to the local police station. They probably won't follow you there. Otherwise, drive off the road and head for the nearest untraversable terrain. When terrain or obstacles prevent you from driving further, exit your vehicle and quickly move on foot to the nearest covered position. If they choose to follow, they will be forced to exit their vehicle also, at which point you can effectively engage them. Once outside your vehicle, the vehicle itself can still be used for cover. The motor compartment provides the best protection.

When being suspiciously followed by another vehicle, crack the driver's window and spray OC out the opening. The slipstream will deliver it directly to the pursuing vehicle. Even if their windows are rolled up, the OC will be sucked into their vehicle and "encourage" them to find something else to do!

Remember, in firing at a motor vehicle, you are considered to be using deadly force, even if there was no intent on your part to harm the occupants. Indeed, it will prove difficult to convince a jury that you meant no physical harm to the occupants of a car at which you launched a number of rounds, ineffective as those rounds are likely to be. Even if you are successful in wounding the driver of a moving motor vehicle, the vehicle may go careening down the road out of control as a direct result, with predictable injurious consequences. You may well find yourself civilly liable (or criminally culpable) for the resultant mayhem and damages. In addition, in your attempt to wound the driver, you may unintentionally injure other people in the car who are not criminal suspects.

Car doors will stop most handgun bullets most of the time, or at least slow them down to non-lethal velocities. Even car glass will often deflect pistol bullets striking at an angle. The only targets on a car soft enough to succumb to handgun hits are the tires and the radiator. Hits to either of these locations will slow the vehicle and may stop it eventually but the vehicle will in no case be stopped immediately. Hitting the radiator will generate a steam cloud that can be distracting to the driver. The resultant overheating will eventually disable the vehicle but it will take some time.

Hitting the tires will not instantly stop the vehicle, but will slow it down. Tires do not explode when hit. It will take several minutes for the hit tire to go completely flat. The front tires are a more profitable target than the rear tires because the vehicle is difficult to steer with flat front tires.

Moving targets

When using a handgun, *don't try to lead moving targets.* At the speed at which most people are capable of moving and at the distances at which handguns are best employed, leading is counterproductive and unnecessary. You have the best chance of hitting an animated human target if you keep your front sight on center of mass of the target and track it as you carefully press off each shot. This holds true whether he is stationary, running toward you, away from you, at an angle or rapidly changing directions. However, when tracking the target, take care not to become so engrossed that you fail to notice innocent bystanders in your line of fire.

Multiple targets

Engage multiple targets alternately until they are all out of the fight. Don't shoot one guy several times while the others have not been engaged at all. Hit them all once quickly, then go back and reengage anyone who is still a threat. Generally, the closest target or the target who otherwise poses the greatest threat should be engaged first. However, don't spend precious seconds punctiliously prioritizing threats. Start shooting immediately, even if you have not had the opportunity to prioritize the targets.

Wounding shots

Don't attempt to only "wound" the person at whom you are shooting by deliberately aiming for an ostensibly non-vital portion of the body, such as a limb. Shooting at such tricky targets often results in misses (and all the inherent issues they engender) and even the shots that do hit are seldom effective in decisively stopping the attack. Your only legitimate goal in using your firearm is to stop a deadly attack as quickly as possible, and hits to non-vital areas of the body are just not effective for that purpose. Worry about your health, not his. *If you are not justified in ending the person's life, you are not justified in shooting at all.*

If you are hit

When you are hit by incoming fire or otherwise wounded, try to remain on your feet, reestablish your shooting position immediately and continue to defend yourself. Ignore your wound(s) for the short term. You must continue to accurately fire at your attackers until they are no longer a threat. You will not be able to defend yourself after you lose consciousness. Tend to your wounds only after you are out of danger. Gunshot wounds are seldom fatal instantly. When they are fatal, the person affected usually loses consciousness quickly. Therefore, if you're still conscious after being hit, you have probably not been fatally wounded. *The best "first aid" for gunshot wounds is immediate and accurate fire at the person(s) who caused your wound.*

Common tactical errors

Standing in one place too long. As long as you keep moving, rapidly and unpredictably, any attacker will have great difficulty putting a successful attack plan together.

Failing to take full advantage of available cover. Ninety-five percent of people who reach cover uninjured ultimately survive the encounter. You must be cover-conscious all the time and *the time to think about cover is before you need it.* When you use cover, use it skillfully. Have a plan. If you leave your position without having located the next one, you will find yourself out in the open chicken walking (slowly and aimlessly walking about in the open) or, when the bullets start flying, frantically looking for cover. You will be an easy mark.

Chapter 2: Personal Tactics

Lack of objectivity. In the heat of serious fighting, it is easy to forget why you are there and what you are trying to accomplish. For example, it is not always necessary to destroy your adversaries. It may be better to circumvent them and escape. Don't allow yourself to get sidetracked. Don't take unnecessary risks. Keep your ultimate goal (your physical survival) in mind.

Letting obstacles slow you down. If you let them, obstacles will slow you down and make you an easy target. Get past them quickly, exposing as little of yourself as possible.

Losing your balance. If you lose your balance, you will probably be hit before you can regain it. Therefore, watch your footing and pick up your feet when you move. If you are knocked down or stumble, recover quickly and keep moving.

Accidental discharges. Like losing one's balance, an accidental discharge in the middle of a fight will be so startling that it will take you out of the fight for several seconds. Keep you trigger finger in register until you're on target and you have decided to fire.

Machine-gunning the target. Sometimes called "spray-and-pray," this is the technique of fools. Your prayers will go unanswered! Handguns neither hold enough ammunition nor fire fast enough to make "machine-gunning the target" likely to be effective. Machine-gunning with a handgun will quickly leave you with an empty gun and an undisturbed target. The successful way to use a handgun is to carefully aim every shot, starting with the first one.

Leading moving targets. In pistol matches, when the "mover" moves at a known velocity, always moves perpendicular to the shooter and is at a known range, leading is sometimes necessary to keep all bullets within a small circle. However, in real gunfights, where your target zigzags, changes directions and velocity and is usually at an unknown range, leading is an exercise in futility. Instead, aim for center of mass and track the target as you carefully press off each shot.

Gawking. Tunnel vision is a real problem and you must be aware of it. You must move your head and be looking all around constantly.

Dithering. No wasted motions. No indecision. No stopping in the middle. In a fight, you must be a continuous whirlwind of motion.

Relaxing too soon. Don't make convenient but foolish assumptions, such as assuming that a person who is gone or off his feet and down is no longer dangerous. Don't leave cover prematurely. Keep looking. Don't assume it is over just because there is a pause.

Using your handgun as a club. You will make it easy for your opponent to take the gun away from you and the blow may well damage your weapon enough to make it inoperable. Also, the gun may discharge when it and your strong hand hit your opponent, wounding the suspect or someone else in the process.

Manually cocking the hammer of your handgun in an effort to scare the suspect. The weapon can easily discharge unintentionally.

Close confrontations

If you discover a person in your home that you did not invite in, you are probably justified legally and certainly justified tactically in confronting him at gunpoint. However, given only that a person is in your home uninvited, deadly force is probably not yet justified. After all, that "burglar" could be your neighbor checking your house out because he noticed your door was open. It could be a police officer or a fire fighter who has responded to the wrong address. It could be a gas company employee checking out a reported gas leak. In any of these examples, you may be required to hold a gun on the individual as you try to ascertain his or her true identity and intentions. We are usually required, both by law and our own moral make up, to allow even a potentially threatening suspect (when confronted) the opportunity to leave in peace. However, in allowing them the opportunity to turn and leave, we also necessarily allow them the opportunity to attack.

There are four potentially disastrous eventualities that invariably haunt this type of confrontation.

- You may allow yourself to be maneuvered into a situation where the suspect gets close enough to successfully attack you before you can effectively stop him with gunfire. A point is often made here that, even if there is a good chance the suspect could close the distance between him and you before you could fire multiple times, he will be dissuaded from trying it, because he would probably be shot (at least once) in the process. Don't depend on it! Many suspects, in addition to being criminally homicidal, are also suicidal. They fully expect to get shot and they think they don't care. For these individuals, fear of death or serious injury is not an effective deterrent.

Chapter 2: Personal Tactics

- You may lose control of yourself or your weapon and your weapon may thus discharge when you did not intend for it to do so. The result of such an unintentional or "accidental" discharge may well be a dead or seriously injured suspect whom you never intended to shoot.

- You may fire ineffectively. That is, you may miss altogether, or you may hit with some but not enough, rounds. Your opponent may thus not be stopped quickly enough to prevent him from injuring or killing you.

- You may fire your weapon intentionally and justifiably, but some of your bullets may miss or over penetrate the intended target and continue downrange and ultimately impact on someone or something you never intended to shoot.

What is the proper way to confront a dangerous criminal at close range and, if necessary, hold him or her at gunpoint? Many officers, even today, routinely approach within several feet of individuals whom they believe are armed, point their handgun at them and instruct them to put their hands up. During those confrontations, many of us have every confidence that we can fire when we see the suspect go for his gun or knife. We foolishly believe that our shot(s) will stop him or her before he would be able to finish his move. Unfortunately, that is just wishful thinking, and we get away with it only because (so far) none of those offenders have called our bluff.

Reaction time is the time it takes for a person to start to move after the perception of danger. In this age of electronic timers and high-speed photography, we have discovered that pure reaction time for most people is two- to three-tenths of a second. In other words, if you see the need to discharge your firearm or make any protective move, a quarter of a second will elapse before you even as much as twitch! Martial artists have always known that the one who acts first usually wins. The one who reacts usually loses, unless he or she has allowed himself enough room to absorb the first blow. The reason is that the one who reacts is always at least a quarter of a second behind and a lot can happen in a quarter of a second.

What all this means is this: if you are confronting, at close range, an offender who has a gun, knife or club in his hand, it makes little difference where he is pointing it or how he is holding it. And, it makes little difference if your gun is already pointed at him. In such a circumstance, you are in the process of committing suicide! By the time you see him move and fire your first shot in response, he will already have closed the distance and struck you. The reason is that he acted first and in reacting you were at least a quarter of a second behind him. If you were trying to talk or shout commands, your reaction time was even slower, up to three-quarters of a second. Moreover, *it will almost certainly require multiple accurate handgun bullet impacts to stop the suspect definitively and even then it will take several seconds, usually longer.* Taking all this into account, it may be as long as three or four seconds between the time you decide to draw your gun and shoot and the time the suspect has been hit a sufficient number of times to stop him. In four seconds, most people, from a dead stop, can sprint at least eight meters. In four seconds, most people can draw a concealed handgun and fire several shots at a person fifteen meters away and have no trouble hitting them. Four seconds is an eternity!

How can you minimize your exposure to risk in a situation like this?

Turn the "close" confrontation into a "distant" confrontation as quickly as possible. Close confrontations with potentially dangerous people are something you should avoid to begin with, but, if you find yourself in one, rapidly create distance by moving away from him.

Put obstacles (as well as distance) between you and him. Force him into a convoluted path.

Seek cover. If guns are involved, get to cover as quickly as possible.

Use verbal commands. Tell him to get back, stay away and keep his distance.

Don't block his only exit. When cornered, desperate people are very dangerous.

The only way you are going to achieve an acceptable degree of safety for yourself during a close confrontation with an armed individual when you allow him or her to make the first move, is to confront him at gunpoint and at extended range (at least eight meters) and from a strong position. That is still no absolute guarantee of survival but at least it can be done in relative safety.

When you are in involuntary physical contact with a criminal suspect:

Your first priority is to protect your gun(s). The best way to do that is to get your hand on your gun and get it drawn. Generally, whoever gets their hand on the grip of the gun first gets the gun. Make sure it's you! If you find yourself in a wrestling match, you must concentrate on gaining or regaining control of your weapon.

Chapter 2: Personal Tactics

Get your gun in your hand and get it pointed at the suspect as quickly as you can.

If the suspect does not release you immediately and it looks as if he is trying to get your gun or otherwise harm you, **shoot him immediately.** Even a shot through his knuckles or into his knee or foot will probably cause him to release you and allow you to regain your balance, disengage and get distance.

Chapter 3

Defensive Weapons

The United States Constitution does not guarantee "innocent people" a fair trial. It guarantees everyone a fair trial. Likewise, virtuous people are not guaranteed the right to free speech and respectable people are not guaranteed the right to the private ownership of firearms. *Those rights are guaranteed to all free citizens.* It is their birthright. Government employees are not permitted to presume to bestow "rights" upon only the people they like. It is not the job of government employees to "grant" or "regulate" rights at all. It is their job only to protect those rights. In other countries, government employees routinely bully, intimidate and tyrannize the people. In this country, they are expected to protect and serve the people.

Of course, some (perhaps most) government employees have never had the forgoing explained to them and they often act accordingly. However, a single reading of the Constitution, including, of course, the Bill of Rights, will leave little doubt as to the intentions of the authors, the Founding Fathers, and the value they placed upon individual rights and freedoms. Those rights and freedoms are under constant attack by many government officials, both elected and appointed, who have far more intellectual kinship with Marx and Lenin than they have ever had with Washington and Jefferson. Crypto-Marxist politicians and bureaucrats are thus the plague of our generation. *We can never relax.*

Most everyone has the capacity to protect themselves and their rights. The bad news is that although every ambulatory person has some capacity to forcefully resist a criminal assault, without extensive training in the fighting arts, such resistance is often pitifully ineffectual. Even with training, many people discover that they are too physically small or weak, infirm or reticent to successfully abrogate a determined physical assault by a bigger and stronger person. They need help.

That help often takes the form of a personal defense weapon. These weapons are known as "force multipliers." That is, they increase the amount and the effectiveness of one's reactive force, in some cases (as with firearms), instantly escalating it to the level of deadly force. Non-firearm weapons can be effective too, but the key is to find a weapon that combines effectiveness with lawfulness, convenience, carryability, speed, ease of use and safety. Physical violence is a form of communication, and there are many dialects. As with all communication, you must be able to make yourself understood, and you must have the last word!

Regardless of what weapon(s), if any, you choose, *professional training and continuous practice are essential.*

Common personal defense weapons

In the following section I will outline the advantages and disadvantages of some of the more common personal defense weapons including aerosol sprays, electronic restraint devices, impact/pressure weapons, knives and guns.

Aerosol sprays. Three of the irritant agents that are available in vaporous aerosol spray form are CN, CS, and OC. CN and CS aerosol agent sprays have been used for many years and are still available but have all but been eclipsed by the new OC formulas. OC is so much more effective than either CN or CS that the latter are no longer used by most police. We recommend only OC. However, be advised that some localities have banned the use of all aerosol incapacitation agents.

"OC" aerosol devices may be used to control or subdue disorderly or violent individuals or animals when lesser methods have proven ineffective or are not practical under the circumstances.

The active agent in OC is tincture of oleoresin capsicum. Basically, it is little more than ground-up red peppers suspended in a solvent and propellant. As indicated above, OC is so much more potent and effective than either CN or CS; it has effectively rendered these older chemical agents obsolete. However, the eyes, mouth or mucous membranes must still be hit by the spray for it to be immediately successful. OC is not effective on everyone in every situation and one must never think of it as a legitimate substitute for a defensive firearm.

Fox Labs 11 gram pepper spray.

Chapter 3: Defensive Weapons

We do not recommend the OC products that use an alcohol propellant as they can cause burns when ignited. We do recommend non-flammable formulas in a "fogger" rather than a "streamer" version. A fogger produces a wide spray, which is generally more effective for defensive purposes than is the narrow squirt of a streamer.

OC spray has the advantage that it does not require you to have physical contact with the suspect, as do electronic restraint devices. OC can be effectively sprayed at a distance and a one-second spray is sufficiently persuasive in most cases.

The effects of CN, CS, and OC are temporary. None are believed by the mainstream medical community to be permanently harmful, although this issue is still actively debated.

ERD (electronic restraint device). An ERD is a hand-held electronic defensive weapon that interrupts the neuro-muscular impulses of the person to whom it is applied. *This interruption usually causes temporary disorientation, loss of balance and an overall dazed condition.* The effect lasts several minutes but there is generally no permanent injury or disability. Most ERDs have a maximum power output of 50,000 volts with a pulse rate of 16-18 cycles/sec. They produce an approximate power output of .35 joules (watt/sec).

These hand-held incapacitation devices are now fairly effective for their intended purpose. Older and much less effective versions became all the rage several years ago in the police business. Unfortunately, they proved about as effective as the older aerosol tear gas. Sometimes they work; sometimes they don't. Modern units are much improved. Be aware that there are a number of cheap, junky devices being sold on the open market. Most of them are just gimmicks. They are notably underpowered. Truly effective ERDs are generally sold only through police supply outlets. As with aerosol or chemical incapacitation agents, possession of ERDs is highly regulated in some localities.

Modern ERDs have proven very useful in subduing and controlling combative and resisting criminal suspects while reducing the risk of inflicting or receiving serious injury. Although ERDs have been shown to be effective against most people most of the time, they are not effective on some individuals. The length of a correct ERD application seldom needs to exceed eight continuous seconds.

The negative medical implications associated with the correct use of ERDs usually consist of minor friction abrasions, scratches and contusions. However, if the ERD is improperly applied, such as to the eyes, groin or in, or on, an open wound or sore, serious bodily injury can result. Such inappropriate use of the ERD will likely subject the user to criminal and civil sanctions.

Unfortunately, ERDs require continuous physical contact to be efficacious and contact must, as indicated above, be maintained for at least several seconds. That means you must get close to the suspect in order to use an ERD. That is a substantial disadvantage.

The Taser, an ERD that uses projectile darts connected with the main unit via wires, is designed to provide a safe "stand-off" distance between the user and the criminal suspect. Police use it with success.

Batons. We prefer to use the term "baton." Some criminal defense lawyers insist that the word "baton" is just a euphemistic expression for the more sinister-sounding "club" or "bludgeon." That is largely true but the picture that comes into most people's minds when they think of a person being "clubbed" bears little resemblance to the modern striking and leverage techniques used with defensive batons. Overhand blows to the head are usually avoided with the baton in favor of strikes to other parts of the body. Non-collapsible batons can be effective but are generally too long to be carried concealed unless they are camouflaged as a cane or some other inoffensive appliance. Canes and walking sticks are regularly carried by many for just such a purpose.

Extendable batons. There are several extendable batons available which can be extremely effective in the hands of a trained person. They are concealable and can be brought into action quickly. In the collapsed form, the extendable baton is fifteen centimeters long and can, in that configuration,

ASP extendable baton, collapsed and extended (21 inches).

Chapter 3: Defensive Weapons

be used as a "yawara stick." The best ones extend to forty-five centimeters. They extend and lock into the rigid extended position through the application of centrifugal force via the user's wrist action. With practice, it can be done with blinding speed. In fact, it is possible to extend and strike all in the same motion. Thus used, batons can deflect strikes, inflict painful blows, break bones and cause extensive serious injury, even death, so they must be used with mature judgment and appropriate self-restraint. It takes some training and practice but these weapons can be depended upon to overcome most unarmed attackers. If you are willing to get the mandatory training (You will have to devote several months to it), I highly recommend these excellent weapons. A bonus is that in most jurisdictions they are perfectly legal even when concealed.

Yawara stick. A "yawara stick" or "judo stick" is a hand-held impact weapon. It is a small cylindrical staff two centimeters in diameter. It is held in the fist and either end can be used for striking. It is an effective weapon in its own right but lacks range and is thus suitable only for close confrontations.

Flexible baton. There are some "flexible" batons available. The shaft is actually a coiled spring and the unit "whips" as it is being used. We do not recommend them because the flexible shaft wraps around the target as it comes in contact with it. The resulting blow is not nearly as effective as with a stiff shaft.

Persuader. Another popular concealable impact/pressure weapon is the five-inch hand-baton. Called the "persuader," it looks like a thin yawara stick with a small eyebolt on one end. The one I prefer is available from Lethal Force Institute and is called the "Dejammer." The body of the baton is of a small enough diameter so it can function as a range rod. That is, it can be inserted down the barrel of most any service handgun. It is thus very handy in checking for and removing barrel obstructions (such as stuck bullets). It is also handy for driving out stuck cases from chambers. It doubles as a key-ring holder, which means that one's key ring and keys will be held by an eyebolt on one end of the stick. One can then use the stick as a handle and flail the face, hands or forearms of an attacker with the keys. This can be a powerful

Ayoob dejammer.

33

and effective maneuver. It is, in my opinion, the only really useful defensive maneuver this instrument is capable of.

There are a number of commonly taught leverage holds where the persuader is brought into contact with the wrist bones of an attacker. When pressure is applied, it is possible to take him down through pain-compliance. It also is used against bones of the head and shoulders. However, with an actively resisting opponent, these moves are all difficult to apply correctly, tedious to maintain and often are not effective at all. Many determined attackers will find them impotent and easily escapable.

Many people carry a persuader because it is a convenient way to carry one's keys. The stick is inserted into the waistband on the left side with the keys hanging out over the top edge of the belt. However, if you stick one in your waistband as a key holder, you may not want to use a shiny, black one. If a police officer sees you remove the stick from your belt, he might mistake it for the barrel of a blue steel revolver. In fact, it is a bad practice to quickly reach under your coat or in the direction of your waistband any time you are in the company of police officers. If you must, do it slowly and tell them in advance what you are doing.

Knives. For too long, knives were overlooked as effective defensive weapons, but not any more. I have had the opportunity to work with several notable knife-fighting instructors and have become convinced that the Philippine and Indonesian fighting styles with knives are superior to the various fencing styles that have traditionally seen common use in this country. With twenty hours of intensive training, almost anyone can become devastatingly effective with a knife using these Far East methods. Don't overlook this option! In fact, I recommend carrying a blade as a complement to a pistol.

Most people are best served by a strong sharp knife that cuts powerfully and deeply. Such a knife is effective and difficult for an opponent to take away. Weak flimsy knives (like most kitchen and household blades) are a death trap, because they tend to break when put

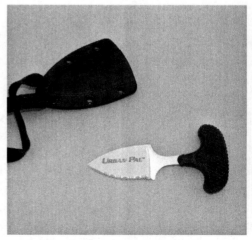

Cold Steel "Urban Pal" push knife with neck sheath.

Chapter 3: Defensive Weapons

to heavy use. Folding lock-blade knives are particularly nice, because they are so easy to carry concealed and are quickly deployed. Switchblade knives are not recommended, as they have a bad habit of deploying in one's pocket on their own initiative! Excellent fighting knives are available from Cold Steel.

Cold Steel also manufactures several excellent "push knives." The blade sticks out from between the fingers as the hand forms a fist. The handle fits securely in the palm of the hand. The sharpened edge can face up or down at the option of the user. The fighting style must be altered because of the way these particular knives are designed. However, they are astonishingly effective and retainable. Because of their short blades, these little knives are also generally legal to possess and carry.

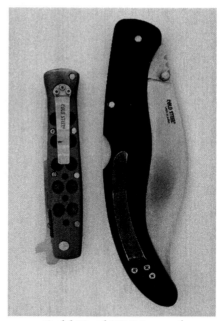

Cold Steel Ti-Lite and Vaquero Grande.

Knives are most productive when you have one, your attacker does not have one, and he does not know you have one until it is too late. By the time he figures out what is happening, he will discover himself in the middle of a serious reversal! I do not recommend becoming involved in knife-against-knife altercations unless there is no viable alternative. When facing a person with a knife, you will have to resign yourself to the fact that you are going to get cut, perhaps ruinously. It doesn't matter how good you are or how bad he is; both of you will probably get cut. The "winner" just gets cut slightly less than the "loser." If you have the option, *confront with a gun any attacker who is armed with a knife.* That's what guns are for!

Nowhere do state statutes and local ordinances vary more widely than when they declare what kind and size of knife is "legal." For example, according the many state and local statutes, most common kitchen knives are illegal even to possess, much less to carry. Some laws prescribe a blade-length limit. Some laws make double-edged knives illegal. Most municipalities have laws prohibiting "switchblade" knives, but the accompanying descriptions are usually inexplicit and absurd. If you decide to own and carry a defensive knife, keep it discreetly concealed so its technical legality (or lack thereof) never becomes an issue.

An intrinsic disadvantage with all impact weapons and knives alike is, like ERDs, they all require close contact. None of the aforementioned weapons afford much standoff distance.

Guns. Despite the forgoing, we must say that nearly every martial artist, regardless of his particular specialty, will readily admit that the firearm is still the ultimate defensive weapon. In general, firearms offer you the best opportunity for survival in any defensive situation. However, training is still essential. The fact that you have a gun no more makes you "armed" than the fact that you have a violin automatically makes you a "musician."

The twin advantages to firearms as defensive weapons are:

- *Strong stopping power*
- *Stand-off distance*

No other weapon comes close in either category.

The disadvantage of firearms is that *they are intrinsically deadly* and the wounds they produce are typically permanently disabling, disfiguring or lethal. Few people recover completely from gunshot wounds. Hence, it is not possible to shoot someone "a little bit." OC, ERDs, even impact weapons and blades can be applied in "less lethal" quanta. Not so with firearms.

Shotgun. A shotgun is very powerful, intimidating and versatile (owing to the large variety of ammunition available). Pointing a shotgun at someone nearly always gets his or her attention and compliance without delay! Some jurisdictions restrict the ownership of handguns and military rifles, but, in those same jurisdictions, shotguns are virtually unregulated. That's the good news. The bad news is that shotguns are big, heavy, unwieldy and inconvenient. They cannot be easily carried for long periods, and they have a high profile. It is nearly impossible to carry a shotgun concealed. They are also difficult to use in confined places and are not particularly retainable. If you are in a covered, stationary position in a house, a shotgun is an excellent defensive weapon. Moving through the house with a shotgun, however, is tactically unsound because the weapon can be easily taken away from you, particularly when you approach outside corners or attempt to open doors. A handgun is a better choice for such maneuvers. It is possible to carry a shotgun in a vehicle or keep one handy at home. Thus, it is not, in reality, an instant, defensive weapon. It is better thought of as a supplementary or backup weapon, albeit

Chapter 3: Defensive Weapons

a good one.

Shotguns are available in single-barrel single-shot, double barrel, and single-barrel repeating models. Repeaters are the universal first choice for defensive shooting. Most people choosing a shotgun for self-defense will be best served by a twelve- or twenty-gauge pump or autoloader, police model (eighteen-inch barrel, composition stock and forend, extended magazine tube, standard bead sight or some other rugged fixed sighting system). Twelve-gauge is the universal first choice with regard to defensive shotgun caliber, for average and large-sized males. However, small-statured people, including most women, are often better served by a twenty-gauge shotgun.

Remington 11-87 in low ready.

Buckshot ammunition for the defensive shotguns consists of several large, lead spheres packed into a single cartridge. The spheres are the projectiles, and they tend to spread apart after leaving the muzzle, creating what is called a "pattern." Buckshot was originally designed for deer hunting, but it is also effective on unarmored human targets out to a range of twenty-five meters. Buckshot is available in several sizes, 000, 00, 0, 1, 2, 3, and 4. The lower the number, the larger the pellets. The larger the pellets, the lower the number of pellets that can be fit into the cartridge. Buckshot in 00 (double-ought) size has proven effective and is recommended for most defensive purposes. In twenty-gauge, the biggest size of buckshot available is number three.

On those occasions where increased range or significant penetration is needed, the rifled slug is called for. The rifled slug cartridge (unlike buckshot) features a single solid projectile. It is destructive, capable of great penetration and extended range. A shotgun slug is effective and useable out to seventy-five meters, but the down-range danger area extends much farther than that for buckshot. In addition, slugs will usually penetrate to the interior of motor vehicles. Buckshot seldom does.

Rifle. Military centerfire rifles and some centerfire sporting rifles are excellent long-range weapons. In 5.56x45mm (223 Rem), 7.62x51mm (308 Win) and

7.62x39mm (30 Soviet) calibers, they are very destructive, intimidating and accurate. There are many excellent rifle choices in all three calibers. Other calibers are available, but the common military calibers mentioned above are the best choices because ammunition is plentiful and easily available. Unlike a shotgun, rifles are accurate and useable at ranges up to two hundred meters and beyond.

Rifles are longarms and thus have the same drawbacks as shotguns, inasmuch as they are big, heavy and long. Add to that the fact that most centerfire rifle calibers are capable of great penetration, even at extended ranges, making their use risky in any congested area. An exception is the 5.56x45mm (223 Rem) cartridge, whose penetration potential is actually less than that of many pistol cartridges. Rifles are excellent military weapons and are carried by all the armies of the world.

Robinson Arms RA-96 in Desert Snake Skin camo by Les Leturno.

A pistol-caliber carbine is a longarm that fires 9mm, 40 Smith & Wesson, 10mm, 45 ACP or some other kind of pistol ammunition. The rifle may be lever action, bolt action, slide action or auto-loading. Longarms, even short ones, which fire rifle ammunition, such as 7.62x51mm, 7.62x39mm, or 5.56x45mm, do not fit within this definition. Pistol-caliber carbines are very accurate but lack the range, power and penetration capability of rifles.

As mentioned above, neither shotguns nor rifles are particularly retainable in close-quarters situations.

Handgun. *Of all firearms, handguns are probably the most useful in the domestic defensive role.* They are made for those situations where an innocent person is attacked suddenly at close range and without warning or provocation. In fact, the nature of personal attacks is such that there is usually very little warning and the attacker is usually close (even in physical contact) before the victim knows he is in trouble. If the victim cannot escape or summon help in time, he must act decisively and quickly if he intends to survive. Handguns are made for just such a situation.

Chapter 3: Defensive Weapons

Any sensible person, who knew in advance he was going to be attacked, would probably arm himself with a shotgun or rifle and then vacate the area. In fact, a really wise person would try to avoid the entire affair in the first place. He would certainly not knowingly enter into a serious fight armed only with a handgun. *A handgun is an instantly reactive defensive firearm. It makes a poor offensive weapon.* No handgun even approaches the power or effectiveness of a shotgun or centerfire rifle. Handguns sacrifice power in exchange for convenience and relatively small size.

A handgun has the advantage of being able to be comfortably carried concealed on one's person. In addition, it can be brought into action quickly, is retainable, can be ready for use almost instantly, is easy to keep hidden in the home, is difficult to parry and is reliably powerful enough to stop most attacks within seconds (assuming an appropriate caliber and good technique). Handguns thus have a lot of advantages. In fact, for most people, the handgun is one of the few personal defense weapons that make any sense at all.

It will take at least twenty hours of intensive training under a competent instructor to get you to the point where you are ready to competently own, safely store, travel with, maintain, carry concealed and effectively use a defensive handgun. It may feel reassuring to have one around, but, *without adequate training, it is mostly a masquerade.*

SIGARMS P229R-DAK in register.

We carry pistols as a way to deal with *unexpected* threats. As such, carry pistols need to be slim, slick, smooth, short and easy and convenient to carry concealed. In addition, a carry pistol needs to have an adequate reserve of ammunition and be powerful enough to stop a fight even if several opponents must be neutralized quickly. Defensive pistols, indeed all defensive firearms, also *need to be loose enough to continue to operate reliably in spite of exposure to sweat, grit, lint and continuous neglect.* No pistol is going to be nearly as effective (as accurate, as powerful) as a rifle or shotgun, but, unlike rifles and shotguns, we can have a pistol on our person (concealed) nearly all the time. *Pistols are convenient, but not particularly effective.*

As noted above, utility or defensive rifles and shotguns cannot be carried on the person concealed (in most cases), but we keep them nearby as a means of dealing with *expected* threats, albeit threats that may still come at any time and from any direction. Like pistols, defensive rifles and shotguns thus must be thought of as *reactive or defensive* weapons. Sometimes, rifles and shotguns must be employed at what are normally considered pistol ranges, where retention is a critical issue. Hence, defensive rifles and shotguns must be short, slick and handy, but robust in much the same way a defensive pistol must be robust. Rifles and shotguns are *effective, but not particularly convenient*, even in the best configurations.

Given the above, we must face the fact that any suitable, defensive rifle or pistol is *never going to yield better than mediocre accuracy*. Accuracy and reliability are mutually antagonistic. Of course, the inherent accuracy of any good rifle is more than sufficient for the purpose to which we're putting it. Greater accuracy is certainly possible, but tighten a gun up to yield great precision, and you turn it into a moody, temperamental prima donna, not something you would want protecting your life. *I am happy to give up superfluous accuracy in exchange for dependable reliability.*

Finally, we use hyper-accurate scoped rifles as *a way of dealing with threats that are not only expected but are also known and identified.* These weapons are not "reactive" and thus are not particularly suitable for dealing with unknown and unlocated threats, be they expected or unexpected. These are temperamental sniper rifles, requiring anal maintenance and gentle treatment. They do have their place, just not in domestic, defensive, reactive shooting.

In order to stay alive long enough to finish the fight, you're going to have to deploy your weapon (blade, pistol) quickly, then cut and shoot decisively, perhaps at multiple targets at various ranges, with *sufficient accuracy to stop the fight and sufficient speed to allow you to seize and hold the agenda.* We have to equip ourselves to fight, not play games!

Soft body armor. On the passive side of the equation, there is body armor. There are two kinds: hard and soft. Hard body armor is usually designed to be worn externally (over clothing). It is heavy and stiff, usually being made of overlapping steel or ceramic plates. It finds its most frequent and suitable use on the modern battlefield. Some current versions will even prevent penetration by high-powered military rifle bullets.

Soft body armor is made from layered sheets of woven Kevlar or other high-tensile-strength fabric. Kevlar is a special textile that, when sufficiently layered, will prevent penetration by handgun bullets. Soft body armor made

Chapter 3: Defensive Weapons

of Kevlar fabric is flexible, comparatively light, and allows the free passage of air. Complete coverage of both chest and back weighs less than five pounds and is designed to be worn concealed *under* clothing and thus not be obvious to casual observers. This undercover armor can be worn continually with reasonable comfort. However, soft body armor is designed to stop only handgun bullets. It will not reliably stop penetration by knife blades, and *it will not stop most centerfire rifle bullets.* If made thick enough to stop rifle bullets, it would be too bulky and uncomfortable to wear.

The big attraction of soft body armor is the fact that it can be comfortably worn all day, not show from the outside, yet still provide real protection from handgun bullets. The best soft body armor units are the ones that correctly balance protection with wearability and comfort. The unfortunate fact is no matter how good the protection, if the armor is uncomfortable, the owner will not wear it.

Experienced users prefer soft body armor that covers the chest and back and is worn over an undershirt, but under the dress shirt. The V-neck style is the most comfortable, because it does not bind on the wearer's neck when he bends over. Groin protectors are also available and may sound like a good idea, but they are uncomfortable and, for the most part, unwearable. It takes about five minutes to put on, adjust, and conceal undercover body armor. It is not designed to be put on quickly.

Good soft body armor breathes. That is, air is free to pass back and forth through the panels. When encased in plastic bags or treated with waterproofing chemicals, soft body armor can become sticky in hot weather. The waterproofing is ostensibly to protect the Kevlar fibers from moisture. Moisture will slightly degrade the ballistic properties of the Kevlar, but usually not enough to worry about. The extreme solution of waterproofing the entire panel produces a vest that is so uncomfortable the owner may not wear it at all.

Raincoats, jackets, dress vests, sport coats, suit coats, even umbrellas have been made from Kevlar. Dress vests and jackets are practical, but the rest of these products are gimmicky and useless. *Unlike undercover armor, a jacket with Kevlar panels can be put on and taken off quickly and is thus a handy travel partner.*

Levels of protection provided by soft body armor have been categorized, and each unit of soft body armor from any reputable manufacturer is clearly labeled with regard to the protection level to which it is certified. It is always tempting to acquire the highest obtainable level of protection, but remember that you will pay a price in bulk, discomfort and lack of concealability. Like most things in life, choosing a protection level is going to entail a compromise. In this case it is between protection and wearability. Fortunately, protection from most all handgun rounds is available in units that are reasonably comfortable.

If a bullet hits the armor and does not penetrate, your life will probably be saved, but you will inherit an ugly bruise. There are few recorded incidents of any permanent bodily damage so long as the projectile does not actually penetrate the armor. Soft body armor will provide some protection against knife slashes, but less against knife thrusts. A thrust from a knife blade or ice pick will often penetrate soft body armor far enough to cause a fatal wound.

It is important to remember that soft body armor simply provides an extra measure of protection. It does not make you invincible, and wearing it is not an excuse to take foolish chances. Keep in mind that many vital areas of the body, including the head, neck, groin, legs and arms are not normally protected.

You can take a hit and stay on your feet and continue to fire if you are wearing soft body armor, and the offender's bullet strikes your body in a protected area. This has been conclusively demonstrated in many actual shootings. Soft body armor not only prevents penetration of the bullet (and thus saves your life), but it also allows you to remain upright and conscious, so that you are able to continue to take appropriate defensive actions.

Good body armor is part of every professional gunman's (male or female) ensemble. It has saved many lives. It is strongly recommended. Manufacturers are making it lighter, thinner, more wearable and more protective all the time.

Choice. The weapon or weapons, if any, that you choose to own and perhaps carry will depend on your perceived level or risk and your willingness to master the weapon(s) you select. Ideally, you should master several. Indeed, it is a bad idea to have a favorite weapon. Mastering a number of weapons will enable you to defend yourself effectively in a broad spectrum of situations. "He never would have touched me, if only I had had my _____ (favorite weapon)," is a feeble excuse used mostly by career losers.

For example, while at a "practical" shooting match, I watched contestants who were required to shoot a number of targets with their handgun while moving through a series of barricades and obstacles. Toward the end of each bout, the contestant was required to take a gun from the body (actually a mannequin) of a fallen enemy soldier, load it and then hit an easy target several meters away.

Chapter 3: Defensive Weapons

It was amazing to see these supposedly experienced shooters fumble awkwardly with the unfamiliar weapon.

Some could not figure out how to load it. Others got it loaded but could not make it fire. And of the ones who could get it to fire, most required five, six, even seven shots to hit the undemanding target. Many fired all eight shots and still could not hit it. With their own gun, the target would surely have been hit with the first shot. But this little foreign weapon baffled and confounded these "top" shooters to such a degree that they were not able to use it effectively. They all had become too attached to their favorite weapon and too unaware of others they may someday be compelled by circumstance to use. Shame on them!

Whatever weapon you choose, buy quality and get the best training you can find. Extravagance is justified in this instance. Economize elsewhere.

Chapter 4

The Stealth Existence

If you're going to own a gun for defensive purposes and particularly if you're going to carry it on your person or in your vehicle, you need to understand that attracting to yourself the attention of either the criminal justice system or wrongdoers is equally undesirable. It is to your advantage that you lower your personal profile to the greatest extent possible. We call it "*The Stealth Existence*," and every gun owner and gun carrier should be an avid practitioner.

Criminals and governments alike tend to pick on people who stand out from the crowd. "Standing out" is something many of us associate with success. However, being conspicuous and eye-catching in public is not to your advantage, particularly if you are carrying a gun. The key is to make it a habit to "blend" with the background thereby making you "invisible."

In nature, animals use camouflage to conceal their presence. The consistent use of camouflage is an important survival skill in our world too! It may be helpful to think of yourself as the pilot of a military aircraft. If you "fly high," it may make you feel good but you will quickly pop into a number of radarscopes and unfriendly people will at once begin launching missiles at you. Smart pilots stay low under the radar. It isn't as glamorous as flying high, but you'll safely get to your destination without attracting attention to yourself or, hopefully, even being noticed at all.

There are some ways you can raise your profile without even realizing you're doing it. Police, particularly state police, look for "profile indicators" and "suspicion enhancers" that are normally associated with people involved in the illegal drug culture and other illegitimate activities. You probably don't know what they are and probably would not fit a drug profile anyway. However, there are certain things you should not have in your possession (or at least visible) particularly while driving.

1. Rolls of duct tape
2. 35mm film canisters
3. U-Haul boxes

4. Large numbers of $100.00 bills

5. Accumulations of fast food wrappers

6. Accumulations of rubbish and garbage in your car

7. Long hair on males

8. Tattoos

9. The smell of alcohol coming from the inside of the car

10.   Unkempt, ungroomed appearance

11.   Snotty, cocky attitude

12.   Excessive talkativeness

13.   Excessive nervousness

14.   Inconsistent answers to questions

Most of the above-listed items and behaviors are not illegal but they are often carried and exhibited by drug couriers and other criminals. Any one item by itself may not generate a great deal of suspicion. But in combination, they could lead to an interminable traffic stop by the police and many probing questions.

Here are some other ways to stay under the radar:

1. Get into the habit of dressing in such a way that you would be difficult to pick out of a crowd. Be nicely and appropriately dressed, but wear clothing similar to what everyone else is wearing. While in public, don't wear flashy outer garments, high-profile hairstyles, loud or contrasting colors or ostentatious jewelry. Practice being "functionally invisible."

2. When in public, wear an inexpensive watch.

3. Drive a respectable, clean car (particularly on the inside), free of safety violations that blends well with the traffic common to the area. Avoid loud or contrasting colors, particularly red. Don't drive sports cars or muscle cars.

4. Don't put contentious bumper stickers or window decals on your car or home, particularly those espousing controversial or unpopular political or religious opinions. Keep your name off lists.

5. Don't get personalized license plates. Use the plates that are issued. *Change license plate numbers every year.* Don't keep the same number year after

Chapter 4: The Stealth Existence

year.

6. Make it a practice to be difficult to physically locate. Your home, like your car, should blend well with others in the area. Receive your mail and packages at a private mailroom rather than at your residence. Have an unlisted phone number.

7. Acquire a document shredder and get into the habit of routinely shredding invoices, telephone bills, letters, envelopes, old checks, bank statements, credit card invoices and anything else which you are going to discard but that may contain important numbers and other personal information about you, your finances, your travel, your associations or your personal habits and preferences. *Don't let those documents go out intact in the garbage.*

8. *Shred all expired credit cards and phone cards.* Don't just cut them once or twice. Destroy them completely.

9. *Don't make 1-800 and 1-900 phone calls from your home phone,* particularly when responding to advertisements or placing orders with mail-order establishments. If you do, your home phone number and address will end up on scores of sucker lists.

10. If your home or business computer runs uninterruptedly, *don't leave it hooked up continuously to a phone jack or high-speed connection.* Many people do this and let a software program function as a telephone answering machine. However, under these circumstances, savvy hackers can easily gain access to your computer and all your files. If you do use a continuous computer phone-line or high-speed hook up, use a separate, "dumb" computer and a separate phone line. Keep only your communications software on the dumb computer, never important files. If this is not possible, investigate hardware or software firewalls and anti-virus software.

11. *Carefully protect your social security number, your driver's license number, license plate numbers and your date of birth.* These are important personal identifiers and criminals can sometimes use this information to steal your identity. Some people, such as your employers and your bank, have a legitimate need to know these numbers, but few others do. Don't carry on your person anything containing your Social Security Number and instruct your employer and your bank to protect them too. *If asked for this information by people who have no right to it (such as sales clerks), tell them you don't have it memorized or provide them with a bogus number.*

12. Protect your name also. When filling out unimportant forms, such as when you register at a motel, use your first initial only, misspell your surname and enter a bogus number for your license plate.

13. . *Don't talk with telemarketers.* There is no such thing as a legitimate telemarketing operation. *They are all scams!* When they call, never tell them whom they are talking with and never confirm the number they just called. As soon as you realize it is a telemarketer on the other end of the line, hang up immediately. *Never give them any information whatever.*

14. Stay away from places where people get into fights, like bars, picket lines, political rallies, protests, hospital emergency rooms, religious "revival" meetings and anywhere else people are likely to be at emotional flash points. Avoid all crowds, particularly those with an agenda. If you witness a fight or a fight in the making, leave immediately.

15. *Keep your guns locked away in a gun safe,* except for those you need in a high state of readiness. Don't show your gun safe to anyone and don't discuss the contents of your safe with anyone who doesn't need to know. The contents of your gun safe needs to be a secret.

16. If you subscribe to gun magazines, political magazines or newsletters or any other kind of publication that could be considered controversial, read them as soon as they arrive and then *promptly throw them away.* Don't allow them to accumulate in your home.

17. . Be careful with the extent of your political involvement. Writing letters to government officials, letters to editors of newspapers and magazines and letters to elected officials, particularly letters of complaint or letters containing implied threats, carries with it considerable risk. The same can be said for becoming associated with what the government calls a DSM (Deviant Social Movement). Prolific letter writers and those who are otherwise attracted toward high-profile political involvement eventually end up being watched more closely than the average citizen. Voting can probably be done with little risk. *Political involvement at higher levels unavoidably raises your profile.*

18. *Don't have intimate conversations or liaisons with people you don't know well.* "Qualify" all those who want to become your close friend or seek to establish a romantic relationship with you. Make sure you know exactly with whom you are dealing. Don't get into vulnerable positions with strangers and always keep sensitive information about you to yourself and

Chapter 4: The Stealth Existence

sensitive documents appropriately secured. Those who are overly casual in this regard are the ones who get mugged, fleeced and date-raped.

19. Be careful about giving to charities, political parties, churches or any other group soliciting contributions. The names of charitable contributors routinely go on lists. Today's "charity" may become tomorrow's terrorist front organization. If you must contribute to a charity, *give in small amounts only, exclusively in cash and always anonymously.* Again, *keep your name off lists!*

20. Constantly be looking for and identifying exits. Whenever you enter any building, *locate all exits immediately.* Same for parking lots, highways or anywhere you might find yourself. Always know how you're going to get out of there fast, if and when necessary.

Remember that among sociopaths, kindness and openness are always interpreted as weakness and vulnerability. Thus, among people you don't know, "Courteous to everyone. Friendly to no one." are the words to live by.

Practicing the stealth existence should require only a small alteration in life style. However, it can pay big dividends in helping you avoid contact with criminals, be they in the public or the private sector.

Chapter 5

Self-Defense

"Violence" is the employment of force with the intent to injure or abuse. *Physical violence, physical fighting and battery all mean the same thing.* In a rational person, violence has only six possible motivators: anger, control, fear, revenge, theft and sex.

Fear is the only legitimate and lawful motivation for violence. The other five are all criminal.

Legitimate self-defense consists of reasonable defensive actions taken by a person in an attempt to protect himself or another innocent person from an imminent unlawful battery. The threat can be by means of either deadly or non-deadly force.

The correct and lawful self-defense response, which will involve an escalation of force, will be dictated by the perceived degree and type of unlawful force being imminently threatened or being applied by a criminal. Legitimate self-defensive actions on the part of an individual citizen may, if circumstances warrant, include deadly force.

Unlike a battlefield situation, where a soldier's deadly-force decision is based on *appearances* alone, your deadly force decision must be based on the *behaviors* exhibited by the offending individual(s). Unlike *appearances* (which cannot be changed rapidly), *behaviors* can change quickly, so you must have a great deal of control over yourself and any weapons you may have. You must be able to act immediately and decisively using a type and an amount of force reasonably required to keep you from getting hurt. However, you must be prepared to de-escalate as well, if the offender's behavior merits it. Most of all, *you:*

1. *Must not let out-of-control emotions cause you to escalate force inappropriately or use an amount or type of force that is clearly in excess of what is reasonably required.*

2. *Must refrain from continuing to apply force after the attack has been stopped and where the additional or continued application of force is plainly pointless and serves no legitimate purpose. When the attack has been stopped, continued disengagement is the only correct action.*

On the other hand, when your life is threatened, you must act quickly and decisively using sufficient force to stop the unlawful violence without delay and in such a way that it is unlikely to continue or resume. Afterward, disengagement can be accomplished safely and reengagement will be doubtful.

There are four elements relating to the attack and the attacker that must *all be present simultaneously* in order for there to be a situation where potentially deadly self-defensive actions on your part are warranted. They are:

1. Ability

2. Opportunity

3. Manifest intent (imminent jeopardy)

4. Preclusion

Ability. Ability is simply a deadly capacity on the part of the attacker. It usually manifests itself in the form of a weapon of some sort but not always. Serious injury, even death, can be inflicted by many individuals using no weapon at all. However, it is a requirement that the person against whom you are considering applying deadly force must be *able* to kill you or inflict serious bodily harm. Threats alone do not suffice, unless he has the *ability at hand* to carry them out. If you were attacked by a person much larger than yourself, or by someone using martial arts techniques, or several individuals at the same time, you may reasonably conclude that he or they have the ability to seriously injure or kill you even though they may be technically unarmed. Disparity in size, age, strength, sex, cultural conditioning and the level of aggressiveness of the involved parties are all-important matters when considering the element of ability.

Opportunity. In addition to having a deadly ability, the attacker must also be in a position to bring the destructive powers of his ability to bear effectively upon you. The question here is: were you within the effective range of his weapon(s)? For example, a knife or bludgeon is harmless in the hands of someone standing twenty meters away from you, yet either can be deadly if the person is standing within arm's reach or is several meters away but closing fast. On the other hand, *any firearm is considered deadly at any range.*

Manifest intent. You are in imminent jeopardy when the attacker clearly indicates by words or actions that he intends to kill or seriously injure you and further that he intends to do so at once. *His deadly intent must be manifested in some conspicuous and describable manner.* You are not permitted to use deadly force to defend yourself against uncorroborated or nebulous threats. The danger

Chapter 5: Self-Defense

to you must involve deadly force or the clear potential thereof.

The deadly threat must also be imminent. It must appear that the circumstances were sufficient to arouse the legitimate fears of a reasonable person and that you acted under the influence of those fears, not in a spirit of vengeance or criminal assault.

Intent is after all a mental process. We therefore cannot perceive intent directly. We can only infer it from a person's actions or words. Accordingly, one shouldn't say, "He intended to kill me." The unfortunate fact is you don't know what was going through his mind at the time. The correct way to phrase it is, "It looked as if he was going to kill me." That way you correctly identify your motivating factor as his (offensive and threatening) *behavior*, which you can plainly see. Always refrain from presuming to have an ability to read his mind.

Intent is not strictly necessary for imminent jeopardy to be present. You can, for example, be placed in deadly danger by an individual acting with extreme recklessness but who may have no specific intention of harming you.

No one is expected to wait to take defensive actions until he has absolute and incontrovertible knowledge that a threat is real. However, *there must be an overt act coupled with the threat.* It does not matter if your attacker's "weapon" later proves to be a toy, unloaded or even non-functional. So long as you had good reason to believe (reasonable belief) that the weapon was real and functional and that he intended to use it to harm you forthwith, your defensive actions will likely be considered reasonable and appropriate. *Remember, you will be judged only with regard to what you knew and reasonably believed to be true at the time.* You will not be judged based upon facts and circumstances of which you had no awareness.

Preclusion. Preclusion simply means that other reasonable options were precluded. In other words, *you used deadly force only as a last desperate resort.* The police (or jury) must be persuaded that, under the circumstances, you had no logical or reasonable alternative but to use deadly force to defend yourself. *Generally, the more self-restraint you display, the more reasonable your actions will appear to the authorities.* Police investigators should see your actions as judicious, restrained, reasonable and retrogressive. They should believe you made legitimate efforts to abate the situation, including the use of verbal challenges and even non-lethal force before finally resorting to the use of deadly force. Conversely, they should see your attacker's actions as precipitous, unwarranted, barbarous and unconscionable.

Some states require preclusion as a component of legitimate self-defense. They have passed "mandatory retreat" laws. In general, these laws require a person to retreat from an attack, rather than use deadly force to repel it, even when the person attacked otherwise has a right to be where he is. Generally, mandatory retreat laws apply only in public places and not in the victim's own home.

What the police and the courts will expect to see if you are claiming legitimate self defense as the justifications for your actions are: *avoidance, disengagement, escape and continued avoidance (evasion)*. The following will help you understand these terms.

Avoidance (general). You should be the kind of person who stays out of bars, stays away from fights, does not associate with people who get into fights, does not insert himself into situations in which he was not otherwise involved, etc. You should be *even-tempered and slow to anger*. People like that don't accumulate arrest records and are not known to the police as troublemakers.

Avoidance (specific). You should be able to explain to the police what you did to specifically avoid the situation in question. Did you have a plan to get out of there? Did you get out of there at the first sign of trouble?

Disengagement. You should be able to explain to the police what you did to de-escalate the situation and disengage from the attacker. *It is extremely important that you are not seen as an instigator, an aggravator* or as the one who goaded the other person into action. You should also be able to explain how you applied only the force reasonably necessary and ceased the application of force as soon as the attacker was stopped.

Escape. You should be able to explain to the police how you made a reasonable effort to escape rather than engaging or reengaging the attacker. At every point, you should choose disengagement and escape (as long as they can be accomplished safely) rather than continuing the engagement.

Continued avoidance. You should be able to explain to the police what steps you took to insure that you did not have to reengage the attacker.

Shoot to kill. This tired and flippant expression is perpetually on the lips of people trying to make any species of legitimate self-defense look and sound inherently uncivilized. Any time a citizen shoots in self-defense, someone will surely ask, "Did you shoot to kill?" This question always suggests dishonesty or ignorance on the part of the person asking it.

Even when we shoot another person in self-defense, death is not our goal. *Our*

Chapter 5: Self-Defense

goal is stopping the attack quickly, thus preserving our own lives and health. After the attack has been stopped, the perpetrator may die or may not. In fact, most perpetrators don't die even when they have been shot. A good answer to this question is, "I shot to keep from getting killed (or seriously injured). I shot to live!"

Shooting someone with the intention of only wounding him is always a bad idea. If your life is in danger, you need to apply deadly force as effectively as you can. If you are considering shooting someone only to wound him, you probably shouldn't be considering shooting at all.

Necessary or "objectively reasonable" force. That is the degree and type of force that is reasonably required to successfully effect legitimate self-defense, the defense of another innocent person, a lawful arrest or any other lawful objective.

Only the facts and circumstances known to, or reasonably believed by, the user of force at the time in question can be used to determine the "reasonableness" of his use of force. Intentions, details discovered after the fact and unmanifested agendas are not entered into the formula.

Thus, *a person's wrong intentions will not make an otherwise reasonable use of force unreasonable; nor will a person's good intentions make an otherwise unreasonable use of force legitimate.* Accordingly, subsequent judgments with regard to the appropriateness of a person's use of force in self-defense require careful consideration of the following:

1. The relationship between the amount and type of force actually used and the apparent need presented,

2. The relationship between the stated intent of the user of force and the extent of injuries actually inflicted, and

3. *The presence or absence of a good-faith effort on the part of the person employing force in self defense to control his own emotions and to disengage and preserve his own safety as dispassionately as possible.*

It should be noted that hate crime legislation makes "wrong intentions" a crime in and of itself, even if the person's actions were otherwise lawful and appropriate.

Objectively reasonable belief (probable cause). This is the logical, rational and articulable confidence in the truth of an allegation not immediately or conveniently susceptible to rigorous proof. *Such confidence, however, must have* *a factual basis and be founded only on unprejudiced and articulable knowledge and sensible conclusions.* Subsequent judgment as to the objective reasonableness of a person's belief shall be based on the totality of the evidence, information and circumstances known to the person at the time in question. A person may not justify a use of force with facts discovered *after* the force was applied.

When a person has reasonable grounds for believing, and does in fact believe, that the danger of his being killed or seriously injured is imminent, he is permitted by law to act in self-defense, based on those appearances, even to the extent of using deadly force. This is true even if it turns out that the appearances were misleading and the person was thus honestly mistaken as to the real extent of the danger. It is for the police or the courts to decide whether appearances of danger at the time were sufficient to justify the particular defensive actions that were ultimately taken.

Chapter 6

Use of Force

In legal terms, force is physical means or the threat of physical means used to compel an individual to do something he is not otherwise inclined to do.

Force is differentiated by type and degree:

- Type of force describes the method or weapon(s) involved.
- Degree of force describes the strength and enthusiasm with which the force is applied.

The most important force differentiation is between "deadly" and "non-deadly" force.

Deadly force

Deadly force is force of such a degree or type that it is likely to cause, or has caused, *death or serious bodily harm.* Some types of force, such as those involving an intrinsically deadly weapon like a firearm or a knife, *are always considered to be deadly* and thus cannot be applied to a "non-deadly" degree. Force involving a lesser weapon, such as a fist or knee, is not considered to be inherently deadly, but can be applied to such a high degree that it becomes deadly. This is particularly true when there is a wide disparity of size, strength or age between the person applying the force and the recipient of the force.

A threat to cause death or serious bodily harm (e.g. via the brandishing of a firearm) so long as the actor's purpose is limited to creating an apprehension that he will use deadly force if necessary, does not, in and of itself, constitute an employment of deadly force.

Non-deadly force

Non-deadly force is that degree or type of force that is not intended and is unlikely to cause death or serious bodily injury.

De-escalation of force. De-escalation of force is a decrease in the intensity and/or magnitude of the force being used.

When a criminal offender appears to be complying with a police officer's or armed citizen's lawful commands, the officer or citizen may, so long as control is maintained, respond by reducing the amount of force being applied, thus indicating to the offender that if he continues to comply, his cooperation will be rewarded through the lessening of force (as in pain-compliance). When indicated, the de-escalation of force does not mean that the officer or citizen becomes complacent or risks losing control.

In cases where maintenance or even acquisition of control is unlikely or ill advised, de-escalation could refer to full-scale disengagement and withdrawal — a wise move in many cases.

Escalation of force. Escalation of force is an increase in the intensity or magnitude of the force being used.

Escalation of force on the part of criminal offenders should always be met by a corresponding, but superior, escalation of force on the part of the person defending himself, but only until disengagement is accomplished. Escalation of force that is substantially beyond what is reasonably necessary to keep oneself (or another innocent person) from being harmed is always unlawful. Citizens may thus take reasonable actions to defend themselves but, unlike police officers, citizens have no continuing obligation (or authority) to restore order or arrest offenders.

In legitimate self-defense, we only escalate force *as a response* to an unlawful escalation of force on the part of a criminal offender.

Excessive force. Force beyond what is reasonably required to successfully affect legitimate self-defense or any other lawful purpose is excessive force. *Excessive force is unnecessary force and is always unlawful.*

Retaliatory force. Force that is unnecessary and is used as a reprisal is retaliatory force. *Retaliatory force is always unlawful.*

Unnecessary force. Unnecessary force is force that is uncalled for and that serves no legitimate purpose.

Chapter 7

When Confronting Criminals

Victimization is the act of making someone the object of a crime. For criminals, victimization is both a goal and a craft. *Criminals do not practice fighting. They practice victimization.* In fact, fighting is something they will usually avoid. Thus, a displayed willingness to fight on the part of a potential victim will nearly always cause the criminal to pause and then move on to another potential victim. On the other hand, cowering, freezing, panicking and other displays of psychological weakness on the part of potential victims will inevitably target the individual and embolden criminals.

In order to avoid being a victim of a crime, we all must think in advance about crime and how we may be victimized. Foolishly telling oneself that victimization is something that can never happen is assuring that it will. *A healthy dose of suspicion and cynicism, combined with an adequate grasp of fighting skills and a conspicuously resolute willingness to use them, are all necessary for those of us who plan on not being victimized by criminals.*

For criminals, the most important of their victimizing skills is the ability to screen many potential victims quickly and select the ones with whom they will likely have the greatest success. Not surprisingly, they always search out the weakest and most vulnerable "prey."

Sophisticated criminals victimize people in a financial way. These are the charlatans and gigolos. Less sophisticated criminals victimize people's property. These are the vandals and petty thieves. The lowest of the low victimize people with physical violence. These are the muggers, bullies, abusers, rapists and child molesters. However, these are also the ones with which we are most concerned, because, although they are repulsive bottom-feeding degenerates, they are still dangerous. They have no honor. They are, without exception, cowards, but they are still human predators, and they harm their victims regularly. Victimizers may not be well armed, well trained or skilled in any other way. But *they are willing to attack* and that gives them a critical advantage, which even seasoned fighters and gunmen often fail to overcome.

When selecting victims for physical violence, criminals inevitably use the following terms to describe the most eligible candidates:

- Vacillating
- Inattentive
- Confused
- Hesitant
- Self-consumed
- Careless
- Anxious
- Fearful
- Faint-hearted
- Lacking energy
- Weak

As one might expect, candidates displaying the following characteristics are immediately rejected.

- Commanding
- Vigilant
- Deliberate
- Assertive
- Extroverted
- Discerning
- Confident
- Tenacious
- Bold
- Energetic
- Strong

There is little doubt that the way criminals perceive individuals dictates how they will interact with them and how they will be categorized:

- As candidates for victimization, or
- As people not to be messed with.

Chapter 7: When Confronting Criminals

The following sections will cover specific aspects of confronting a criminal.

Concealment of a weapon. This type of "concealment" describes the practice or custom of carrying a gun or other defensive instrument (concealed) upon the person. There are three levels of concealment:

Casual: Casual concealment is the preferred method for the discreet carrying of defensive handguns for most of us under most circumstances. The weapon is secure from casual observation but can be drawn and reholstered (and reconcealed) quickly, should the need arise. The act of bending over may reveal the weapon's outline under clothing (called "printing"), and a sudden gust of wind may blow a coat or vest flap to the side, momentarily exposing the gun to direct observation. These kinds of circumstances obviously need to be monitored carefully. Otherwise, the gun should remain undetected by all but the meticulously observant.

When carrying a pistol concealed in a waistband holster, be careful when sitting in vinyl chairs. The outline of the gun will often imprint into the chair. When you then get up, the pistol's imprint is left behind and is often plainly visible.

Rigorous: Rigorous concealment is required only if one wants to eliminate all possibility that the gun he is carrying could be inadvertently detected, even by the observant. Rigorously concealed guns are usually small and are buried under several layers of clothing and are thus not readily accessible. Several holster makers have produced "rigorous" concealment arrangements that enhance accessibility but are not always comfortable or convenient for daily use.

Total: Guns that are totally concealed will never be inadvertently exposed and will probably remain undetected, even during a pat-down or a personal search. Totally concealed guns are usually taped directly to the body or concealed within a bodily orifice. This is, of course, the stuff of which spy novels are made, and it is otherwise of little interest to most gun owners.

Brandishing firearms. *When a person is holding a pistol or longarm in a firing grip and with a stance that is normally associated with shooting, the gun is considered to be brandished.* It is not necessary that the gun be pointed in any particular direction, that a finger be in contact with the trigger or that the gun be loaded in order to meet the requirements of the definition. The position of the manual safety lever, if any, or the presence or absence of a magazine is also irrelevant.

When a firearm is brandished in the direction of a person, that person (and all other persons near him who are aware of the gun) has been "assaulted" by the person holding the gun. Since a gun is involved, the assault will usually be judged as aggravated.

So long as it is not grasped by the wearer, a holstered sidearm, even if it is exposed, is not considered to be brandished. Likewise, a longarm carried slung over the shoulder or neck, so long as it is not grasped in a firing grip, is not considered to be brandished.

One is legally permitted to brandish a firearm only in a situation where there is reasonable cause to anticipate potentially deadly danger. An example would be any situation in which a person reasonably believes that a potentially violent criminal offender (e.g.: burglar) is in the area. One may point firearms at suspected criminal offenders and hold them at gunpoint only when there is good reason to believe they are dangerous and would likely initiate a deadly attack if it were not for the presence and posture of the firearm.

You should realize that, on occasion, innocent persons might have your firearm pointed at them. It may be the result of mistaken identity or an innocent person may be in the same area or on line with the criminal offender in question. This is regrettable, but it is sometimes unavoidable. For this reason *you must always have your firearm under precise control* so that tragic unintentional shooting injuries or deaths can be avoided.

After your gun is "brandished," there are no "good" options left. They should have all been exhausted before that point was reached.

Pointing a firearm in someone's direction and actually discharging it in that person's direction are not the same thing and do not require the same legal justification. There are situations in which you are perfectly justified in confronting a person at gunpoint (assaulting them with a brandished weapon), but are not yet justified in firing. An example would be confronting a (thus far) non-aggressive and non-violent burglary suspect in your home. Just because you point a gun at someone doesn't mean you have to fire, but it does mean that *you must be prepared to fire.* Don't try to bluff with a firearm! If you are not prepared and willing to fire, you need to reconsider gun ownership.

Verbal challenge. Verbally challenging a person whom you believe to be dangerous is recommended when you:

- Already have a gun brandished.
- Are confronting the person at a safe distance and from a strong position.

Chapter 7: When Confronting Criminals

- A deadly attack upon you is possible, but does not appear to be imminent.

A verbal challenge is designed to get the suspect's attention and arrest his movements as he focuses his attention on you and your posture with your weapon. Of course, if you are confronting a person at gunpoint, it means the person is a criminal suspect, and there is reasonable cause for you to foresee serious bodily harm to yourself or others.

The recommended verbal challenge is, **"Police! Don't move!"** That is followed immediately by, **"Drop your weapon!"** These are common police challenges. There is a good chance that the suspect has heard them before. If he believes you are a police officer, he will likely assume you are armed, and that assumption will, of course, be confirmed when he sees your gun in a confrontational posture. If he believes you are a police officer, it is unlikely that he will continue with his attack, far less likely than would be the case if he believed you to be merely a frightened householder. It is also improbable that arriving police officers will shoot you if they believe you are one of them.

If a criminal suspect responds to your verbal challenge by stopping and looking in your direction, the best thing to do is order him to leave the area. If he believes he is being confronted by armed police officers, he will usually be more than happy to comply. *It is strongly recommended that you not try to arrest the suspect(s) or hold him or them at gunpoint until police arrive.* Trying to communicate with arriving police officers with a gun in your hand and a dangerous felon nearby is extremely hazardous. When holding a criminal suspect at gunpoint, don't allow your front sight to get above his navel. Keep your front sight low enough so that you can see his hands and so that he cannot duck out of your vision.

Don't get involved in a conversation with suspects. Only issue commands and make them short and abrupt. Don't converse with him and don't reply to any of his questions. *Watch your language.* To be particularly avoided are racial slurs and death threats. If there is more than one of you confronting the suspect, stay close together and cover each other's blind side. Don't allow the suspect to get between you.

When it comes to the security of your home and family, you need to start by thinking about all the threats that are likely, and then develop a plan. A family security plan is something with which everyone in the family must be familiar. In general, if your home is invaded, wake up first! Be sure you are fully awake before you get your hands on your defensive firearms. Next, get your gun!

You want the option of a lethal response as quickly as possible. As indicated before, for most people, the best storage option for defensive handguns kept in a bedroom is a quick-access lock box.

Once you're fully awake and have your gun in hand and ready, get yourself into a strong position relative to the bedroom door. Your spouse, executing your plan, should get into his or her own position.

Chapter 8

First Aid for Gunshot Victims

Single gunshot wounds from most calibers of handgun ammunition are rarely fatal. In fact, of ten people brought to a typical hospital emergency room with gunshot wounds:

Six will be "treated and released."

Three will be treated, kept overnight in the hospital and released the next day.

One will be kept in the hospital for more than one day and a small percentage of that group will ultimately die.

Eighty-five percent of penetrating torso wounds don't even require surgery. The ones that do require surgery usually involve torn and severed blood vessels and therefore require the services of a vascular surgeon.

The fatality rate from gunshot wounds is only three percent. However, *when a person is struck by multiple bullets over a short period of time, the fatality rate goes up dramatically.*

What all this means is that, when you or a family member are wounded by a criminal using a handgun, the greatest source of danger to the person who has been shot is not the wound itself. He will likely survive that. The greatest source of danger is the criminal who still has the ability to inflict additional wounds. *Your greatest enemy in this case is being distracted by your wounds and thus failing to deal decisively with the original threat.*

Rifle and shotgun wounds are generally much more serious than handgun wounds and the fatality rate is therefore much higher. But the principle is the same. *Threatening individuals must still enjoy your highest priority.*

When all immediate threats have been

Emergency Bandage

neutralized, you must attend to your own or someone else's wounds. The thing to remember is: *plug the holes.* Then, evacuate to a hospital as soon as possible.

External bleeding must be stopped. The best way is through direct pressure. Remember, *the main purpose of a bandage is to apply pressure to the wound.* The current Israeli battle dressing (available through most medical supply houses as "The Emergency Bandage") is the best bandage or dressing available. Your kit should include a half dozen.

CPR is seldom of any real use with gunshot wound victims, and it consumes one's attention and a great deal of time. Few people upon whom CPR is started are ever successfully resuscitated.

There is little you can do about internal bleeding and most other internal injuries. If the person who has been shot is still alive after a few minutes, they have a very high likelihood of surviving, if they get to a hospital emergency room and a surgeon quickly. People who die from gunshot wounds usually do so within less than a minute. So, if you are conscious enough to remember being shot, you're probably going to be fine, so long as you quickly and decisively deal with the threat FIRST, then deal with your own bleeding and other injuries. If you, through inaction, allow yourself to be shot additional times, your survival probability will decline dramatically.

We offer more in-depth information regarding additional first aid techniques in the DTI course *Tactical Treatment of Gunshot Wounds.*

Chapter 9

Interacting with Law Enforcement Officers

Rights and powers: *Individual citizens have rights. Governments have powers.* Rights and powers are, by their nature, in constant conflict. It is up to the courts to continually define and redefine, commensurate with the Constitution, where individual rights unduly interfere with the government's ability to execute its primary function of preserving public order, and where the powers of government unduly interfere with the exercise of individual freedom and liberty.

Rights are NOT granted to citizens by governments. Rights are granted to citizens by the Creator and are thus inalienable. No government can ever legitimately claim to "grant" rights to citizens. Citizens already possess those rights.

On the other hand, citizens, in possession of their inalienable rights, do grant government its powers. Therefore, the powers of government can be granted and they can be taken away. Governmental powers can also be, and should be, regulated and overseen by an informed citizenry.

Cooperating with the police is often a form of voluntarily imposed, temporary detention. Free citizens, of course, may cooperate or not cooperate with police at their discretion. However, police often use their intimidating presence and persuasive craft to convince free citizens that they are legally required to "voluntarily cooperate." Hence, police may tell a free citizen that he should "come with us" to the police station so that he can "answer a few questions." The police don't always make it clear that *the citizen is under no legal obligation to go anywhere with them (unless the citizen is under arrest), nor is he obligated to answer any questions, make statements, or, for that matter, carry on any conversation with police at all!*

Carrying on a conversation with police without one's lawyer personally present is nearly always a bad idea, as any statements you make in their presence can be used against you. Thus, if police officers confront you and want to "ask you some questions" or ask you to "come with us" to the police station, you need to immediately ask them, "Am I under arrest?" If they answer in the negative, you should tell them that you will be happy to talk with them, but *only at your lawyer's office and with your lawyer present* and that you will call your lawyer right away and make the appropriate arrangements. They will usually discontinue their questioning at that point. If they indicate that you are under arrest, let them take you into custody. Make sure that you do not answer any questions or make any statements from that point forward, until you have an opportunity to talk with your lawyer.

If police officers come to your home of their own volition, it is best not to invite them in. They can talk with you on the front porch. If they ask if they can come in, answer that the conversation is just fine where it is. If you do invite them in, keep them in one place as you talk. *Don't give them a tour of your home!* If they start snooping around, ask them to leave your property at once.

If you are stopped or questioned by the police when you are away from your home, produce identification if asked, be truthful and always polite but:

1. **Don't be chummy or chatty.** This is not a "friendly conversation."

2. **Don't be defensive or emotional.** Don't plead with officers for forgiveness, get into lengthy rationalizations or drone on and on professing your innocence.

3. *If you don't have direct personal knowledge that something is true, the correct response to a question is,* **"I don't know."** Never guess at answers and never speculate. Never answer hypothetical questions. *Don't express opinions, particularly controversial political or religions opinions.* If a police officer is very opinionated about some extraneous subject, don't agree or disagree. Appear to be indifferent.

4. **Don't answer questions that weren't asked.**

5. **Don't keep answering the same question over and over.** If officers persist indicate that, "Your questions are making me confused and uncomfortable, officer. Please don't ask me any more questions."

6. **Don't expand on your answers.** Make each reply as brief as possible. A simple "Yes," "No," or "I don't know" will usually suffice.

7. **Don't volunteer information.**

8. **Don't produce documents** that were not specifically requested.

9. **Don't ask questions.**

10. . **Make eye contact** with the officer and maintain eye contact when you're talking with him. Don't appear to be shifty-eyed or give the impression that

Chapter 9: Interacting with Law Enforcement Officers

you are contemptuously ignoring him.

11. . **Don't get too close to police officers.** Stay out of their personal space. Police officers often interpret people getting into their personal space as an assault.

12. **Don't do or say anything that could be interpreted as a threat.** For example: Don't cock your head, place your hands on you're hips, clench your fists, clench your jaw, spit, cross your arms or stretch. All these behaviors will be interpreted by police as indicators of an impending assault or battery.

13. **Don't get out of your vehicle.** Stay in your vehicle with your hands in plain view, unless or until an officer directs you to exit.

If the police ask you what you are doing there or where you are going, tell them you are "visiting friends." That answer is surely going to be true and in giving it you don't reveal specifics. *Never tell them you are "on business."* They will want to know immediately what business you're in.

When the police ask you to produce identification, produce only what is required and be careful about reaching into pockets quickly. Move slowly and tell them which pocket you're going for before doing so. *Don't show them the inside of your wallet, credit cards, cash or any other document except those which are specifically asked for.*

If the police ask you for permission to talk with your children without you being present, politely tell them that you don't want them talking with your children under any circumstances. Instruct your children not to talk with police unless they are with you.

I am not advocating non-cooperation with police. What I'm advocating is smart cooperation. If you are suspected by police of committing a crime, you need not and should not "cooperate" in your own prosecution! Despite what they may try to tell you, *you are **not** required to become a witness against yourself.*

As any trail lawyer will tell you, the problem with "telling your side of the story" to police, members of the news media or anyone else is that *you will never tell the same story twice.* Inconsistencies will creep into each "version" of your story every time you tell it, no matter how careful and truthful you are. Police, prosecutors, news people and plaintiffs' attorneys alike will seize upon such inconsistencies, no matter how small and inconsequential, in an effort to make you out to be a liar. It is best to tell your story only once and only after consulting with, and with the assistance of, an attorney. That way, there will only be one version.

Protected speech

The framers of our Constitution decided that certain critical social relationships are more important to the health of a civilization than is even the pursuit of justice. Thus, communication between you and certain other persons enjoys protection from the probing eyes of the criminal justice system. There are four people with whom you may talk in which the conversation enjoys some, but not absolute, protection:

1. **Yourself.** Under our Constitution, *you cannot be compelled to become a witness against yourself.* You are not, therefore, legally required to incriminate yourself by answering questions posed by police. Your private thoughts are your own, and you don't have to reveal them to, or discuss them with, anyone.

2. **Your spouse.** Communication between your spouse and yourself is also protected. Your spouse, under most circumstances, cannot be compelled to testify against you. *Spouses may voluntarily testify,* of course, but such testimony cannot be demanded.

3. **Your lawyer.** Conversations with your lawyer and any of his employees or associates are protected. You may freely discuss all elements of your case with him. However, there are limits. For example, your lawyer is not permitted to assist you in the planning of, or the commission of, a crime. Consequently, if you revealed to your lawyer that you were planning to harm a witness, your lawyer would be legally required to report that portion of the discussion to the police.

4. **Your clergyman.** The priest-penitent relationship is also protected. Therefore, conversations between you and a member of the clergy of any mainstream religion enjoy protection. In addition, members of the clergy of all major religions are sensitive about the traditional sanctity and confidentiality of the priest-penitent relationship. Thus, an ethical clergyman will refuse to compromise that confidentiality, even if ordered to do so by the court.

Most members of the clergy are also trained counselors and may be of great assistance in your time of need. Their ability to help you emotionally will probably be far greater than that of your lawyer or even your spouse. It is therefore a good idea to initiate a relationship with a member of the clergy even

Chapter 9: Interacting with Law Enforcement Officers

if you are not a member of a church or don't attend church regularly.

It is important to note that in most jurisdictions there is no protection of communication between:

- Patient and doctor (even if the doctor specializes in mental health)
- Parent and child
- Sibling and sibling
- Employer and employee
- Teacher and student
- You and members of the news media (despite what they may try to tell you)

Thus, *there is no such thing as an "off the record" conversation with any of the aforementioned.* If you say something incriminating and it is overhead by anyone (except your lawyer, spouse or clergyman), it can be used against you in court because that person can be compelled under penalty of law to reveal the contents of the conversation.

Hate crime: Hate crime laws explicitly make the lives of one segment of society more important than those of another. When hate crime laws are passed, it is suddenly a more serious crime to harm a member of this or that minority than it is to harm someone who does not fit into a state-defined minority. To make matters worse, with hate crime statutes, one's thoughts, even when they were not manifested into action, are still considered criminal. Thus, *hate crime statutes make it a crime to think thoughts that are not approved by the state.*

In an era of hate-crime legislation, *it is all the more important to keep silent and not make statements or answer questions in the immediate aftermath of a deadly-force event in which you were involved.* Any statements made by you may be used to demonstrate that you were thinking "unapproved thoughts" at the time of the incident and therefore should be prosecuted for a hate crime.

Chapter 10

Arrest and Searches

A "citizen" is a native or naturalized resident of the United States of America who owes allegiance to its Constitution and laws and is entitled to its rights and protection.

Citizens can have four different statuses:

- **Free citizen**
- **Citizen under temporary detention**
- **Citizen under formal detention (arrested), awaiting adjudication**
- **Incarcerated citizen** serving a court-imposed jail or prison sentence

Most of us, most of the time, are free citizens living our lives only under the restraint of law and thus enjoying a high degree of personal freedom. We are restrained from nothing except that which is obviously harmful to others or ourselves.

When arrested, a free citizen becomes a "citizen under detention awaiting adjudication." At this stage, the citizen may be incarcerated or he may be free on bond. Upon conviction and incarceration, he becomes an incarcerated citizen. At each stage, the citizen loses some, but not all, of his rights. Government entities must still adhere to "due process" when arresting and detaining citizens and even when incarcerated, citizens must be treated humanely and are protected from "cruel and unusual punishment."

An "arrest" is the taking of and detaining in physical custody of a person, by authority of law. In our society, police officers (and others under some circumstances) are authorized to arrest (seize) persons suspected of committing crimes. When a free citizen is arrested, his citizen status automatically defaults to *citizen under detention, awaiting adjudication,* where he will remain until he is either returned to free citizen status or is convicted, and subsequently becomes an *incarcerated citizen serving a court-imposed jail or prison sentence.* Arrests by police officers usually involve the arrestee being immediately restrained via handcuffs or other restraints, searched and subsequently transported to an incarceration facility (jail).

A free citizen is "under arrest" when he is so informed by the arresting officer and is then touched by the officer or "submits to the officer's authority." It is important to know that when you are arrested, it doesn't mean that you're automatically guilty of committing a crime. It simply means that the police believe they have probable cause to take you into custody. For example, if you're involved in a shooting that is a clear case of legitimate self-defense, you still may be arrested by the police who respond to the scene; even though you and everyone else believe what you did was perfectly reasonable.

Upon being informed by the police that you are under arrest, most lawyers agree you should peacefully submit, obligingly allowing the police to do whatever they deem necessary to take you into custody. This can include the application of handcuffs and transport to a local incarceration facility. *When thus arrested and taken into custody, you must never do anything (such as fighting or becoming verbally abusive) that could be even remotely construed as "resisting arrest." Resisting arrest will be a separate charge against you, with its own additional penalties.*

You should never concede to the police or jailers that you "understand the charges against you" or that you "understand your rights." When asked by the police if you understand the charges against you or understand your rights, the answer is *always* **"no!"** If asked what part you don't understand, indicate that you *don't understand any of it.* Aside from that, you should politely but firmly decline to make any statements or answer any questions.

When in jail, police will sometimes approach the incarcerated citizen and try to persuade him to "sign a statement." It is usually described as a "release document" and is lightly dismissed by police as "just a formality." They fraudulently explain, "All we need is your signature and you're out of here!" The thought of getting out of jail is so seducing that many people sign such documents without reading them carefully. Don't do it! *The document is customarily a full confession to a crime or several crimes!* After the document is signed, the citizen is not released. He is immediately rearrested and charged with all manner or crimes to which he has just "freely confessed." Don't fall for that scam. When in jail, contact your lawyer as soon as you can and understand you will probably be there for a day or two before he can get you out. While you are in jail, *never sign anything and have no conversations with police, the press, court officers or anyone else (aside from your lawyer).* Remain silent until your lawyer arrives.

Resisting arrest. Under federal law, *all citizens are required to peacefully submit to arrest by police officers, even if they believe the arrest to be inappropriate.* Resisting arrest is always illegal. Thus, becoming rude, verbally abusive or physically resistive during the arrest process is *always* ill advised. Resisting arrest offers one no benefit and carries with it great risk of physical injury and subsequent additional charges of "resisting," "fleeing" or "assault on a police officer." When police officers inform you that you are under arrest, the *best course of action is for you to submit peacefully, do exactly as you are told and allow them to touch you and apply handcuffs.* It is important that you not do or say anything that could be even remotely construed as "resisting."

Suspect status. When you are in contact with police officers, they may at some point come to believe you are "probably guilty" of committing a crime. At that point you have entered *suspect status.* It may be because of an answer you provided to a question, your demeanor, facial expressions or any of a number of other causes. The evidence may not be sufficient for a conviction, but it is sufficient to make the police suspicious of you. In any event, when you enter suspect status, the officers should stop questioning you and "read you your rights" before continuing.

Any time police officers read you your rights or in any other way indicate that you are a suspect, you should immediately ask for a lawyer to represent you and abruptly and permanently stop any substantive discussion between them and you. *Politely tell them that the interview is over and that you want your lawyer.* When asked if you understand your rights or if you understand any particular right, always indicate clearly that you do not. When subsequently asked what part you don't understand, indicate that you don't understand any of it. *Never indicate that you understand or want to waive any of your rights.*

If the police do not place you under arrest, you should indicate to them that you will be happy to continue the discussion, but *only at your lawyer's office.* If they do place you under arrest, decline to answer all questions from that point forward and, of course, indicate to them that you want your lawyer. *Don't go anywhere with them, unless you have been arrested.*

Police don't routinely read rights to everyone they talk with. In fact, if a police officer approaches you he will probably not immediately read you your rights. Therefore, in order to politely avoid making potentially incriminating statements, when a police officer approaches you and wants to ask questions, ask him first, "Am I suspected of committing a crime?" If he replies with something like, "Everyone is a suspect right now," that obviously includes you, so *assume you are a suspect at that point and proceed accordingly.*

If he indicates that you are not a suspect (as would be the case if you were merely a witness to a crime), you may then answer his questions so long as he confines himself to the case at hand, in which you have no involvement. *The moment you are asked probing questions about your personal life or any other irrelevant questions that make you uncomfortable, consider yourself a suspect at that instant and act accordingly, whether he reads you your rights or not.*

Consent search. In this country, police are not authorized, at their own whim, to forcibly enter a free citizen's dwelling, vehicle or personal space, any time they want and rummage through his personal papers, records and other personal items. In this country we have a right to privacy. Private property may be forcibly entered by police, but only pursuant to a valid warrant, pursuant to "probable cause" or as part of a lawful arrest.

However, the occupant of private property may, if he so chooses, "consent" to a police search. To be valid, such consent must be freely given. Consent may not be coerced or granted in exchange for a promise by the police of special treatment. Unfortunately, sometimes cunning and deceptive police officers try to dupe naive people into "consenting" to a search when freely given consent appears unlikely. The technical legality of this dubious procedure is murky, but such underhanded "consent searches" are still commonly practiced.

If you do consent to a police search, you may strictly limit its scope and duration, and you may unilaterally withdraw your consent at any time. Unfortunately, most police are anxious to conduct a "consent" search and will neglect to make any of that clear to you. Therefore, most lawyers agree, when asked by police for your consent to conduct a search, you should *always* deny permission, politely but firmly and absolutely, so there is no chance that your denial can be misinterpreted.

Thus, during a traffic stop, if an officer says (in a friendly and conversational tone), "You don't mind if I take a quick look through your car, do you?" What he is actually doing is asking you for your permission for him to conduct *an exhaustively thorough, interminable, tedious, intrusive and even a destructive search of every part of your entire vehicle and everything and everyone in it,* although his words will be chosen to artfully conceal his real intentions.

In addition, *if during the search your property is damaged or lost; neither the officer nor his agency will assume any responsibility. They will not offer to make restitution nor will the officer or anyone from his department offer to help you recover and put away your disarranged possessions.* A good rejoinder in a case like this is, "Officer, I really don't want you going through my personal things." That reply is polite, but it would be difficult for anyone to misunderstand. If he persists, continue to repeat your reply. If asked by police to sign any document confirming your consent to a search, politely decline.

In summary, if the police are asking you for *your* permission *for them* to do something, they don't need you. They need a supervisor! *It is best never to grant consent,* thus compelling the police either to obtain a valid warrant or abandon their effort to persuade you to consent. Whatever they do, it is best that you not be any part of it.

Definitions

Battery. Battery is the unwanted and unsolicited touching or striking of one person by another *with the intent of bringing about a harmful or offensive contact.* Batteries may or may not involve weapons. Batteries are usually unlawful when unprovoked, but, like assaults, may be lawful when appropriately employed as a reasonable defensive counter-measure and thus a necessary component of legitimate self-defense. As soon as touching occurs, however slight, a major escalation in the level of force has taken place. Potential force has given way to actual physical force. *Shooting someone, accidentally or intentionally, always constitutes a battery.*

Assault. Most state criminal statutes define assault as *creating the apprehension of a battery.* That is, when one menaces another person in such a way as to create in the other person's mind the reasonable fear of an impending battery, he commits an assault. Unprovoked assaults are usually illegal, but counter-assaults that are employed as a reasonable response to precipitous and unprovoked assaults or batteries by an attacker upon an innocent person are often appropriate as a necessary component of legitimate self-defense. *Pointing a gun in someone's direction almost always constitutes an assault, regardless of intent.* Since a weapon is involved, such brandishing is nearly always "aggravated assault."

Aggravated. When a crime is characterized as "aggravated," it means that the particular example in question is more egregious than the simple form of the same crime. Thus, aggravated assault and aggravated battery usually involve weapons which are capable of causing, or which actually have caused, serious bodily harm or death. The simple or non-aggravated forms of these same crimes usually do not involve weapons and are less serious.

Serious bodily harm or injury. Serious bodily harm describes any physical or psychological injury that causes acute or protracted incapacitation or disfigurement, protracted loss or impairment of the function of a bodily member, organ or mental faculty, protracted unconsciousness, protracted hospitalization, significant or substantial internal damage, or a significant degree of pain, suffering or emotional trauma. Included within this definition are grievous internal damage, serious psychological trauma, and any other injury that requires significant medical treatment or hospitalization.

Examples of serious bodily injury include the following: broken bones or teeth, dislocations, grievous cuts or lacerations, stab wounds, serious burns, bullet wounds, severe abrasions, significant internal damage and any other incapacitating injury. A substantial risk of death is surely a factor to be considered, but it need not be in evidence in order for serious bodily injury to be present.

Serious bodily injury is easy to demonstrate and show *after* it has been inflicted. However, the purpose of legitimate self-defense is, of course, to *prevent* serious bodily harm. If the self-defensive actions selected and implemented by an individual are successful, the serious bodily injury he fears never occurs. So, when subsequently justifying his actions, the user of self-defense must convince those who sit in judgment that serious bodily injury *would have* occurred had he not taken the defensive actions that he did. Ultimately then, when self-defense is successful, "serious bodily injury" is *prevented* and is thus (thankfully) only speculative.

Misdemeanor. A misdemeanor is a criminal offense (crime) for which state or federal statutes provide a sentence of less than one year of imprisonment, usually in a local jail rather than a penitentiary. Misdemeanors are still crimes, but are less serious than felonies. Examples: trespassing and low-value theft.

Felony. A felony is a criminal offense (crime) for which state or federal statutes provide a sentence of death or a term of imprisonment in a penitentiary for more than one year. Felonies are the most serious of crimes, but there are two levels:

- *Forcible felony:* A felony during which the perpetrator uses, is about to use, or threatens to use, unlawful deadly force. Examples: murder, voluntary manslaughter, aggravated sexual assault, armed robbery, aggravated burglary, arson, kidnapping, aggravated battery and aggravated assault.

- *Non-forcible or non-violent felony:* Any criminal offense that qualifies as a felony under state or federal statutes but lacks the element of the use, or threat of the use, of unlawful deadly force. Examples: high-value theft, forgery and unlawful flight.

Homicide. Homicide is killing of one human being by another. Homicide is usually a crime, particularly when there was specific intent on the part of the perpetrator. With intentional homicides, most state statutes differentiate between those that are premeditated and those that are spontaneous (first and second degree murder). There are also several degrees of unintentional homicide that are caused by reckless conduct but where there was no specific intent (manslaughter, reckless endangerment). And, of course there are unintentional homicides brought about by accidental circumstances. Homicides that are purely accidental are regrettable, but are usually not considered criminal.

Of most interest to us is "justifiable homicide," where the homicide was intentional but where a person was acting in legitimate self-defense. When a person claims justifiable homicide, he is saying he did intentionally commit a homicide but *his actions were reasonable under the circumstances.* In other words, it is reasonably foreseeable that, if he had failed to act when and in the way he did, he would have suffered serious bodily injury or death at the hands of the person who was ultimately killed.

Weapon. A weapon is any instrument that can be used by a person to stop, injure, and/or kill another person or himself. Even bodily parts can be considered weapons. Fists, knees, and elbows can all be used as effective weapons of attack or self-defense.

Lethal (deadly) weapon. A lethal weapon is any weapon that is, by its nature, inherently capable of being used to cause serious bodily injury when employed to virtually any degree. Examples: firearm, knife, automobile, ax, baseball bat and poison. In the eyes of the law, it is impossible to shoot or stab someone "a little bit."

Some lethal weapons are designed, built and are intended to be used solely as weapons. They have no other purpose. Examples: defensive handguns and fighting knives. Other lethal weapons, such as an automobile, have purposes other than being used as a weapon. In fact, cars and baseball bats are not even normally thought of as "weapons." However, both can be used in a pernicious manner and when thus used against you must be regarded as lethal weapons.

Grand jury. A grand jury is an official inquest, via a jury convened by the prosecutor, which examines accusations against persons charged with crimes and, if the evidence discovered warrants, makes formal charges on which the accused persons are later tried in court.

In most areas, a grand jury is little more than a rubber stamp for the local prosecutor. Since he usually lacks the resources to prosecute every case he would like, the prosecutor tries to pick which cases he wants to carry forward. The unfortunate reality is decisions with regard to which cases are prosecuted and which aren't are often unduly influenced by local politics. Grand juries are thus put in place in an effort to counter improper political pressures. However, the grand jury is the prosecutor's show, and he usually has the power to manipulate it to conform to his wishes.

When the grand jury rules that an accused is "probably guilty," they return a "True Bill," which commands the prosecutor to prosecute the case in court. If they return a "No Bill," the accused is exonerated at that point, and the prosecutor is directed to drop the case.

Being exonerated by a grand jury is obviously less involved and less expensive than going to trial and being tried before a jury in a court of law.

Coroner's jury. A coroner (or "medical examiner," as the office is known in some jurisdictions) is a public officer, usually a physician, whose duty is to inquire directly or by jury inquest, into the cause of the death of an individual where there is probable cause (reasonable belief) to believe the death in question was due to something other than natural causes.

Many people die each day in this country, and the vast majority of those deaths are from "natural causes," disease or advancing age. Most take place in hospitals and nursing homes. The criminal justice system has no interest in such deaths and they are normally not investigated. *Only when there is evidence that a death was due to criminal activity does the criminal justice system get involved.* It is the coroner's job to examine the body and the circumstances and determine if further investigation is warranted. If the coroner decides there are no suspicious circumstances surrounding the death after all, the criminal justice system has no further interest.

The coroner is sometimes authorized to convene a jury. The jury is asked if the death in question warrants further investigation. If they say "yes," the investigation is expanded. If they say "no," the matter is dropped. A coroner's jury thus acts as a grand jury, albeit at a lower level. Thus, any death declared by a coroner's jury to be a unilateral suicide, due to an unsuspicious accident, or a justifiable homicide pursuant to legitimate self-defense will, at that point, no longer be of interest to the criminal justice system.

A coroner's jury is of interest to us in as much as they can dismiss, at a low and

Chapter 10: Arrest and Searches

inexpensive level, a self-defense shooting. A lawyer representing a person involved in a self-defense shooting will thus try very hard to get the whole matter disposed of via a coroner's jury, rather than allowing it to rise to the next level, which is a grand jury. If a coroner's jury decides that the death in question was the result of a clear case of legitimate self-defense, they will thus rule, and the person who did the shooting is, at that point, exonerated.

Coroner's juries are not common in all jurisdictions. They are found mostly in the east and southeast parts of the country. Where they are present, they can be a valuable prerogative if they are properly taken advantage of by a person involved in a self-defense shooting.

Tort. A tort is a "wrongful act" (which may or may not also be a crime) for which relief may be sought in civil (not criminal) court, via a lawsuit by an injured party, in the form of compensatory damages, punitive damages, or injunction. Upon being found "liable" in civil court (as opposed to "guilty" in criminal court), a person may be required to pay money to an injured party or may be instructed by the court to perform some specific compensatory act.

Civil courts settle disputes between individuals. Criminal courts adjudicate accusations of wrongdoing brought by the government against individuals.

Bail. Bail is the conditional release from police custody of a citizen under formal detention (incarcerated and awaiting adjudication) in exchange for monetary security pledged (held by the court) to insure the due appearance of the citizen in court at the appointed time. When the bailed citizen does, in fact, appear in court at the appointed time, the bail amount is returned to him. If the bailed citizen fails to appear at the appointed time, the bail amount is automatically forfeited and a warrant is issued for his immediate arrest. *Failing for any reason to appear in court at the appointed time is thus always contraindicated.*

Bond. Bond is an obligation to appear in court made binding by a pending monetary forfeit (bail). Bond is also the term that enumerates the amount of the monetary guarantee.

Bondsmen. Also known as bail bondsmen, they are private businessmen who are licensed by the state to guarantee to the court monetary bond for individual citizens under formal arrest who are incarcerated, thus allowing the citizen to be free until his appearance in court without having to come up with the actual bond amount themselves. Arrangements between the citizen and the bondsman are private business transactions, and the bondsman is free to charge reasonable fees for his services. With high bonds, seeing a bondsman is often the only way a citizen can avoid sitting in jail until his appointed court appearance. Bondsmen often employ bounty hunters to locate clients who fail to appear in court.

Temporary detention. This term describes a situation in which a free citizen is confronted and detained for a short time by a police officer for the purpose of determining the person's identity, issuing a summons, etc. The citizen is not actually taken into custody. The assumed outcome of a temporary detention is that the citizen will be returned to "free" status promptly and permitted to go his way. In some cases, however, the outcome is that the citizen is formally arrested. The most common form of temporary detention is a traffic stop. During a temporary detention, the citizen may be restrained or "patted down" (as opposed to a thorough, personal search, which is permitted only as part of a formal arrest).

It is common for officers to attempt a consent search, particularly of vehicles, during a temporary detention. Of course, you will always politely decline consent.

Temporary detentions can only be done in a public place and may only go on for a reasonable amount of time. Most courts have defined a "reasonable amount of time" as twenty minutes. If the traffic stop or other temporary detention lasts longer than twenty minutes, ask the officer, "Am I free to go?" If he indicates that you are, say "Good day sir," and leave immediately without saying another word. If he indicates that you are not free to go, ask him if you are under arrest. If he indicates that you are not, then indicate to him that you want to leave without further delay. Every traffic stop and other form of temporary detention is divided into two phases, the "custody" phase and the "voluntary" phase. During the custody phase, you are not under arrest, but you are not free to go either. During the "voluntary" phase you are free to go at any time, as you are "voluntarily" staying longer than required. As you might expect, the officer will not make it clear to you when one phase ends and the other begins. Police often wait until the "voluntary" phase to ask probing and intrusive questions and ask your permission to search your car. That is when you must indicate that you want to leave and that you don't want to answer questions, carry on any kind of conversation or submit to a search. Your interests are best served by keeping the contact as short as possible.

Citizen's arrest. Under some circumstances, non-police citizens are permitted by law to make arrests and thus take criminal suspects into custody. This occurs most commonly when a citizen is asked to assist or voluntarily assists

Chapter 10: Arrest and Searches

a police officer. Under all other circumstances, *attempting to make a "citizen's arrest" is exceedingly ill advised* as one has little to gain and a great deal to lose when such an attempt is made. Most free citizens have not been trained in the mechanics of arrest or arrest procedure nor do they routinely carry handcuffs, OC spray, police radios and other necessary police accouterments. Making a citizen's arrest thus carries substantial risk of physical injury as well as exposure to civil and even criminal litigation. Accordingly, if you are not a police officer and see someone whom you believe needs to be arrested, the best plan is to go to a telephone and call the police. Do not become physically involved yourself unless such involvement is unavoidable.

Law. *A law is a rule of conduct or action established and prescribed by a duly constituted governmental entity, formally recognized as binding on all citizens and consistently enforced by governmental authority.*

Western Civilization has always prided itself on the fact that we are ruled by unwavering written laws, not the arbitrary and inconsistent whims of conceited kings and potentates. We have thus always considered arbitrary governmental power to be associated with lower forms of civilization. Unhappily, we are now coming full circle. In our time, politicians and bureaucrats who lust after power routinely subvert the rule of law with their cavalier belief that their personal power is and should be, unlimited. Thus, *we are rapidly deteriorating from a civilization that is governed by laws, to one that is governed by agendas.* This is attractive to would-be czars because they can control agendas without having to endure the inconvenience of legislative review.

One consequence is that our civilization has become "feminized" by unscrupulous politicians seeking the loyalty of female voters. Any form of masculine behavior, such as gun ownership or self-defense, has now been declared to be vulgar. Only stereotypical female behavior (by either gender) is now appropriate.

The regrettable result is that the enforcement of "law" has become arbitrary. Political agendas determine which laws are enforced and which are not. Often, agendas themselves are enforced as law, even when there is no law to support them. As a result, ill-conceived "conspiracy," "seizure" and "hate" statutes are routinely exploited in order to advance unlegislated agendas.

Tyrants will always dislike the idea of citizens being privately armed. They abhor the very concept of privacy. Private possessions, private property, private enterprise, private dwellings, private arms, private communication and even private thoughts must all be eliminated before their idea of utopia can come to fruition. They regard the idea of not being able to casually and arbitrarily terrorize us private-sector peons as frightening. Thus, even though gun ownership is "legal," it passionately violates the political agenda of these would-be despots. Accordingly, we see them trying in every way possible to convince us that individual gun ownership is inherently sociopathic, all the time, of course, heavily arming themselves.

They assure us that they want to take away all our guns, "for our own good." They tell us, "You don't need liberty; you need protection." "You don't need individual rights; you need control." Accordingly, we gun owners must, more than ever, maintain a healthy distrust of government and the motives of politicians and bureaucrats, particularly those who come to us with high-sounding rhetoric. *We must resign ourselves to the fact that they are never going to like us.*

Chapter 11

Firearm Safety

If you are going to carry a handgun concealed about your person, or keep any firearm in your home or vehicle with the intention of having it handy and ready for defensive purposes, *you will be handling it often,* probably daily. You owe it to yourself and others to seek out and obtain proper training so that you can learn to store, handle, transport and use it safely, correctly and effectively. If you learn to handle and live with guns safely from the beginning, the appalling consequences of unintentional discharges will likely not touch you or your family.

There are two separate sets of circumstances in which you will need to handle firearms:

- **Administrative**
- **Tactical**

The handling procedures in both instances are nearly identical, but there are some important differences.

Tactical circumstances are those where you are in the middle of a life-threatening emergency. The prime consideration with regard to your weapon is to use it in the best way possible in order to keep yourself from getting hurt. "Safety" is a secondary consideration. Of course, if you shoot yourself because of incorrect gun handling, that will not likely upgrade your survival potential; so correct and safe gun-handling procedures are still important.

Tactical procedures are:

- Drawing and reholstering
- Firing
- Reloading
- Reducing stoppages

In training, tactical procedures are all timed. You are expected to do them quickly and smoothly, because they must be done under tactical circumstances. Under tactical conditions, you may even be forced, for the sake of expediency, to momentarily point your weapon in an unsafe direction or violate some other administrative handling procedure. Sometimes this is unavoidable.

Administrative procedures are:

- Loading
- Chamber check
- Unloading and clearing
- Cleaning

Administrative procedures are done under non-tactical (administrative) circumstances. There are no time limits and the prime consideration is safety, more specifically: *the prevention of accidental discharges and the prevention of personal injury when an accidental discharge does occur.*

Administrative Handling

Accidental discharges. To reiterate: *guns do not go off by themselves.* The probability of a gun in a drawer or in a holster, or lying about on a counter, discharging on its own volition is zero. *It is only when a gun comes into someone's hands that it becomes dangerous.* Modern handguns from reputable manufacturers are all designed with an eye toward human engineering. They have many built-in safety features, some of which you will probably never even be aware. They are as safe as it is currently possible to make firearms. However, they are just machines and are designed, after all, to launch bullets under emergency circumstances. If they were so safe that they never fired, I expect the manufacturers would have trouble selling them! "Safety" is never an absolute reality. It is just a term used to describe a relative state. Remember, once your bullet leaves the muzzle, it has no friends!

Most unintentional discharges result in property damage only, but, if the muzzle is pointed in an unsafe direction, personal injury can also result. This, of course, is the ultimate nightmare. It can be prevented only by the constant observation of the safety rules and continuous presence of mind whenever firearms are handled. *If you are going to have firearms around, you must firmly resolve that you will never allow a mental lapse on your part to precipitate an unthinkable tragedy.* As indicated above, modern defensive firearms are designed primarily to discharge bullets. Once launched, a projectile cannot be recalled. We therefore do not learn how to live with guns by trial and error. Your first mistake may be your last! *Your first accident is the one that must be prevented.*

Chapter 11: Firearm Safety

The memorization of a laundry list of safety rules is no substitute for presence of mind and common sense when it comes to handling firearms. However, four firearms handling maxims must be learned and observed under all administrative circumstances:

- **All guns are always considered to be loaded and immediately ready to fire, all the time, and will be handled accordingly. Unloaded guns are handled no differently than loaded ones.**

- **The muzzle of any firearm must not, at any time, be allowed to point in an unsafe direction.**

- **Fingers are to be kept out of the trigger guard and out of contact with the trigger unless the gun is simultaneously (1) sighted on a target and (2) it is intended that the weapon discharge at once.**

- **When pointing a gun at a target, be sure it is something that you want to shoot and that the area around and behind it is clear and safe.**

When handled for any purpose, all firearms should be treated as if they could discharge at any moment. Therefore, the muzzle must constantly be made to point in a safe direction. We call this *"muzzle consciousness."* Guns do not point themselves. The person holding the gun is always the one who points it and who is responsible for where it is pointed, all the time. If the gun does discharge accidentally and it is pointed in a safe direction, the bullet will expend itself harmlessly or cause only minor property damage. The muzzle must not be allowed to point in the direction of a person, even for an instant, unless, of course, that person represents an imminent deadly threat.

If the muzzle of the weapon of which you are in control inadvertently points at an innocent person, you are guilty of gross negligence, the kind of negligence for which you are unlikely ever to be forgiven. The feeble excuse, "Oh, don't worry. It's not loaded," is unacceptable and will in no way diminish the contempt in which others will and should hold you. It is something you must not ever allow to happen. Whether or not the firearm is actually loaded at that particular moment is utterly irrelevant. Loaded guns seldom harm people accidentally, because they are handled carefully. *It is "unloaded" firearms that, when handled carelessly (because of their supposed status), are responsible for nearly all gun accidents.*

Careless handling is indeed responsible for the vast majority of unintentional discharges, but not all. Guns do malfunction occasionally, even reputable ones, so *even correct gun handling will not prevent all unintentional discharges.* That is why muzzle consciousness is such a basic tenet of correct gun handling.

A safe direction is sometimes hard to find if you are not on a firing range. If you are in your home and direct the muzzle at a nearby interior wall, there may be someone on the other side of whom you are not aware. Better that the muzzle be pointed at something you know would stop the bullet if the weapon discharged unexpectedly. A dresser full of folded clothing, a filing cabinet full of papers, a full refrigerator, a brick fireplace, a masonry wall, toilet bowl, etc., can all provide a safe direction. It is also best that, in general, the muzzle be kept depressed and not horizontal. However, if you are on an upper floor of a motel or apartment building, neither downward nor upward will be a safe direction. A company called BetterBilt now makes a Kevlar gun rug called "Safe Direction." It provides an instant, convenient and portable, safe direction in which to point a pistol and is highly recommended, particularly for those who routinely travel with guns.

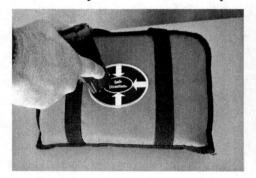

Safe Direction range bag.

Whenever a gun comes into your hand that has not been under your direct continuous control, it must be checked before anything else is done with it. *You need to know what you're holding.* While observing the safety rules, the chamber should be opened in order to ascertain whether or not the weapon is loaded. It is not sufficient that the weapon had been cleared or checked recently. If it has been out of your control or sight, you must check it again as soon as it comes into your hand.

Notice that I'm not suggesting you always unload a gun as soon as you pick it up. You may want it loaded. What you need to do in every instance, however, is to immediately ascertain exactly what you're holding in your hand. Once you've done that, you can proceed with your routine.

When you hand a gun to someone else under administrative circumstances (non-tactical procedures), courtesy, good sense and safety demand that the weapon be cleared and the action be open (if possible). Keep in mind that *unloaded guns are handled no differently than loaded ones,* and weapons are checked every time they change hands. Exceptions to the forgoing may, of course, be made

Chapter 11: Firearm Safety

under tactical circumstances.

Any time you touch the trigger of a firearm, you must expect that it will discharge at that instant. Whether you believe the weapon to be loaded or not, keep your fingers away from the trigger unless you intend for the weapon to discharge at once. The trigger is the "go button" and no modern reputable firearm in proper working order will discharge unless pressure is applied to the trigger.

Unintentional discharges can be prevented by practicing the principles of safe gun-handling and using assiduous common sense. However, there are no guarantees. Ultimately, guns are potentially dangerous machines and, as with any potentially dangerous machine, *the risks of having them around must be balanced against the risks of not having them around.*

Unintentional hits

When you launch a bullet in self-defense, or for any other purpose, your bullet may not hit what you intended for it to hit, but it will certainly hit *something*. It will not conveniently dematerialize the instant it passes its intended target or somehow attain escape velocity and go into permanent, equatorial orbit! It will continue downrange until it strikes something stout enough to stop it. Whatever it strikes, it will damage or wound. And you are going to pay for whatever damage is done. As far as the legal system is concerned, *you* are the new owner of whatever your bullet lands on!

Whenever you are firing intentionally, whether at the firing range or in actual self-defense, *there is little room for doubt as to what you're shooting at and what else may be struck in the process.* No matter how desperate your situation, you are not justified in shooting at shadows, shooting at unidentified movement, or shooting through doors or walls. You must be in a position to testify that you knew exactly what you were shooting at and where your bullets were going. Remember, you relinquish control over the bullet the instant it clears the muzzle. For this reason, *we never fire carelessly or recklessly.* The consequences of unintentional hits are too catastrophic to risk. You must refrain from shooting until or unless:

- *You are confident you are going to hit your target and nothing but your target.*
- *You are sure of your target beyond a reasonable doubt.*

Of course, you will never be *absolutely* sure of anything! If you wait for absolute certainty, you'll never shoot. When shooting for recreational or training purposes, you need a reasonable degree of confidence that your targets and backstop will harmlessly contain all bullets launched. When shooting in an emergency, you need a high degree of confidence that all bullets launched will strike the people they need to strike and no one else.

Misses are triply disastrous.

- They don't stop or even slow the attack.
- They endanger innocent people and property, and by extension your financial future, career, etc.
- They rapidly draw down a limited reserve of ammunition, leaving you with even fewer rounds with which to solve your problem.

The only socially responsible thing to do, no matter how monstrous the predicament, is to shoot with precision.

Safe Storage

If there are a number of guns in your house, there is rarely any reason to have more than one or two readily accessible. *The rest of the guns should be kept continuously locked in a gun safe.* This will certainly prevent thievery and unauthorized access, but more importantly, it will remove the temptation for you to move around the house looking for intruders. The knowledge that your guns and other high-density valuables are securely locked in a safe that no burglar will be able to get into will eliminate most reasons for you to leave your bedroom. In addition, police arriving at your home in the aftermath of a shooting or for any reason will not be able to determine the contents of the safe. They will not be able to open it and confiscate your guns without a warrant.

Lock box attached to a headboard behind a sliding door, with a push button combination that is easy to open in the dark.

Chapter 11: Firearm Safety

Gun safes are available in a variety of sizes and styles from several excellent manufacturers and are highly recommended.

If you have a gun safe, never discuss its contents with anyone who doesn't need to know and don't open it and show its interior to anyone. *The contents of your safe must remain a closely guarded secret.* If there are people who have been made aware of the contents of your safe, their statements to the police may be used as a basis for the police to obtain a warrant to search your safe. The police will then have legal access to your safe and may subsequently impound and carry away everything in it.

When storing handguns in a safe, or anywhere else for that matter, don't hang the gun by a peg inserted through the trigger guard. If the gun drops or is pushed on the peg so that the peg strikes the trigger, the gun could discharge and keep discharging as it recoils and the trigger repetitively strikes the peg. *The best way to store guns is in the shipping container in which they came, or in a gun rug or other padded case or hard box.*

It may seem like an obviously stupid thing against which to forewarn, but don't place your handgun in an oven. Believe it or not, many people have placed their guns in kitchen ranges and ovens, in an attempt to quickly get them out of sight. What happens is that they are promptly forgotten and then at some later time the oven is turned on. When this happens, the ammunition in the pistol's magazine will burst, usually destroying the gun beyond any possibility of repair. If there is a round in the chamber, it may actually fire or "cook off" and may cause personal injury or significant property damage.

Even if the gun is not loaded, the heat in the oven will melt plastic parts such as grip panels and may deleteriously affect the temper of the metal, making it soft or brittle. The gun may thereby be rendered unsafe to shoot and thus be effectively ruined. *So, never put your gun in an oven, even temporarily.*

Trigger lock

A trigger lock is an external device that clamps around the trigger guard of a firearm and thus prevents the trigger from being touched until or unless the lock is removed. Part of the device normally protrudes inside the trigger guard, in some cases in actual contact with the trigger. Trigger locks are produced by a number of manufacturers and most feature a key lock.

There are several negative issues associated with trigger locks that, as with magazine safeties, completely negate any conjectured "safety" benefit they may provide:

- They require a great deal of imprecise manipulating in order to get them on and off a gun. You are required to get your fingers dangerously close to the trigger during both installation and de-installation. During both procedures, the gun invariably points in multiple unsafe directions.

- They cannot be removed quickly, so they are only appropriate for weapons in storage mode. All guns in storage mode should be locked in secure containers anyway, in which case the trigger lock becomes a pointless redundancy.

- The "one-size-fits-all" approach taken by manufacturers means that any trigger lock you purchase is probably not designed to precisely fit your particular gun.

- Any external device that positions a part of itself inside the trigger guard of a firearm is a veritable invitation to an accident. In fact, *many accidents occur when people try to install trigger locks on loaded guns.* As they manipulate the gun and the trigger lock simultaneously, the trigger is invariably touched, and an accidental discharge occurs at that moment.

On balance, trigger locks have caused far more accidents than they have ever prevented. I highly recommend against their use. However, if you do decide to use one:

- Never attempt to install a trigger lock on a loaded gun.

- Never install a trigger lock on a gun that is unloaded but that you intend to load after the trigger lock is installed.

- Never install a trigger lock on any gun that you expect to be able to put to use quickly. Consider any gun with a trigger lock installed to be in storage mode.

Instead of trying to install some after-market "safety" gimmick (like a trigger lock) on the gun itself, it makes much more sense to lock up the entire gun in a secure container designed for this purpose, such as gun safe or quick-access lock box. That way:

- The direction of the muzzle can be readily controlled during the entire process,

- Excess manipulation can be avoided, and

- It is not necessary to get fingers anywhere near the trigger.

Trigger Shoe

A "trigger shoe," as the term suggests, is an after-market clamp-on pad that fits on the front of the trigger of a handgun or longarm. It is usually secured via a setscrew, and its purpose is to provide a wide contact surface for the trigger finger. Trigger shoes are popular within certain target-shooting circles.

Installed on any defensive firearm, however, *trigger shoes are inherently unsafe*. The trigger shoe extends laterally beyond the dimensions of the trigger guard. For this reason, a trigger shoe may cause an accidental discharge during the reholstering of handguns or the slinging or mounting of longarms. In addition, trigger shoes often come loose, slip down and subsequently jam the trigger against the bottom of the trigger guard, producing a gun that cannot be made to fire.

On all defensive firearms, trigger shoes are both worthless and extremely hazardous. They are not recommended.

Chapter 12

Accidental and Unintentional Discharge

When a firearm discharges unintentionally, we have an accidental discharge or "AD." In some circles, it's referred to as an unintentional discharge or "UD." Other places, it's called a negligent discharge or "ND." *In almost all cases ADs are a direct result of operator error.* In some rare cases, ADs result from defective firearms or ammunition. Among professional gunmen, ADs are exceptionally uncommon but since an AD can theoretically happen at any time *it is extremely important for anyone who handles a gun to keep the muzzle continuously pointed in a safe direction.*

Another class of accidental discharge occurs as a direct result of imprudent or negligent storage of firearms. When unauthorized people (usually children) get their hands on improperly stored firearms, ADs occur, frequently with tragic results.

In the eyes of most courts, there is no excuse for an accidental discharge, whether it is at the hands of the gun owner himself or as a result of inappropriate storage. *Police, judges and juries have scant patience with careless gun owners.* People who have accidents with guns are seen as either thoughtless or foolhardy.

Accidental discharges during gunfights are not only hazardous for everyone in the area (including yourself), they are also tactically disastrous. An accidental discharge will invariably startle you to the point where you will be out of the fight for a number of seconds recomposing yourself. During that time, you will be settling yourself instead of paying attention to the fight.

It is all too common among gun owners to experience the discharge of a firearm in the absence of the operator's intention or his conscious decision to fire. Such unintentional discharges usually result from the involuntary contraction of the muscles controlling the fingers. The involuntary contraction is caused by:

- The "startle effect"
- Loss of balance
- The "sympathetic grip" or "inter-limb interaction"

Muscles of the hands and fingers will contract involuntarily if a person is startled by a precipitous or unexpected noise, visual event or physical contact. In addition, an unanticipated postural disturbance will predictably generate the same phenomenon. In both cases, the person will involuntarily squeeze anything (a pistol, for example) he is holding in his hand.

A person exerting force with one hand (for example: grasping a suspect's lapels or attempting to open a car door) will experience a simultaneous and involuntary contraction of the other hand. This is the sympathetic grip, sometimes called inter-limb interaction.

The higher the level of anxiety, the more pronounced these effects become. At high levels of anxiety, an average person can involuntarily press the trigger of a firearm with an amount of pressure well in excess of fifty pounds! No handgun, shotgun or rifle, trigger cocking or otherwise, will stand up to that kind of pressure. If the person's finger is in contact with the trigger of a firearm he is holding and he is subsequently startled or loses his balance or grabs something with his other hand, *the weapon has a high probability of discharging, without any intention or awareness on the part of the person holding the firearm.*

It is particularly important to be aware that unintentional discharges of firearms caused by the startle effect, loss of balance or inter-limb interaction are not restricted to cocked revolvers, Colt/Browning pistols or longarms with the manual safety off. As you can see in the forgoing cases, the effect is common in cases involving uncocked revolvers, uncocked trigger-cocking autoloaders and virtually every other type of firearm ignition system.

In addition, you need to realize that muscular contractions caused by the aforementioned phenomena are beyond the voluntary control of the average person. No amount of training can abrogate it. If you have your finger in contact with the trigger of your firearm or out of contact with the trigger but still inside the trigger guard and the critical combination of circumstances occur, you will experience an unintentional discharge!

There is only one way you can prevent unintentional discharges when you have your gun in hand in an exciting environment:

Keep your trigger finger in the register position until you:

- Have a sight picture on a target that you want to shoot
- Have decided to fire and want the gun to discharge straightaway

I recommend the "universal cover mode" (depressed ready) for all situations where your gun is drawn, but you have not yet decided to fire. In the universal

Chapter 12: Accidental and Unintentional Discharge

cover mode, the handgun or longarm is held in a ready position, with the muzzle low enough to allow you to observe the entire situation and the trigger finger in register. In these situations, you should keep as much distance from the potential source of danger as the tactical situation permits. Getting close to dangerous people is usually contraindicated.

In potentially lethal confrontations, exciting intervals, prodigious physical exertion, physical contact with criminal suspects and the handling of guns under dynamic conditions are circumstances that should, of course, be avoided. When they are unavoidable, don't become a victim of your own gun handling. Handle your guns correctly. This nation doesn't need more inept people with guns. *This nation needs competent gunmen who don't have accidents and who don't miss.*

Chapter 13

Modes

Defensive firearms have four different modes: storage, transport, carry and engagement. A thorough understanding of firearms modes is necessary for any student of defensive shooting.

Safety and readiness are always mutually antagonistic. The more safe a gun is, the less ready. The more ready, the less safe. Any defensive firearm must be kept in a condition that is a reasonable compromise between the two extremes, commensurate with the circumstances and the job the gun is expected to do. Modes can then be changed, upgraded or downgraded, as changing circumstances warrant.

Storage mode

Storage mode is appropriate for weapons being prepared for non-accessible long-term storage, such as in a gun safe or any other storage situation where rapid access is *not* a requirement. In storage mode, the gun is unloaded and the magazine is removed or voided if it cannot be removed. All springs should be at rest so the hammer is down (dropped) on an empty chamber.

Transport mode

Transport mode is intended for weapons that are kept close at hand but not carried on the person, such as would be the case of a shotgun or rifle carried in a car. Since it is not being carried on the person, the weapon is not under the owner's direct control, but it is still intended to be readily accessible and available for defensive purposes on short notice. In transport mode, the chamber is empty. The bolt (slide) is all the way forward (in battery) and the hammer is down (the gun has been dry fired), as is the case with storage mode, but a fully charged magazine is inserted and locked in. The manual safety (if the weapon has one) is in the "off" position. The gun is thus inert, but it can be quickly rendered ready to fire by simply reciprocating the bolt or slide. With shotguns, transport mode is also called the "loader's safe" condition.

Carry mode

Carry mode is appropriate only if the weapon is being continuously carried on the person and is thus under constant, direct control. A pistol in a holster or a rifle or shotgun slung on a shoulder should be in carry mode. In carry mode, the weapon is immediately ready for use. *A round is in the chamber and a fully charged magazine is inserted and locked in.* The correct carry condition for defensive pistols that are designed for carrying is fully loaded with the manual safety (if the weapon has one) in the "on" position.

Since most shotguns do not have a military-specification manual safety, shotguns are not carried loaded. The same is true with most commercial rifles. Since these weapons are not carried with a round in the chamber, they must be loaded as they are mounted. *Thus, with most shotguns and some commercial rifles carry mode and transport mode are the same.*

Engagement mode

Engagement mode is the condition of the weapon when it is held at eye level, or mounted in the case of a longarm, pointed in the direction of a threat and may have to be fired at any instant. The only difference between carry mode and engagement mode with firearms equipped with a military-specification manual safety, is that the manual safety is pushed from the "on" position to the "off" position as one goes from the former to the latter.

With most handguns, carry mode and engagement mode are the same since nothing need be done to the pistol (except pressing the trigger) in order to get it to fire when there is a round chambered. With pistols equipped with a manual safety, such as the Colt/Browning system guns, the manual safety must be pushed off in order to go from carry mode to engagement mode.

At the end of a day of training, be it with handguns, rifles, shotguns or several weapons, I ask all students what condition or mode they want their weapons in as they prepare to leave the range. The important point here is that it is solely the student's decision within certain parameters. When weapons are put away, longarms are first. Handguns (one's last-ditch defense) are always the last to be put away except for those who regularly carry pistols concealed. Those individuals holster their weapons (in carry mode) and leave the range that way.

Those who do not choose to carry their pistols off the range in a holster will

Chapter 13: Modes

secure them in a case in either storage or transport mode.

The purpose for "mode drill" is to help students to organize their thinking so that poor judgment and blunders, born of confusion, can be reduced.

Chapter 14

Defensive Handgun Operator Systems

There are, for most practical purposes, only two basic types of defensive handguns:

- Revolvers
- Autoloaders

Among revolvers, there are only two types:

- Single-action
- Double-action

There are three basic divisions within the autoloading pistol category:

- Colt/Browning system
- Continuous-motion system
- Trigger-cocking system

Within the trigger-cocking system, there are three subcategories:

- Two-stage decocking
- Single-stage decocking
- Self-decocking (DAO)

Double-action revolver system. These trigger-cocking guns can be manually cocked and then fired; however, manual cocking is contraindicated in most defensive shooting. Double-action revolvers are probably the easiest of the handguns to learn how to use and carry safely. Owing to their simplicity of operation, they are the least likely to discharge unintentionally. *Carelessness with firearms is a dependable recipe for catastrophe in every instance, but double-action revolvers tend to be more forgiving (to a point) of negligent handling than are most autoloaders.* Though waning in popularity, the double-action revolver is still an excellent defensive handgun and will be the first choice of many people for a long time to come.

Single-action revolver system. These guns are now obsolete and are, for the most part, no longer suitable for carrying or defensive shooting. There was a time when they represented the state of the art but they are now better suited to museums than to carrying for defense. *They are revolvers with no trigger-cocking provision.* The hammer has to be manually cocked for each shot. They are still manufactured, but there are none that I recommend for serious use.

Colt/Browning autoloader system. This system is currently found only on the Colt autoloaders, various Colt clones and the Browning Hi-Power. This once-popular system is rapidly losing ground to the other autoloaders. These guns are single-action, slide-cocking but not trigger cocking. They feature a two-position manual safety mounted on the left side of the slide. Although it is technically possible to manually cock the hammer, there is no decocking lever and thus no safe way to lower it on a live round, so *keeping the gun with the hammer forward on a loaded chamber is not considered a viable option, as manually lowering the hammer onto a chambered live round is not considered a prudent or safe procedure.* In fact, the only prudent and recommended procedure for carrying this gun is with a live round chambered, the hammer cocked and the manual safety on.

Continuous motion autoloader system. Heckler & Koch (H&K) is the sole manufacturer of guns featuring this system. These guns are slide-cocking and squeeze-cocking but not trigger-cocking. The hammer is cocked and decocked via the motion of a "squeeze-cocker" which is a spring-loaded lever integrated with the front of the grip. There is no manual safety. These pistols are no longer marketed in the United States. There are many still in circulation, but their popularity has diminished greatly.

Trigger-cocking autoloaders with two-stage manual decocking. This system is found mainly on Smith & Wesson, Beretta and Ruger pistols. Mechanically, various brands may be slightly different but from the standpoint of the operator, they are identical. These guns are trigger cocking and feature a two-position manual decocking lever mounted on the rear of the slide (usually featuring dual levers, one on each side of the pistol) and correctly operated via the user's strong-side thumb. With most of these guns, the operator pushes the decocking lever down to decock and sterilize, and up to enable. *The lever must be manually pushed in both directions.* These guns are trigger-cocking and slide-cocking.

Smith & Wesson, Beretta and Ruger autoloaders have traditionally used the trigger-cocking two-stage decocking system, but recently they have all introduced their pistols in single-stage decocking (like the SIG) and self-decocking

Chapter 14: Defensive Handgun Operator Systems

(like the Glock) versions. In addition, the magazine safety, long standard equipment with Smith & Wesson autoloaders, is no longer a feature on some of their pistols, namely their Sigma and P99 lines. Beretta has also introduced several pistols in .380 Auto caliber that are two-stage decocking, but the decocking lever is reversed from the conventional pattern. That is, pushing the lever up decocks and sterilizes while pushing the lever down enables the gun to fire.

Trigger-cocking autoloaders with single-stage decocking. We see this system on SIG, Walther, Taurus and certain new models of the Smith & Wesson, Beretta and Ruger autoloaders. This system features a spring-loaded decocking lever, but the lever cannot be used to sterilize the gun. The lever must be manually pushed only in one direction (down), but it cannot be maintained there. It springs back as soon as it is released. Therefore, the user pushes the lever down to decock, then simply releases it and lets it reposition itself back to the enabled position. There is no manual safety aspect associated with it and therefore no manual safety with this system.

To accomplish this, Beretta, Ruger and recently Smith and Wesson have simply spring loaded the slide-mounted decocking lever on their two-stage decocking pistols. From outward appearances, the two models otherwise look identical. Other manufacturers (SIG) have mounted the single-stage decocking lever on the pistol's frame, but this sometimes places the decocking lever and the slide-release lever in such close proximity that the user can confuse the two.

Trigger-cocking autoloaders that are self-decocking. A relative newcomer on the handgun scene, this system has become enormously popular in a short time and is probably destined to be the most prevalent of all the systems. Glock is currently the major manufacturer of guns using this system, however, Smith & Wesson, Beretta, Ruger, Taurus and SIG have now introduced versions of their autoloader line using this system. Springfield Armory has introduced its XD series, which looks like and works like a Glock. This system is a trigger-cocking autoloader with no manual safety (except for the Beretta which features a safety on some models). Although these pistols are technically slide-cocking, the hammer automatically decocks itself every time the slide goes forward, so every shot (first shot and all subsequent shots) are via the trigger-cocking mode. In other words, it is self-decocking or automatic decocking. It is a system that is simple and easy to learn with a minimum of things to remember.

An additional benefit inherent to self-decocking autoloading pistols with an external hammer is that the hammer actually helps push the slide forward.

This enhances feeding reliability and positive ejection.

In my opinion, the trigger-cocking autoloaders are the best choice for most people seeking a suitable defensive handgun. The trigger-cocking system provides an acceptable compromise between the speed of the first shot and the user's control over the trigger during subsequent shots. It must be remembered that, in the vast majority of times a defensive handgun is brandished and pointed in the direction of a criminal suspect, *it will ultimately not be fired.* This is because the presence and posture of the gun often modifies a prudent suspect's behavior in a way that makes shooting unnecessary. That is, of course, a desired result.

A defensive handgun must, of course, be designed so that it can be fired rapidly, but it must also be designed so that the user can control it precisely, even under stressful circumstances. The venerable Colt/Browning system offers the user a fast first shot, but it is difficult to start to press the trigger on these guns, then subsequently change your mind and not fire.

Defensive handgun manufacturers have coined the term double-action only or DAO to describe self-decocking autoloading pistols. It is an awkward and illogical term that has created a great deal of confusion among new gun owners, but we're probably stuck with it.

The two terms double and single-action are so muddled that they have now become inexplicit and virtually useless for the purpose of any accurate description of an autoloading handgun operating system. The terms are still useful only in differentiating revolver types. Indeed, save when talking about revolvers, experts now avoid these terms altogether.

These two terms first came into use in the nineteenth century. Before the invention of the first trigger-cocking revolvers, all revolvers had been single-action; that is, they only fired one way. The hammer was first manually drawn back using your thumb until it locked into the full-cock position, then the trigger was pressed allowing the hammer to fall forward, and the gun to subsequently discharge. With the introduction of the first trigger-cocking revolvers came the term "double-action". It meant that the gun could still be fired in the conventional way involving manually cocking the hammer, but it could also be fired in a second way, simply by pulling the trigger when the hammer was forward. The two different methods of firing the pistol gave rise to the term double-action.

Lamentably, when these terms were later applied to the autoloading pistols, confusion burst forth. Since the terms double-action and trigger-cocking had

Chapter 14: Defensive Handgun Operator Systems

been so closely connected (with revolvers), people started to confuse the two terms and even use them interchangeably. But, they do not mean the same thing. For example, the Glock autoloading pistol is trigger-cocking, but it only fires one way and is hence also single-action. You see the problem. Today, trigger-cocking autoloaders are classified by the method of decocking, and, as stated above, the terms single and double-action have been dropped altogether.

I should add that single-action revolvers, because they are difficult to use in the modern defensive context and slow to reload, are now obsolete and will be mentioned in this text only in passing. Indeed, even with double-action revolvers or any trigger-cocking handgun, nearly *all defensive shooting is done via the trigger-cocking mode* because manually cocking the hammer takes too much time and, with the hammer cocked, the trigger is sensitized and the gun is thus prone to unintentional discharges. *Manual cocking is thus contraindicated for nearly all defensive shooting.*

Advantages of double-action revolvers

- Revolvers are simple for the average person to understand and learn to operate safely.

- Revolvers are forgiving of careless handling and are unlikely to precipitate accidental discharges and other mishaps when issued to large numbers of officers of widely varying intelligence, disposition, ability, motivation and knowledge.

- Revolvers are not ammunition sensitive. Revolvers will fire any cartridge that can be chambered. Feeding is not a factor.

- The gun itself is inexpensive and only a short time is needed for initial familiarization.

- Revolvers can be properly maintained at the user level without disassembly. In fact, disassembly at the user level is discouraged.

- Either the Isosceles or the Weaver stance will work well.

- Revolvers are inoffensive and conventional in appearance.

Disadvantages of double-action revolvers

- Stoppages with revolvers are difficult and inconvenient to remedy in the field. In most cases the gun is rendered impotent in the short term.

- Revolvers are temperamental and not particularly durable. Continuous neglect and lack of maintenance will readily render the gun inoperable. In addition, revolvers are not tolerant of dirty or rough environments, nor are they designed for heavy use. Armorer level maintenance is required every five thousand rounds or so.
- Revolvers have a small ammunition capacity, usually no more than six rounds.
- Reloading is slow, awkward and uncertain.
- Revolvers are bulky for their ammunition capacity and power.
- Revolvers cannot be sterilized. If they are loaded, they will fire.

Advantages of self-decocking autoloading pistols

- Self-decocking autoloading pistols are simple for the average person to understand and learn to operate safely, not as simple as a revolver, but adequate.
- Most stoppages can be quickly and easily remedied in the field. The gun can usually be returned to service in a few seconds.
- Autoloaders are more durable and less environmentally sensitive than are revolvers. Autoloaders are designed for military use and are thus robust and tolerant of dirty and rough environments as well as lack of maintenance and heavy use. Armorer-level maintenance is rarely required.
- Autoloaders have a large ammunition capacity, larger than most revolvers.
- Reloading is fast and reliable.
- Autoloaders are compact and flat, less bulky than revolvers and easier to carry concealed.

Disadvantages of self-decocking autoloading pistols

- Self-decocking autoloaders are not as forgiving of careless handling as are revolvers. Correct handling procedures are critical. Accidents will predictably occur among those who are not trained adequately.
- Autoloaders are ammunition sensitive. Ammunition must feed reliably and must be powerful enough to dependably cycle the action.

Chapter 14: Defensive Handgun Operator Systems

- An autoloader is usually more expensive than a revolver of similar size and caliber. Initial familiarization takes longer.

- *Autoloaders are not a good choice for the mechanically inept.* Field stripping into major components is required for adequate user-level maintenance. Correct reassembly is, of course, required before the pistol can be returned to service.

- The Weaver stance is best. Because of the shape of the grip and other factors, the isosceles stance is awkward and difficult to correctly assume.

- Autoloaders are more militaristic in appearance than are revolvers, although autoloading pistols are now much more accepted by the public than they were just a few years ago.

- Self-decocking autoloaders cannot be sterilized (in most cases). If they are loaded, they will fire.

Additional advantages of all autoloaders

- Colt/Browning system and continuous motion autoloaders are fast on the first shot, faster than any trigger-cocking pistol.

- Manually decocking autoloaders are trigger-cocking for the first shot, but are fast on follow-up shots, since the hammer remains cocked.

- Two-stage, manually decocking autoloaders can be sterilized, as can Colt/Browning system and continuous motion system autoloaders.

Additional disadvantages of all autoloaders

- Vastly more complex learning process. More controls and critical sequences to become familiar with. More training required. Even among the well trained, accidents are still more common with these pistols than with revolvers or self-decocking autoloaders.

- Unforgiving of careless handling and incorrect procedure. These pistols may be suitable for professional gunmen, but are surely not a good choice for the casual gun owner. *They are a particularly bad choice of the careless, inept and nonchalant.*

Comparison of Handgun Systems

	Speed/accuracy	Ease of operation	Safety
DA Revolver	Fair	Superior	Excellent
Colt/Browning Autoloader	Excellent	Good	Fair
Continuous Motion Autoloader	Superior	Good	Poor
Two-stage Decocking Autoloader	Good	Poor	Fair
Single-stage Decocking Autoloader	Good	Fair	Fair
Self-decocking Autoloader	Good	Superior	Good

Chapter 15

Cycle of Operation and Parts

All defensive handguns have a cycle of operation. A revolver uses a revolving cylinder to successively position individually chambered rounds in line with the barrel. The mechanical energy necessary to rotate the cylinder and cock the hammer is provided by your finger as you pull the trigger. As you pull the trigger, the hammer is drawn back and the cylinder simultaneously rotates in order to bring the next chamber in line with the barrel. Just before the hammer reaches its release point, the cylinder reaches its exact alignment with the barrel (indexes) and is locked in position. The hammer is subsequently released and falls forward. You must then fully release the trigger prior to pulling it again for the next shot. Under spring pressure, the trigger returns to its original position and the cycle is ready to repeat itself.

The autoloading pistol's cycle of operation taps a small portion of the energy released during the discharge of the gun. This energy is converted into mechanical motion, the objective of which is to extract the just-fired cartridge case from the chamber, eject it from the pistol, replace it with a fresh (live) cartridge (held in reserve in a spring-loaded magazine), recock the hammer (on slide-cocking guns) and reposition all other internal parts so that the gun may be fired again immediately. The slide is the part of the weapon that moves back and forth to accomplish all of the above. All autoloaders harness a portion of the energy released during firing to impart rearward motion to the slide. In some cases, it is impulse inertia; in other cases it is gas inertia. The effect is the same. The slide moves backward and then forward, making the gun ready to be fired again and the cycle of operation is poised to be repeated.

The entire cycle of operation is accomplished within a fraction of a second and, upon discharge, the weapon is instantly ready to fire again. However, all steps are critical and must happen in the correct sequence. Any interruption in any of the steps and the gun will experience a stoppage.

The cycle of operation for autoloading pistols has seven steps.

1. Feeding

2. Chambering

3. **Locking**

4. **Firing**

5. **Unlocking**

6. **Extraction**

7. **Ejection**

Feeding. While the slide moves forward under spring pressure, the bolt face contacts the top round in the magazine and forces it out of the magazine and forward into the chamber. The extractor claw positions itself on the cartridge's extraction ring.

Chambering. The round is pushed all the way into the chamber until it "headspaces."

Locking. The gun's mechanism locks the round in the chamber by mechanically locking the barrel and slide together (battery), so that, while the propellant powder is burning and there is high pressure in the chamber and barrel, the chamber will be sealed and remain so until after the bullet has progressed all the way down the barrel and out the muzzle. After the bullet exits, the pressure is relieved as excess compressed gases are vented into the air. If the chamber were to unlock before the bullet reached the muzzle, or if the gun were to fire before locking was complete, the rear of the cartridge case would rupture and hot gases and molten particles of cartridge case would spew forth from the rift between the barrel and the slide and cause the gun to malfunction and possibly injure the shooter or others nearby. All modern autoloaders have a mechanical safeguard, usually an automatic disconnector that prevents the gun from firing if locking has not taken place or is incomplete.

The forgoing describes pistol actions that employ a mechanical locking system. However, with some pistols the necessary momentary adhesion of the slide and the barrel is accomplished in other ways. Examples are the gas-retarded blowback system and the unretarded blowback system. Both are uncommon in defensive pistols chambered for serious calibers.

The typical autoloading pistol will fire when its slide is slightly out of battery (less than an eighth of an inch), but this often results in a misfire and a second blow of the hammer or the invocation of immediate action (stoppage reduction) is then required to get the pistol firing again.

Firing. The movement of the trigger mechanically releases the hammer from

Chapter 15: Cycle of Operation and Parts

its cocked position (the trigger also draws the hammer back to the cocked position on trigger-cocking pistols). The hammer then falls and strikes the firing pin. In turn, the firing pin goes forward and strikes the primer in the chambered cartridge. The primer compound burns and ignites the main reserve of powdered propellant in the cartridge case. The bullet is forced forward by the expanding gases behind it and begins to engage the rifling in the barrel and is subsequently accelerated down the length of the barrel and out of the muzzle.

Some pistols don't have traditional hammers. Instead, they employ a spring-loaded firing pin, called a "striker."

Unlocking. After the bullet has cleared the muzzle, the chamber is mechanically unsealed; the barrel and slide separate and free movement of the slide is restored.

Extraction. The slide is forced backward, compressing the recoil spring. The extractor (attached to the slide) withdraws the expended cartridge case from the chamber and continues to pull it backward. On slide-cocking autos, the rearward movement of the slide also recocks the hammer.

Ejection. The expended cartridge case continues to be drawn backward by the movement of the slide until it is pulled into a metal spike called the ejector. The ejector strikes the case on the opposite side from the extractor. The case then rotates out of the extractor claw and flies through the ejection port and free from the gun.

The entire cycle of operation takes place very rapidly, in the neighborhood of a thirtieth of a second. Since even the fastest shooters can seldom physically manipulate their trigger finger fast enough to cause the pistol to fire at a rate in excess of six rounds per second, one usually need not worry about outrunning the gun with rapid shots. The cycle of operation will have long since been completed before the shooter is able to even begin the finger movements necessary for a second shot.

Definitions

Double-action only. DAO is an awkward industry term applied to autoloading pistols that are self-decocking. Self-decocking pistols need not be manually decocked, because they decock themselves automatically every time the slide goes forward.

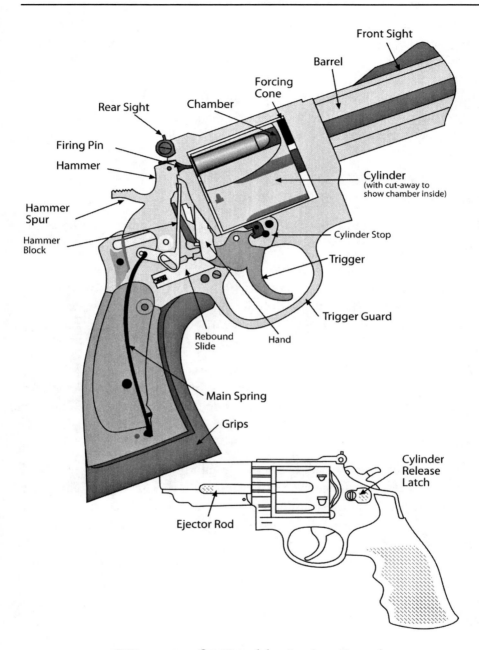

Diagram of a Double-Action Revolver

Chapter 15: Cycle of Operation and Parts

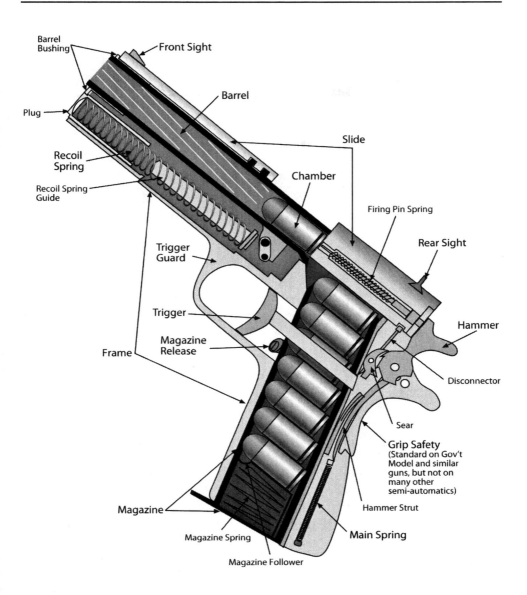

Diagram of an Autoloading Pistol

Barrel. The barrel is the discharging tube of a gun. The barrel is directly forward of, and continuous with, the chamber. Pistol and rifle barrels have spiral grooves on the interior surface, called "rifling," for the purpose of spinning the bullet as it is propelled forward. Gyroscopic stability is thus imparted to the bullet by the rifling, causing the bullet to retain its orientation and line of travel, predictably following a smooth trajectory, rather than an erratic path. Shotgun barrels usually do not have rifling and are thus called "smoothbore."

Battery. Battery is the full forward and locked position of the slide on an autoloading pistol or the full forward and locked position of the bolt of an autoloading rifle or shotgun. When the slide or bolt is thus "in battery" it is all the way forward and locked. When not locked forward, the bolt is "out of battery."

If the slide is more than an eighth of an inch out of battery, a disconnector mechanism on most autoloading pistols will prevent the hammer from falling even if the trigger is pressed. However, the trigger mechanism will often allow the hammer to fall when the slide is only slightly out of battery. When such "out-of-battery" hammer blows occur, the resulting dent in the chambered cartridge's primer is often light and off center and the cartridge often thus fails to fire (misfire). A quick second press of the trigger will usually fire the recalcitrant round, because, when the hammer falls the first time, it pushes the slide the rest of the way forward.

Most manually-decocking pistols will permit such a second trigger pull and subsequent second hammer fall. Most self-decocking pistols will not. Where a second drop of the hammer is not possible, the slide must be manually recycled. This will reset the firing mechanism, extract and jettison the suspicious round and chamber a fresh round, thus rendering the pistol, once again, immediately ready to fire.

Chamber. The chamber of a firearm is the place where the cartridge is held as it is fired. The barrel is directly forward of, and continuous with, the chamber. Revolvers have a revolving cylinder that contains several individual chambers (usually six). Autoloading handguns have only one chamber. A fresh cartridge is fed into it with every shot by means of the reciprocating action of the slide, known as the cycle of operation. *A gun is considered loaded if a live cartridge is chambered.* If a cartridge is not chambered, the gun is not considered to be loaded, even if there are still cartridges within the gun itself, such as would be the case in an autoloading pistol that has its slide forward, the chamber vacant, but a charged magazine inserted into the magazine well. *Loaded guns are*

Chapter 15: Cycle of Operation and Parts

immediately ready to fire. Unloaded guns are not.

Clear. A gun that is both unloaded and has all other ammunition removed from it is called "clear." Guns that have been cleared (with all springs at rest) are in "storage mode."

Decock. Decocking is the act of causing the hammer of a pistol to fall from the full-cock position to a safe forward position, without the weapon discharging. Once a manually-decocking autoloading pistol has been fired, there has to be some reliable way of getting the cocked hammer forward without a discharge so that the gun can be quickly and safely returned to the holster or so it can be held on a criminal suspect for long periods without the danger of an accidental discharge. These handguns are designed to be manually decocked quickly and safely *without having to touch either the hammer or the trigger.* Manual decocking is accomplished via the manipulation of a decocking lever or via the relaxing of the squeeze-cocker, depending upon the pistol being used. The manual decocking lever is either single stage or two stage. Manual decocking on those guns that require it should always take place before:

- *Moving with the firearm*
- *Holding a suspect at gunpoint*
- *Reholstering*

Decocking is automatic in some handguns such as the double-action only (DAO) system. On these guns, the decocking process is self-operating, with no lever to be manipulated.

On other autoloading pistols, such as those of the Colt/Browning System, there is no manual decocking provision at all because these pistols are designed to be carried with the hammer at full cock. Using one's fingers to attempt to lower the hammer on one of these pistols is a very treacherous proposition, as there is no fail-safe or convenient way to do it, and it requires that both the trigger and the hammer be touched at the same time. Thus, the *manual decocking of Colt/Browning System pistols is not recommended, nor is it necessary.* The maneuver is only attempted by those who do not understand the Colt/Browning system.

With SIG autoloaders, when the gun is manually decocked, the hammer does not go all the way forward as it does with most of the other autoloaders. It stops in the "register" position (which looks like half cock). This is correct, and it is the way this particular system operates. Not all SIG autoloading pistols are manually decocking. Recently SIG has introduced their line of pistols in self-decocking (DAO) versions. Even more recently, SIG has introduced the "K" trigger system, which is also self-decocking, but features a trigger that is shorter and lighter than those on their first DAO pistols.

With Smith & Wesson, Beretta and Ruger autoloaders, the hammer actually drops all the way forward, as in firing, but the weapon is mechanically prevented from discharging because the firing pin is blocked. Just the same, be careful where the muzzle is pointed during the decocking process. Defective weapons have been known to discharge during manual decocking. The phenomenon is rare, but it has happened.

It is important on all manually-decocking pistols to use the decocking lever and never try to lower the hammer by holding it back with your fingers, then pressing the trigger and attempting to slowly ease the hammer forward. *This unsound procedure is a literal invitation to an accidental discharge.* In addition, in the case of certain (old) SIG models, the gun may be rendered not drop safe.

Decocking lever. Also called the decocker, the decocking lever is mounted either on the side of the frame or the side of the slide of manually-decocking autoloading pistols. The lever is usually on the left side, but many models feature ambidextrous (one on each side) decocking levers. The decocking lever can be either spring-loaded, hence single stage or it can be two stage and thus have to be manually pushed in both directions. In the latter case, when the decocking lever is in the down position, it renders the pistol sterile in addition to decocking it. Thus, some have suggested that the decocking lever on these particular guns is also a safety lever. Indeed, one may call it a safety lever but it is difficult to use it as such. This is because the motion of pushing the lever up to the enabled position quickly with one's thumb (the only finger that will be able to reach it) is awkward and untrustworthy. Thus, the vast majority of people who carry these pistols do so with pistol in the engagement mode (which, for these guns, is also the carry mode) rather than with the decocking lever in the down position which renders the pistol sterile. The "sterile carry," as it is called, has few advocates.

To further confuse matters, Beretta, for one, has manufactured two-stage manually-decocking pistols with the decocking lever positions reversed. That is, pushing the lever up decocks and sterilizes. Pushing it down enables the gun to fire.

Disconnector. All the modern autoloaders have a mechanical linkage, usually called a disconnector, which prevents the pistol from firing until the slide

Chapter 15: Cycle of Operation and Parts

is fully in battery. This is a passive safety system that insures that the gun will not fire if the barrel and slide are not locked together. It also prevents the gun from firing more than one shot for each pull of the trigger. That is, the trigger must be released to the point of reset before it can be pressed again for another shot. The effect is to prevent the pistol from firing full-auto.

Enabled. A gun that is "enabled" is in "engagement mode" and is ready to be fired. The manual safety, if the weapon has one, is in the "off" position. "Enabled" is the opposite of "sterile."

Ejector. The ejector is little more than a stud or spike placed in the path of the expended cartridge case as the case is drawn backward by the extractor. When the rear of the cartridge strikes the ejector, the whole cartridge or cartridge case is pried loose from the extractor and flung free of the pistol.

Ejection port. The ejection port is an oblong opening cut into the side or top of the slide. It provides an open path for the ejected cartridge case to clear the gun and fall to the ground.

Extractor. All autoloaders have extractors. The extractor is usually a spring-loaded lever with a hook or claw on the forward end. The extractor fits into the slide and the claw positions itself in the extraction ring on the rear of the chambered cartridge. Most autoloading pistol cartridges have an extraction ring cut into the base. The claw hooks into the extraction ring during feeding and when the slide subsequently moves backwards, it pulls the cartridge backwards and out of the chamber.

Firing pin. The firing pin of any firearm is a spring-loaded metal shaft with a point at the front end. When the gun fires, the firing pin is struck from behind by the hammer and subsequently moves forward striking the primer of the chambered cartridge, causing ignition and ultimately the discharge of the bullet from the barrel. On most pistols, the hammer and firing pin are separate parts. With some pistols, such as Glocks, the hammer and firing pin are combined in one continuous unit called the "striker."

On all modern reputable pistols, the firing pin is locked in place and unable to move forward unless and until the trigger is pressed and held to the rear. Such a firing pin locking system is necessary to render the pistol drop safe.

Half cock. Some guns, particularly autoloading pistols, have a half-cock notch on the hammer. When the hammer is drawn back manually, it can come to rest in a position between all the way forward (down) and full cock (cocked).

This half-cock notch is provided as a redundant safety mechanism, the purpose of which is to intercept the hammer and prevent it from falling all the way forward in the unlikely event it is unintentionally jarred off the full-cock notch. *Handguns that have a half-cock notch should not be carried or stored with the hammer in half-cock.* Half-cock was not intended as a carry option and should not be used as such.

Some have advocated the half-cock hammer position as a valid carry option for the trigger-cocking autoloaders. Some holsters carry these guns in such a way that the decocking lever can be inadvertently pushed down as the pistol is holstered. These guns are correctly carried with the decocking lever in the up (enabled) position. This can be a dangerous condition because the operator, assuming that the decocking lever is up, may try to shoot suddenly and discover too late that the gun won't fire because, when the decocking lever is in the down position, it renders the pistol sterile.

One way to address this problem is to carry this particular pistol with the hammer in half-cock. This is accomplished by manually drawing the hammer back to the half-cock notch after the weapon has been loaded. With the hammer in half-cock, the decocking lever is more difficult to move out of position and will thus resist accidental migration. In addition, the half-cock position of the hammer shortens the trigger movement necessary for the first shot. This procedure is not something that should be considered unless there is a real problem with the manual decocker inadvertently migrating to the down position as the gun is carried in the holster.

A particularly dangerous maneuver is trying to manually position a hammer in half-cock that has had its spur removed. It is usually impossible without first pressing the trigger in order to start the hammer backwards. An obvious invitation to an accidental discharge, this routine is strongly discouraged.

There may be some confusion here when we discuss SIG autoloaders. As mentioned before, the correct decocking of a SIG actually fixes the hammer in what appears to be a half-cock position (called "register"). This is as it should be. The thing to remember is that *using the decocking lever will decock the gun properly and position the hammer correctly. Manually manipulating the hammer, before or after decocking, will likely put it in an incorrect position or cause an accidental discharge.*

With some autoloaders, there is a rare, but well-documented, condition called "false half-cock." The edge of the sear actually rests on the lip of the half-cock notch rather than the shelf itself. The hammer appears to be somewhere between full and half-cock. In this condition, the slightest jarring can cause the hammer to slip off and fall all the way forward causing a discharge (on older guns which do not have a trigger/firing pin interlock). *False half-cock usually occurs as a direct result of the operator manually manipulating the hammer.* I have seen cases of false half-cock documented only on the older Colt/Browning Autoloader System guns but it may be possible with other guns as well.

Hammer. All handguns have hammers, although the hammer and firing pin are amalgamated into a striker in some. All handguns require that the hammer be cocked (drawn back against spring pressure) prior to firing. Sometimes the hammer is external and exposed and sometimes it is internal and contained within the confines of the gun itself. The hammer is a spring-loaded lever or linear striker that is first cocked, then released and allowed to fall forward. When it does, it falls on the firing pin that, in turn, goes forward and dents the primer of a chambered cartridge. The primer compound then ignites, burns and thus kindles the main reserve of powdered propellant. The powdered propellant burns and generates gases that rapidly expand and thus generate sufficient pressure to force the projectile from the cartridge mouth, into the barrel and ultimately out of the muzzle. The firing pin may be integral with the hammer itself, or separate.

No firearm can discharge unless the hammer (striker) has first been cocked. The hammer can be cocked in any one of four different ways:

- Manual-cocking
- Trigger-cocking
- Slide-cocking
- Squeeze-cocking

On some guns, the hammer can be cocked manually, via your thumb. Single-action revolvers, for example, can only be fired via manual cocking. All other handguns need not be cocked manually in order to fire, although some may be at the option of the operator. *Manual cocking is almost always contraindicated in defensive shooting* because it takes too much time and sensitizes the weapon's trigger to the point that you cannot exercise adequate control over it.

The hammer on most autoloaders is recocked by the reciprocating action of the slide every time the slide moves through its cycle. The slide cycles automatically every time the weapon is fired. Thus, the hammer is recocked or slide-cocked every time the weapon fires and every time the slide is reciprocated manually. On some autoloaders, the hammer remains in full cock after the slide reciprocates. On others, the hammer automatically drops forward or into a halfway (register) position.

On trigger-cocking handguns (revolvers and autoloaders), the hammer can also be cocked by pulling of the trigger. Pulling the trigger on these handguns draws back (cocks) and automatically releases the hammer, thus discharging the weapon. This is referred to as the trigger-cocking mode of firing.

In continuous motion system autoloaders that are equipped with a squeeze-cocker, the hammer is cocked (and decocked) via the motion of a spring-loaded squeeze-cocking lever that is integrated into the front of the grip. Thus, squeezing the grip cocks the weapon and relaxing the grasp decocks it.

Loaded. *A firearm is loaded only when there is a live round in the chamber(s).* The terms "loaded" and "armed" mean the same thing. Magazines, be they integral with the gun or removable, are not "loaded." They are "charged." One charges the magazine then loads the gun. Likewise, magazines are not unloaded. They are "voided."

Magazine. In an autoloading pistol, the magazine is usually a removable spring-loaded rectangular container that holds the reserve of cartridges. The spring is compressed below a follower that pushes up on the bottom round. The magazine fits within the grip of the weapon (called the "magazine well") and is locked in place. Loading an autoloader involves inserting a charged magazine (a magazine filled with live cartridges) up into the magazine well until it locks in place. The slide then must be manually pulled all the way back and released. As it springs forward and ultimately into battery, it will strip the top round off the magazine and whisk it into the chamber. With a round now chambered, the gun is loaded. Remember that most autoloaders will fire the chambered round, even if the magazine has been removed. Therefore, *simply removing the magazine does not unload an autoloading pistol.*

Pistol magazines are charged manually, one round at a time, prior to being inserted into the pistol. In most cases, magazines cannot be charged while they are in the gun. Several charged magazines should be carried when one carries the gun, providing the means for expeditious reloading.

Some magazines, when charged with as many rounds as it is possible to get into them, will not feed the first round reliably because of excessive compression of the magazine spring. Check the owner's manual and charge the magazine only with the number of rounds indicated, even though it may be technically possible to exceed that number. In any event, *if it is not possible, with finger pressure alone, to push the first round down into the magazine at least a quarter of an inch, there is not sufficient clearance for reliable operation.* The magazine has one too many rounds in it.

Pistol magazines are not "clips." The term clip is often incorrectly used to refer to a pistol magazine, but it actually refers to a metal bracket used to hold cartridges in a row for the purpose of charging a magazine. Clips of ammunition are commonly used to charge military rifle magazines.

Most shotgun magazines and some pistol magazines are not removable. They are integral with the weapon itself and must be charged by inserting cartridges directly into them.

Magazines are an indispensable but perishable component of any autoloading pistol. They must be maintained and cared for just like the rest of the pistol. A watchful eye should be kept on their condition and when they wear out, they must be promptly replaced. In fact, it's a good idea to maintain a generous inventory of quality extra magazines for your pistol.

Magazine safety (magazine disconnect). Some pistols, such as most of the ones manufactured by Smith & Wesson, come equipped with a magazine safety. This is a passive safety device that prevents the pistol from firing a chambered round when there is no magazine inserted in the pistol. Thus, removing the magazine effectively sterilizes the weapon. If you have one of these guns, don't allow your dependence upon the magazine safety to lull you into sloppy gun-handling practices.

A magazine safety is a mechanical linkage that prevents the weapon from firing when the magazine is removed or not completely inserted, even if there is a round in the chamber. This may be a desirable feature in some situations, but it is definitely undesirable in others. Realizing this, manufacturers have made the device easily removable. The trouble is, it is impossible by merely looking at the pistol to tell whether the device is in place or not. So, *even if the pistol you are handling is supposed to have a magazine safety, do not assume that it does, or even if it does, that it is working properly.* It may not work, or it may have been removed. Most autoloading pistols do not come from the factory with magazine safeties.

The presumed advantages of having a magazine safety on a pistol are that it:

- Sterilizes the pistol when the magazine is removed. One possible use for this would be to enable uniformed police officers to temporarily disable their sidearms when closing to physically subdue a dangerous but unarmed suspect. In all but a few extraordinary cases, there is no equivalent need for a legally armed citizen.

- Enables a person to sterilize his pistol as he is physically fighting with an attacker and the attacker is about to gain control of the gun. Of course, any such attacker may bring his own gun and there is nothing to prevent him from picking up a jettisoned magazine and inserting it back into the pistol.

- Enables a gun owner to store his pistol with the magazine removed in an attempt to prevent an accidental discharge if an unauthorized person gets his hand on the gun. The weakness in this argument is that the mere separation of the magazine from the pistol is not an adequate safeguard against such a discharge, as anyone finding the unsecured pistol may also find the unsecured magazine and subsequently combine them, allowing the pistol to fire. A better precaution against unauthorized access is the proper and secure storage of both the pistol and magazine, in which case a magazine safety becomes a pointless redundancy.

Disadvantages of magazine safeties and reasons why many people disable this device:

- The pistol will not fire if a magazine is not fully seated. Often the magazine in a pistol that is being carried for defensive purposes is inadvertently unseated. This may occur upon first inserting the magazine or later if the magazine-release button is unintentionally depressed as the weapon is being carried. Under these circumstances, the pistol will not fire and the owner doesn't know it and won't find out until the pistol is desperately needed to defend his life. In a worst case, the unseated magazine may casually fall free from the pistol and thus not be immediately available for reseating.

- *The pistol is unavoidably inoperable during much of the reloading process.* In addition, if magazines are damaged or unavailable, the pistol becomes useless. Many consider this a formidable liability that negates any conjectured "safety" benefit of this device.

- Pistols equipped with magazines safeties require the insertion of an empty magazine in order for one to dry fire. To gain expertise with a pistol, "dry

Chapter 15: Cycle of Operation and Parts

practice" is mandatory. During such practice sessions, inserting a magazine introduces the possibility of introducing a charged magazine, instead of an empty one and thus the possibility of an unintended discharge. Inserting an empty magazine during dry practice also precludes manually cycling the slide to allow resetting the trigger.

- Magazine safeties can be circumvented. Inserting a finger into the empty magazine well of a magazine-safety-equipped pistol can activate the trigger and enable to gun to be fired. In addition, if one starts to press the trigger of a magazine-safety-equipped pistol, then removes the magazine, the pistol will fire.

- Dependence on a magazine safety can be and has been used to excuse sloppy and unsafe gun handling and storage. *Storing an unsecured pistol with a round chambered is unsafe and improper, whether the pistol is equipped with a magazine safety or not.* No exceptions to the gun-handling procedures enumerated herein are made for magazine-safety-equipped pistols.

In summary, magazine safeties provide precious little in the way of "safety" but do substantially jeopardize the health of the user. Accordingly, *numerous police agencies as well as the military have stipulated that their duty handguns not be equipped with magazine safeties,* and many independent gun owners as well have removed the device from their pistols.

Manual safety. A manual safety is a two-position lever or button that is intended to be physically operated by the shooter. When in the "on" position, the manual safety prevents the gun from firing even when the trigger is pressed. When in the "off" position, the gun is enabled and pressing the trigger will cause it to discharge normally. Thus, when guns equipped with manual safeties are carried on the person, the weapon is loaded, but the manual safety is in the "on" position. Some autoloading handguns come equipped with manual safety levers. Most do not. Revolvers do not have manual safeties. All longarms do have manual safeties.

All firearms are manufactured with multiple internal safety devices and mechanisms. Most of these are automatic (passive) and the operator of the firearm doesn't need to be concerned with them (so long as they are operating properly) as they operate without any conscious input. Therefore, all guns have "safeties," but most handguns do not have *manual* safeties. Just because a handgun does not have a manual safety, one should not conclude that the weapon is necessarily unsafe.

The one category of defensive handguns that is best known for having a manual safety is the Colt/Browning System pistol. Some Smith & Wesson, Beretta and Ruger pistols have a two-stage manual decocking lever that, when in the down position, prevents the weapon from firing and is therefore mistakenly considered by some to also be a manual safety. However, this lever is very difficult to use as a manual safety and indeed cannot satisfactorily be used as such by most people.

There are some pistols that combine a manual safety with a single-stage decocking lever. These pistols then actually have a three-position manual safety/decocking lever. Most operators find this arrangement too confusing for something intended for emergency service. This "three-position" system is thus highly not recommended for any serious pistol.

There is an important detail pertaining to manual safeties of which every gun owner should be aware. Manual safeties on military weapons meet a military specification. In particular, when in the "on" position, they render the gun drop safe by either physically blocking the firing pin or freezing the firing mechanism. *Military-specification manual safeties are not found on many commercial rifles and most commercial shotguns.* Manual safeties on the majority of commercial longarms are nothing more than a trigger block, so, when the safety is on, *these weapons are still not drop safe.*

On weapons that have them, manual safeties may be used, but they should never be depended upon nor used as a convenient pretext for careless gun handling. *Guns must always be handled correctly, whether the manual safety is "on" or not.*

Grip safety. A grip safety is a spring-loaded lever built into the rear of the pistol's grip. In the rest (extended) position, it blocks the trigger and prevents the weapon from firing even if the trigger is pulled and the manual safety is in the "off" position. When the shooting grip is acquired, the grip safety is simultaneously depressed and hence, deactivated. Therefore, grip safeties are passive safety devices that ostensibly prevent the weapon from firing until or unless the weapon's grip is firmly grasped by the shooter. A few autoloading pistols have grip safeties. Most do not. Most double-action revolvers also do not.

Some shooters with small hands do not consistently depress the grip safety, even when they establish a firm and otherwise correct grip on the pistol. These people should obviously choose a pistol that does not "feature" a grip safety.

Chapter 15: Cycle of Operation and Parts

Drop safety. Most autoloading pistols use a spring-loaded inertial firing pin. That is, the hammer does not directly drive the firing pin through the hole in the bolt face and into the primer of the chambered round. Rather, the hammer simply slaps the firing pin, causing it to fly forward on its own momentum. After it strikes the primer, spring pressure returns it to its withdrawn position. This means that, even if the hammer is resting directly on the firing pin, the other end of the firing pin usually will not be in contact with the primer of a chambered round. Thus, physically striking the hammer will generally not cause a discharge. Autoloaders without hammers, like the Glock, also use a system by which the firing pin (striker) does not "rest" while in contact with an active primer.

In addition, nearly all modern autoloaders have an internal trigger and firing pin interlock linkage that positively locks the firing pin into its withdrawn position until the last few millimeters of rearward trigger movement, making manipulation of the trigger the only way the gun can discharge. Therefore, *the gun will not discharge as a result of being dropped* (via drop-engendered firing pin momentum), regardless of its condition, how it lands, how far it falls or what kind of surface it falls on. That is the good news. The bad news is that *no gun, even today, is absolutely drop safe.* Dropping a gun, particularly on a hard surface, always entails some risk of accidental discharge.

There are some (now out of production) autoloaders that, although otherwise perfectly serviceable, have no passive trigger/firing-pin interlock and are therefore not strictly drop safe and thus can discharge if there is a round in the chamber and the weapon is dropped from a meter or so and lands on its muzzle on a hard surface. The inertia imparted to the firing pin by such a fall can be sufficient to dent the primer and discharge the gun. When it happens, the discharge itself is usually harmless because the bullet customarily disintegrates as soon as it strikes the hard surface. However, it is embarrassing, to say the least! These guns are (for the most part) no longer manufactured, but there are many still in service.

Sufficient momentum to discharge these weapons can be inadvertently imparted to the firing pin in other ways too. For example, it can happen when the slide free falls on a chambered round. This can be accomplished by dropping a round through the open ejection port when the slide is locked to the rear and there is no magazine inserted into the weapon. If the slide is then released, it free falls into battery. In the normal cycle of operation the slide does not free fall. As it goes forward after being forced to the rear by the recoil forces associated with firing, it strips the top round off the magazine on its way back forward. This consumes some mechanical energy and checks the slide's forward velocity. On the other hand, if the slide is allowed to free-fall from its rear position (no magazine inserted), it attains excessive velocity by the time it reaches battery. If there is a round chambered and the slide free falls, the gun (if it does not have a trigger/firing pin interlock) may discharge due to inertial movement of the firing pin.

Accordingly, *correct loading procedure for any autoloader does not involve dropping a live round into the chamber through the ejection port, then releasing the slide and allowing it to free-fall onto the chambered round.* This is a bad practice regardless of the vintage of the autoloader because, in addition to inviting an accidental discharge (on older guns that do not have a trigger/firing pin interlock), it rapidly wears metal off of the front of the extractor claw. After several iterations of this incorrect practice, the claw itself will break off. If this happens during a gunfight, the weapon will be out of action and you will then have to rely on your back-up gun.

The fact that most modern firearms are designed to be drop safe is taken advantage of during range training exercises. *If a student's grip on his gun slips, he is instructed to allow the gun to fall to the ground rather than trying to catch it as it falls.* It is usually safer to just allow it to fall to the ground, rather than grab for it as it is falling and take a chance on inadvertently touching the trigger before he has any control over the direction in which it is pointing.

Master grip. The "master grip" is the normal, strong-hand grip on the pistol's stocks. The master grip is the correct grip to use when the gun is handled for any reason. With the master grip in place, you can easily control the direction in which the pistol is pointed.

Muzzle. The muzzle of a firearm is the front face of the barrel, the discharging end of the weapon.

Slide. The slide on an autoloading handgun is the upper portion of the weapon that reciprocates back and forth on the weapon's frame as a part of the normal cycle of operation. All autoloaders have slides. Revolvers do not have slides.

The slide is spring-loaded via the recoil spring and its normal (rest) position is all the way forward, in battery. The slide can be manually drawn back against the resistance of the recoil spring, but it will spring forward as soon as it is released. On most autoloaders, there is a slide-lock lever that permits you to manually lock the slide in its rearward position for the purpose of inspecting

Chapter 15: Cycle of Operation and Parts

the chamber.

In addition, most autoloading pistols are designed in such a way that, when the last round is fired, the slide does not return to the forward position, but remains locked in the rear position, having been locked there by the follower in the empty magazine pushing up on the slide-lock lever. This is designed to serve as a signal that the gun must be reloaded if firing is to continue. Hence, when you notice during a firing string that the slide of your autoloader is locked to the rear, you may usually presume that the magazine is exhausted and the chamber is vacant. After the empty magazine is replaced with a fresh (fully-charged) one, the slide can be manually released and allowed to chamber a round as it goes forward, thus preparing the gun for the resumption of firing. As a practical matter, slide locking does not always work and sometimes the slide will go forward on an empty chamber after the last round is fired. This can be caused by worn parts, a dirty gun or underpowered ammunition.

Most autoloaders have a slide-release lever. When depressed, it releases the slide that has been locked to the rear, to spring forward. *In most cases the slide-lock lever and the slide-release lever are the same lever.* Pushing it up locks the slide to the rear (after it has been drawn back manually). Pushing it down releases the locked slide to spring forward. When locked to the rear, pulling the slide further to the rear and releasing it also disengages the slide lock lever and allows the slide to go forward.

When manually operating the slide on an autoloader, you must do it with authority. Manipulating the slide gently or hesitantly will lead to malfunctions. The slide must be grasped firmly, pulled to the rear forcefully and released briskly. *Good autoloading pistols are not harmed by positive aggressive handling.*

Sterile. "Sterile" is the opposite of "enabled." When a pistol in engagement mode is deliberately rendered temporarily unable to fire, it is said to be "sterilized." Thus, pushing the manual safety to the "on" position on a Colt/Browning System pistol sterilizes it. Similarly, pushing the decocking lever into the down position of most pistols equipped with a two-stage manual decocking lever renders those pistols sterile.

Trigger-cocking. Trigger-cocking refers to the ability of the handgun to be fired via pulling of the trigger when you start with a gun that has its hammer forward (uncocked). Guns with a trigger-cocking provision need not be manually cocked prior to firing. The action of the trigger cocks and releases the trigger, firing the first shot. This is a handy feature, because you can carry the gun with the hammer forward, yet you can fire quickly by simply drawing the gun and pulling the trigger.

On trigger-cocking autoloaders that are manually decocking, only the first shot is fired via the trigger-cocking mode. Once the first shot is fired (and the slide subsequently cycles) the second and all ensuing shots are fired from a cocked hammer. When you stop firing, the gun must be manually decocked, via the decocking lever, prior to reholstering.

On trigger-cocking autoloaders that are self-decocking (or Double Action Only), the first shot and *all subsequent shots* are fired via the trigger-cocking mode since the hammer decocks itself after every shot. You needn't worry about manual decocking prior to reholstering since the pistol does it automatically.

With double-action revolvers, the first and all subsequent shots are also fired via the trigger-cocking mode. Revolvers have no slide to recock the hammer.

Chapter 16

Defensive Handgun Mechanical Systems

There are five commonly used mechanical systems employed by autoloading pistols to effect the cycle of operation:

- Drop-lock system
- Tilt-barrel system
- Gas-retarded blowback system
- Rotary-barrel system
- Straight (unretarded) blowback system

The purpose of the brief mechanical locking together of the barrel and slide at discharge is to provide a short pause to allow the bullet to clear the muzzle and the internal gas pressure to thus be relieved as compressed gas is ultimately vented to the outside. If the barrel and slide started to separate with the bullet still in the barrel, the unsupported portion of the cartridge case would not be strong enough to contain the pressure within it and would thus rupture.

Most Beretta pistols and Taurus copies use the drop-lock system. H&K is the exclusive manufacturer of pistols using the gas-retarded blowback system, and they have dropped those pistols from their line. H&K's new line of pistols (P2000 series) features a tilt-barrel system. Beretta is currently the exclusive manufacturer of pistols using the rotary-barrel system. Straight blowback is a mechanical system restricted to low-pressure cartridges like the 380 Auto. All other defensive autoloading pistols use the tilt-barrel system, and this system is the most popular.

Drop-lock system. Of all those enumerated above, the drop-lock system is probably the most functionally reliable. In fact, Beretta pistols have displayed such a high level of reliability that this system was chosen by the Pentagon as the official pistol of the United States Armed Forces back in the 1980s.

The system uses two tandem dropping lugs, one on each side of the barrel. During the cycle of operation, the barrel moves straight backward during unlocking but does not tilt. The lugs rotate downward completing the unlocking stage. The slide is then free to move backward the rest of the way necessary to eject the fired case and clear the next round in the magazine. Because there are no locking recesses in the underside of the slide, as is the case with the tilt-barrel system, the slide is completely open on top, thus creating a very large ejection port. This feature all but eliminates failures to eject and related stoppages that plague some other guns with small ejection ports.

The disadvantage with this system centers around the thick steel slabs on each side of the slide flanking the barrel. They are necessary in order to provide sufficient stock in which to cut the locking recesses for the tandem lugs. The result is that the gun is necessarily heavy and wide, not slim like the tilt-barrel guns. Even the compact versions of this pistol are wide and relatively heavy. In 40S&W and smaller calibers, the system is at least workable. In the larger calibers, the pistol becomes so wide that it is no longer practical. This system is thus practically limited to nine millimeter and forty caliber rounds.

In actual practice, Beretta drop-lock pistols have, as noted above, shown themselves to be reliable. Unfortunately, they have not proven particularly durable. Intrinsic to the drop-lock system is excessive parts breakage, which makes these pistols difficult to keep running. They are relatively "high maintenance."

Tilt-barrel system. The tilt-barrel is the most common autoloading pistol mechanical system. The locking between the barrel and the slide is accomplished via lugs or locking surfaces machined into the top of the barrel. These are mated to locking recesses or surfaces machined into the underside of the slide in some cases, into the ejection port in others. Obviously, in order for the barrel to lock to and unlock from the slide, the barrel has to pivot or tilt downward. During firing, the slide and barrel, locked together, move backward slightly until the bullet has cleared the barrel. Then, the rear portion of the barrel tilts downward, unlocking from the slide and allowing the slide to move the rest of the way back. The real advantage is that these pistols are slim, even in the larger calibers, making them eminently suitable for concealed carrying.

There are two variations of the tilt-barrel system: the internal-lock and the external-lock. The differences between them deserve mention.

The internal-lock is the older of the two and is found on Colt/Browning System pistols and on some Smith & Wesson pistols. The locking lugs on the top of the barrel and the corresponding locking recesses on the under side of the slide

Chapter 16: Defensive Handgun Mechanical Systems

are all internal. The result is a rounded slide and a slim contour.

Glock, SIG, S&W Sigma, XD and Ruger pistols feature an external-locking, tilt-barrel system, where the locking surfaces on the barrel and the slide are external and exposed to the outside. The external-lock system is the better of the two from the standpoint of functional reliability because dirt and grime that get into the locking surfaces and into the locking area are free to fall away (or be wiped away) directly to the outside. With the internal-lock system, dirt build up can cause a weapon malfunction, due to the fact that the dirt has no place to go and must be cleaned out manually. Of course, competent weapon maintenance will prevent most malfunctions anyway, but I believe the external-lock system has a distinct advantage in this regard over the internal-locking methodology.

On the other side of the ledger, the internal-locking systems tend to have a curved slide and chamber area and are thus nice for carrying, because of the smooth and gently curved crown of the slide. The external-locking systems need a generous linear contact surface for positive functioning and thus tend to have slides and chamber areas that are square and blocky.

Gas-retarded blowback system. The gas-retarded blowback system is sometimes called gas-delayed blowback. This system actually harnesses some of the high-pressure gases while they are still in the barrel to retard the rearward movement of the slide until the bullet clears the barrel. There is no mechanical locking mechanism between the barrel and the slide, and the barrel is fixed and does not move at all. The slide movement with this system is violent and the ejected cases are thus flung far from the gun. *Because of the fixed barrel, these guns are the most inherently accurate of all the autoloading pistols.*

It is possible to make a gun extremely compact using this system, and these guns are also functionally reliable, but the gases do tend to foul the mechanism and one must do a very good job of keeping this gun clean or it will not continue to function dependably. In addition, the gas-tap hole in the barrel will rapidly become plugged if non-jacketed ammunition is used. Further, the gas system generates a lot of heat, very quickly. *Under rapid fire, these little guns get hot fast;* so hot, in fact, you may not be able to continue holding the gun! This constitutes a significant drawback.

With this system, the chamber has many parallel, longitudinal flutes cut into its inner surface. The purpose is to allow high-pressure gas to seep in and break the case loose in preparation for extraction. Ejected cases are thus characteristically marked with longitudinal grooves and gas smudging, and their reloadability is thus diminished.

Rotary-barrel system. Beretta, wanting to build compact guns and frustrated by the limitations of the drop-lock system, has introduced autoloading pistols built on their new rotary-barrel system. The barrel itself rotates to perform the required locking and unlocking. Even in 45ACP caliber, this pistol is relatively compact.

Straight (unretarded) blowback system. The straight blowback system is impractical for most pistol cartridges because the resultant gun is too big for most practical purposes. Blowback pistols have a fixed barrel and no mechanical locking system between the slide and the barrel. A big heavy slide provides sufficient stationary momentum to keep the chamber sealed until the bullet clears the barrel. As indicated above, this system just cannot be made small or light enough to be practical for most serious handguns. They have been made, but they are little more than submachine guns without stocks.

No major handgun manufacturer uses this system for high-pressure defensive handgun calibers. However, for some low-pressure rounds, like the .380 Auto, practical guns are made using this system. The barrel actually separates from the slide while there is still pressure in the barrel. With low-pressure ammunition, the case itself has sufficient strength to hold together for the instant that part of its rear portion is unsupported.

Chapter 16: Defensive Handgun Mechanical Systems

Comparison Between Mechanical Autoloading Handgun Systems

	Drop-lock	Tilt-barrel	Gas/retarded blow-back	Straight blow-back	Rotary-barrel
Reliability	Extremely	Very	Very	Very	Very
Accuracy	Very	Accurate	Extremely	Very	Very
Size	Slide is wide and bulky	Slide is slim	Slide is slim and the gun is short	Very small when used with low-pressure cartridges, but the system is not useable with high-pressure loads, unless the gun itself is very big and bulky	Slide is slim and the gun is compact
Handling	Smooth under rapid fire	Choppy under rapid fire	Very choppy under rapid fire and heats up quickly, often making the gun too hot to handle	Choppy under rapid fire	Smooth under rapid fire

Comparison Between Mechanical Autoloading Handgun Systems, Continued

	Drop-lock	Tilt-barrel	Gas/retarded blow-back	Straight blow-back	Rotary-barrel
Maintenance	Normal	Normal	Particular attention must be paid to keeping gas system clean and unplugged	Normal	Normal
Ammunition Compatibility	All kinds	All kinds	Jacketed only	Full-power only	All kinds
Availability	Beretta and Taurus	Smith & Wesson, Glock, SIG, Ruger, H&K, Walther, Colt, Springfield Armory	H&K only and now out of production	Only with low-pressure rounds, such as the .380 Auto	Only from Beretta

Chapter 17

Safe Gun Handling

Tactical and administrative are the two separate sets of circumstances in which you will need to handle firearms. The handling procedures in both instances are nearly identical but there are some important differences.

Tactical circumstances are those where you are in the middle of a life-threatening emergency. The prime consideration with regard to your weapon is to use it in the best way possible in order to keep yourself from getting hurt. "Safety" is a secondary consideration. Of course if you shoot yourself because of incorrect gun handling, it will not likely upgrade your survival potential, so correct and safe gun-handling procedures are still important.

Tactical procedures are defined as drawing and reholstering, firing, reloading and reducing stoppages. In training, tactical procedures are all timed. You are expected to do them quickly and smoothly because they must be done under tactical circumstances. Under tactical conditions, you may even be forced, for the sake of expediency, to momentarily point your weapon in an unsafe direction or violate some other administrative handling procedure. Sometimes this is unavoidable.

Administrative procedures are defined as loading, chamber check, unloading and clearing and cleaning. These are done under non-tactical (administrative) circumstances. There are no time limits and the prime consideration is safety. Your objective is the prevention of accidental discharges and the prevention of personal injury if an accidental discharge does occur.

The various administrative processes may seem protracted; however they are not intended to be done under time pressure. The procedures catalogued below are described from the perspective of a right-handed person. If you are left-handed, you will accomplish the same thing but the exact procedure may have to be altered. These procedures are not the only ones currently taught. There are many variations. However, experience has shown these procedures to be very good and reasonably safe. They are the only procedures I currently recommend and the only ones I will permit on the range.

During administrative gun handling, our prime concern is performing whatever procedure we're doing safely. However, you must never let your guard down. When performing all the following procedures, don't get so engrossed in what you're doing that you fail to look around now and then. Don't bend over your gun. Stand upright and keep your head and eyes moving.

Whenever handling any firearm, adhere to the safety rules outlined previously, specifically: *watch where the muzzle is pointed and keep your finger out of contact with the trigger (unless you intend for the hammer to fall at that moment)*. In fact, your trigger finger should be in only one of two positions when the weapon is grasped:

- It should be inside the trigger guard and making contact with the trigger, or
- It should be outside the trigger guard fully extended and contacting the slide (this is the register position). With a revolver, the register position should have the fully extended trigger finger on the frame just below the cylinder.

In certain advanced training, we do teach some "unsighted" shooting. That is, you actually fire the gun without using the sights. This may be advisable in close-contact, defensive situations and constitutes an exception to this rule.

When the trigger finger is extended along the slide or frame, it is said to be in register. The trigger finger should be in register any time the firearm is grasped until:

- You have a correct sight picture, *and*
- You have decided to fire and intend for the gun to discharge at once.

Contrary to popular fiction, there is no logical reason to have your finger on the trigger except when you intend to fire. *Running around with one's finger on the trigger, even in a tactical situation, is flirting with a self-inflicted gunshot wound.* Your finger can move to the trigger from register rapidly. The movement requires only two-tenths of a second. When you are reacting to danger, your finger will be in contact with the trigger in plenty of time for an accurate shot.

Finger in register position.

The trigger finger must find the same register position every time because you

Chapter 17: Safe Gun Handling

must learn the exact distance between register and trigger contact. When not on the trigger, your finger should not be floating in space or positioning itself one place one time and another place another time. *The register position must be consistent.* That way you will be able to consistently find the trigger quickly and smoothly without the danger of an impetuous and disoriented finger clumsily crashing into the trigger and causing an accidental discharge.

Keep in mind that the vast majority of accidental injuries with handguns are self-inflicted! They often happen, not in the middle of gunfights, but while the owner is loading, unloading or otherwise administratively handling his pistol. It happens to the unwary, the careless and the distracted. Yes, you *can* shoot yourself! Therefore, take your time and perform every step carefully and in the correct sequence. Keep your mind on what you're doing. Don't allow yourself to be distracted, and don't shortcut the procedure.

When loading or unloading, don't allow the barrel of your gun to wave all over the place! Keep constant control of it and keep it pointed in a safe direction. Immediately after loading your pistol, either holster it or secure it in some other reasonable way. *Don't load your pistol and then lay it down, unsecured.* A loaded pistol belongs either in a holster on your body or locked in a safe or lock-box.

Secure it in one of those two ways immediately after loading. It is your responsibility to keep your firearm out of the hands of unauthorized people. An unloaded pistol also needs to be locked in a safe. Pistols, loaded or not, need to be out of sight and appropriately secured at all times.

The following section explains the administrative process for double-action revolvers, trigger-cocking two-stage decocking autoloaders, the continuous motion autoloader system, trigger-cocking single-stage decocking autoloaders, the Colt/Browning single-action autoloader system, self-decocking autoloaders as well as strange or unfamiliar weapons.

Double-action revolvers

Pulling the trigger of a double-action revolver to the rear as far as it will go rotates the cylinder and simultaneously cocks and releases the hammer, firing the weapon (if it is loaded). A deliberate motion is required to discharge the weapon (in the trigger-cocking mode). It is difficult to fire a double-action revolver by accident as long as the hammer has not been cocked manually. When the double-action revolver is carried, it must be fully loaded (all chambers loaded) with the hammer down (all the way forward). There is no manual safety.

Independent inventors have devised several add-on manual safety schemes for revolvers over the years, but none has ever been satisfactory enough to cause manufacturers to incorporate any of them into production guns. None are currently available from OEM manufacturers.

In fact, there is nothing preventing a loaded double-action revolver from discharging any time sufficient pressure is applied to the trigger. However, as long as the hammer is forward, the trigger itself, due to its long and heavy pull, will provide the adequate margin of safety necessary to make the weapon safe to carry that way. Pulling the trigger far enough to the rear for the weapon to discharge generally requires a conscious decision and a deliberate act on the part of the operator.

In order for most revolvers to discharge in the trigger-cocking mode (hammer forward), the trigger must move to the rear 1.5 cm (0.59 inch) against 5.9 kg (13 lbs) of resistance. These figures are typical. Trigger pull weight can actually vary from as little as 3 kg (6.6 lbs) to as much as 9 kg (19.8 lbs). Generally factory guns are pretty close to 5.9 kg (13 lbs).

On the other hand, if the hammer is first manually cocked, the amount of trigger pressure required to release it and cause the weapon to discharge is only 1.5 kg (3.3 lbs). As indicated before, such a light trigger break does not provide the necessary margin of safety for carrying. Therefore the double-action revolver cannot be safely carried when it is cocked. In fact, save for rare circumstances, *all defensive shooting is correctly done via the trigger-cocking mode.* Manually cocking the weapon is nearly always contraindicated.

When the hammer on a reputable double-action revolver is all the way forward, you should know that the firing pin is not actually in contact with, nor is it resting on, the primer of the chambered cartridge. The gun's mechanism is such that when the hammer is forward, the firing pin is actually withdrawn from the primer and blocked from contacting it. This means that even a heavy external blow to the hammer would not cause the weapon to discharge. Hence, all modern, reputable double-action revolvers are "drop safe," even when they are fully loaded.

There are some now-obsolete single-action revolvers that cannot be safely carried with the hammer down on a live round because a blow to the hammer could discharge these particular weapons. They were correctly carried with the individual chamber under the hammer empty. Current double-action revolvers and even most modern single-action revolvers now have a passive mechanical

Chapter 17: Safe Gun Handling

firing pin block interlocked with the trigger, which prevents the firing pin from going forward of the firing-pin hole unless the trigger is pulled all the way to the rear and held there during the entire hammer fall. The mechanical strategy used to block the firing pin is slightly different with different brands of revolvers. However, all reputable brands now use a reliable system. Unless you are mechanically inclined, it is not especially important that you understand exactly how it works in each instance. Suffice it to say that it does work, so *it is therefore not necessary to carry modern double-action revolvers with the chamber under the hammer empty.* This is an obsolete custom practiced only by the uninformed. Some gun manufacturers who still recommend this practice probably do so out of fear of lawyers and lawsuits, not out of concern for the owner's safety. *When the modern double-action revolver is carried, all chambers should be loaded.*

Lowering the hammer (decocking). If the hammer has for some reason been manually cocked and you do not intend to fire the gun immediately, it must be lowered to its forward position before the weapon can be safely handled or carried. A loaded and cocked double-action revolver will discharge with very little encouragement, so great care must be exercised as the weapon is handled in that condition. The hammer should be safely lowered as soon after the gun is picked up as possible. *Double-action revolvers do not have decocking levers so the hammer must be lowered manually.* Here is the correct procedure for safely lowering the hammer from its full-cock position:

- With the weapon pointed in a safe direction and the trigger finger in register, place another finger between the cocked hammer and the chamber under it. This will prevent the hammer from falling all the way forward when pressure is applied to the trigger. Do not release the hammer (press the trigger) before its forward movement is thus positively blocked by a finger. If the hammer falls forward unretarded, the weapon will discharge (if it is loaded).

- Apply pressure to the trigger until the hammer is released and falls forward onto your finger. As soon as the hammer falls, remove your finger from the trigger. The trigger/firing pin interlock will prevent the weapon from firing as long as there is no pressure on the trigger, even if the hammer falls the rest of the way forward.

- Slowly draw the hammer back slightly (manually) and remove your finger from under it. Then gently allow the hammer to move the rest of the way forward.

With finger in register, pull back the hammer and place a finger underneath.

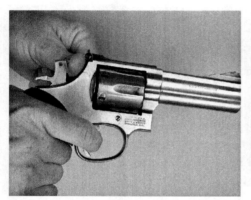 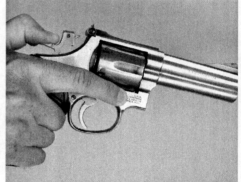

Next, press the trigger until you feel the hammer move forward. Keeping your finger off the trigger, gently allow the hammer to move all the way forward.

Once the hammer is released as described above, even if the hammer spur slips from under your finger and the hammer subsequently falls forward of its own accord, it will do so harmlessly, so long as the trigger is not touched. Nonetheless, the hammer should be lowered slowly as an additional precaution because there are some weapons that are defective or lack required safety features.

Unloading and clearing. Like most appliances, guns are designed for right-handed people with average to large-sized hands and fingers. The procedures enumerated below are thus from the perspective of a right-handed person with at least average-sized hands. People who are left handed or have small hands and short fingers will have to struggle with some of these techniques, and may indeed have to modify them. Many left-handers simply elect to do the techniques right handed. Others do everything left handed, but obviously have to alter the manner in which they do it.

Chapter 17: Safe Gun Handling

With the hammer forward, trigger finger in register and the muzzle pointed in a safe direction, unlock the cylinder by manipulating the cylinder release. The hammer must be forward. If the hammer is cocked, the cylinder cannot be released on most revolvers. Swing the cylinder away from the frame and unload the weapon (remove all rounds from the individual chambers). Simply turning the weapon upside down should allow the rounds to fall out of the chambers by their own weight. However, if the ammunition has been in the weapon a long time, one or more individual rounds may stick and not come out. In that case, gently pushing the ejector rod should break them free. Live rounds should fall free from the chambers and out into your right hand.

If the revolver has been stored loaded for a long time, you may not be able to get the rounds out of the chambers at all, even with the help of the ejector rod.

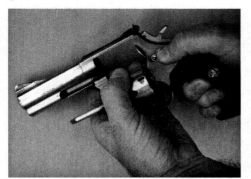 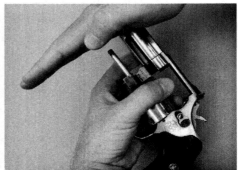

Press the cylinder release and swing out cylinder. Point the muzzle up, if needed. Use the ejector rod to remove the rounds.

In that case, the gun needs a trip to the gunsmith before anything else is done with it. In this case, the ammunition is probably old and unreliable and the gun itself may well be inoperative.

Be absolutely sure all rounds have been removed from the cylinder before declaring that the revolver is unloaded and clear. Examine each individual chamber carefully to be sure it is vacant. It is easy to leave a chamber loaded by mistake particularly in poor light. Some instructors advise students to count the rounds removed from the weapon to be sure all ammunition is accounted for. Such counting of loose rounds, however, is ticklish, dubious and often results in dropped rounds. It is my advice to dispense with counting and rely instead on a thorough physical examination of all chambers.

Try not to allow live rounds to fall on the ground. If they fall on a hard surface, they will be scuffed and may not chamber properly when you try to load them the next time. In rare instances, they have even been known to detonate. If they fall in the grass, dust or mud, they are likely to get dirty, wet or lost. If you do allow them to drop, try to arrange for them to fall on a soft surface like a bed or a padded chair.

Loading. Now that the weapon is unloaded, it can be loaded, if desired. Here are the steps:

1. With the hammer forward, trigger finger in register and the muzzle pointed in a safe direction, grasp the gun by the grip with your right hand. Lay the right side of the weapon in the palm of your weak hand. If the hammer is cocked, lower it and unload the weapon via the above procedure before proceeding.

Hold the revolver close to your body. That way, if you drop rounds during the loading process, they will fall into the palm of your left hand and can be quickly recovered and loaded back into the weapon. If the weapon is held away from the body, dropped rounds will fall all the way to the ground.

2. Unlock the cylinder by manipulating the cylinder release. The cylinder release is just forward of the hammer on the left side of the revolver. Some off-brand weapons locate it elsewhere. It works differently on the various brands of revolvers: It is pushed *forward* with Smith & Wesson revolvers, pulled *back* with Colts and pushed *in* with Ruger revolvers.

3. Swing the cylinder out of the frame as far as it will go and hold it there with your left thumb and your two left middle fingers. Left-handers must push the cylinder out with their right thumb and hold it out with the two middle fingers of the right hand.

4. Take the appropriate number of live rounds into your right hand and load each chamber individually until all chambers are loaded. Make sure each round is pushed forward as far as it will go. It is good to get into the habit of rotating the cylinder during the loading process in the *opposite* direction that it rotates during firing. This is to insure that if it becomes necessary to fire before the cylinder is fully charged and the partially charged cylinder must thus be pushed into the frame in preparation to shoot, the first chambers to rotate under the firing pin will be loaded. Otherwise, you would snap the hammer on several empty chambers before hitting a loaded one.

With the Smith & Wesson and Ruger revolvers, the open cylinder is pushed with the left thumb (rotated clockwise) to position successive chambers for loading. Revolvers manufactured by Colt and some others rotate clockwise

Chapter 17: Safe Gun Handling

during firing, so the cylinder is rotated counter-clockwise during loading.

Speed loaders by HKS and Safariland make it possible to precisely and quickly load all chambers simultaneously. Their use is highly recommended.

5. With your left thumb, push the fully charged cylinder back into the frame until it locks in place. Then, rotate the cylinder in either direction until it locks in index and will not rotate further. This indexing of the cylinder is not imperative and the weapon will fire even if you forget. In fact, in reloading we even don't bother with it because it consumes time. When not under time pressure you will probably want to do it just to lock everything up.

Do not slam the cylinder out of, or back into, the frame. Such cylinder slamming is both unnecessary and ruinous to the gun. It will bring about misalignment of the yoke, which will cause the cylinder to bind on the forcing cone thus impeding its normal rotation and sometimes cause it to seize completely.

Loading using a speedloader.

The revolver is now loaded, ready to carry and ready to fire. *It is correctly carried with the hammer all the way down* (forward) on a live round (loaded chamber). Remember, *a double-action revolver cannot be safely carried, handled or stored with the hammer cocked.* If you are carrying it in a holster, sweep the blade of your hand between the grip of the revolver and your shirt to be sure the gun did not drag part of your shirt into the holster with it. Also be sure that the gun is completely and firmly seated in the holster.

Trigger-cocking, two-stage decocking autoloading pistols

What follows may seem complex but with sufficient practice these handguns can be mastered. Nevertheless, they are more complicated than double-action revolvers and they do require more practice. Some Smith & Wesson, Beretta, Ruger, H&K and Taurus trigger-cocking autoloaders fall into this category.

Decocking. When the decocking lever is down, the hammer is always down, because pushing the decocking lever into the "on" (down) position automatically decocks the weapon. In addition, when the decocking lever is down, the trigger is disconnected and the pistol is thus sterile. Thus, pushing the decocking lever down sterilizes, as well as decocks, the gun. If carried with the decocker down, it must be pushed up as the weapon is being drawn from the holster so that you will be able to shoot when the weapon comes on target. Because of the design and location of the decocking lever, most people find pushing it up during the draw to be clumsy, dubious and difficult to master. The maneuver is prone to failure. The majority of veteran shooters, including myself, therefore, carry this autoloader with decocker in the off (up) position.

When the decocking lever is in the up position, the gun is enabled. The hammer may be down or cocked and the firing pin is unlocked. Actually, as with the double-action revolver, there is an additional passive firing-pin lock interconnected with the trigger that continues to block the firing pin until the trigger is pulled and held to the rear during the entire hammer fall. This insures that the weapon will not fire unless the trigger is held all the way to the rear during the entire hammer fall. This is a passive safety device that functions automatically.

When the hammer is down on a live round and the decocking lever is up, the weapon is about as safe as a double-action revolver in the same condition, since pulling the trigger all the way through is necessary to cock the hammer, release it and discharge the weapon. As with the revolver, the firing pin is not actually in contact with the primer of the chambered round when the hammer is all the way forward and the trigger is also all the way forward.

To summarize, the trigger-cocking two-stage decocking autoloader is properly carried with the hammer down, live round chambered, fully-charged magazine inserted and the decocking lever up. That is the correct "carry mode" for this particular gun.

Decocking lever down (on).

Decocking lever up (off).

Chapter 17: Safe Gun Handling

Two-stage decocking autoloaders are slide-cocking. The hammer is automatically recocked with every shot during the normal cycle of operation. *That means that only the first shot will be trigger-cocking; the second and all subsequent shots will be from a hammer that is already cocked, having been recocked by the movement of the slide.* When the hammer is thus cocked, the trigger will be in its rear position near the rear of the trigger guard. When the hammer is down, the trigger is in its forward position ready for the trigger-cocking mode on the first shot. In other words, the trigger has two positions and changes positions from the first shot to the second shot. So, when you stop shooting (assuming you have not shot the weapon dry and locked the slide to the rear), *before the weapon can be reholstered, or even lowered from the fire position, it must be decocked.* Decock the weapon only by using the decocking lever. Do not try to lower the hammer manually.

To reiterate, *attempting to decock the pistol by manually lowering the hammer on a live round is extremely dangerous and is not recommended.* As we have seen, this procedure is sometimes necessary with a double-action revolver. It is not necessary and should not be attempted with an autoloader. Some off-brand trigger-cocking autoloaders (not listed among the systems described above) do not have a decocking lever. Decocking is accomplished through maneuvers that require you to simultaneously manipulate the trigger, the hammer or both. It is invariably an uncertain process that can and often does easily lead to an unintentional discharge. Often, before manually lowering the hammer, you are required to engage a cross-bolt firing pin block that is difficult to reach and operate with any of the fingers of your gun hand.

The weapon cannot therefore be quickly decocked and rendered safe to carry with only the gun hand. Both hands are required. I consider this a severe liability because both hands may not always be available. If you then forget to disengage the cross-bolt safety after decocking (again, using both hands), the weapon will not fire when it is urgently needed. In my opinion, these guns are inherently unusable, unsafe and not recommended for any serious purpose. *We recommend only those trigger-cocking autoloaders that come equipped with a fail-safe decocking system that can be easily operated using only one hand and that do not require you to touch the hammer or the trigger during the decocking process.*

It is extremely important that you train yourself to depress the decocking lever and decock the weapon as soon as you stop firing and before you lower the weapon from the firing position. Like the double-action revolver, this weapon cannot be safely handled, carried or holstered when it is cocked. Attempting to do so is an invitation to an accident.

As soon as the weapon is decocked, *the decocking lever must immediately be pushed back up* rendering the weapon ready to fire again (enabled). You should not be holding a weapon in your hand that will not fire. If you neglect to push the decocking lever back up again, you will holster a sterile weapon. When you draw it the next time, you will pull the trigger, expecting the weapon to fire, but it will not. You may be killed before you realize that you carelessly left the decocking lever down the last time you decocked.

Unlike double-action revolvers, these weapons can be in a number of different conditions ranging from clear to loaded and ready to fire. The conditions described in the following section are the ones with which you should be familiar.

Unloading and clearing. During the entire unloading and loading processes, *keep the pistol in your strong hand and in the master grip.* If you grip the gun any other way, you will lose awareness of where it is pointed. So long as the master grip is maintained, the direction that the muzzle is pointed can be continuously controlled.

1. Regardless of the weapon's actual or presumed condition, hold it by the grip and with the muzzle pointing in a safe direction and your trigger finger in register.

2. Turn into your gun, so that you are holding it close to and directly in front of your navel. Make sure that the muzzle continues to point in a safe direction.

3. Push the decocking lever down, thus safely decocking (if the hammer was cocked) and simultaneously sterilizing the weapon. The hammer must be forward and the decocking lever down before proceeding any further. The decocking lever remains down during the entire unloading and clearing procedure.

4. Depress the magazine release button and allow the magazine to fall out of the weapon and into your hand. Then, put the magazine off to the side, in your pocket or waistband.

5. Grasp the slide with your left hand to the rear of the ejection port, taking care that your hand does not cover the pistol's ejection port. Rapidly pull the slide all the way to the rear and then release it and let it spring all the way forward again. That will eject the live round if one was in the chamber.

The strong hand holds the weapon's grip (trigger finger in register). The weak

Chapter 17: Safe Gun Handling

hand grasps the slide at its rear portion where the grooves are, to the rear of the ejection port. Be sure to grasp the slide with the meat of the hand and all four fingers. Don't just pinch it between the thumb and index finger. A pinch grip on the slide is not sufficiently secure and the slide may thus slip. It is also important to grasp the slide to the rear of the ejection port, not forward of it. *The ejection port must be completely in front of the hand and not occluded.*

If the slide is grasped incorrectly, i.e., too far forward, it is likely that your little finger will drape itself in front of the muzzle. A number of shooters have blown their little fingers off for this reason. It is also possible for an incorrectly

Point gun in a safe direction, then turn your body towards the gun.

placed hand to be injured if it obstructs the ejection port. Sometimes, a round of ammunition can ignite during the unloading process sending hot particles of brass out through the ejection port. Therefore, be sure to grasp the slide correctly. Also, *be sure to direct the ejection port down and away from your face as the slide is pulled rearward.* There should be no direct line between the ejection port and your face.

As you are pulling the slide to the rear, be careful to leep your left arm or elbow clear of the muzzle. It is easy to allow this to happen, particularly if you are holding the gun close to your body. *All body parts must be kept to the rear of the muzzle.*

The round that was in the chamber should be allowed to fall to the ground. Do not try to retrieve it directly into your weak hand by placing your weak hand over the ejection port. As indicated above, with some autoloaders the primer of the chambered round can strike the tip of the ejector or a sharp corner of

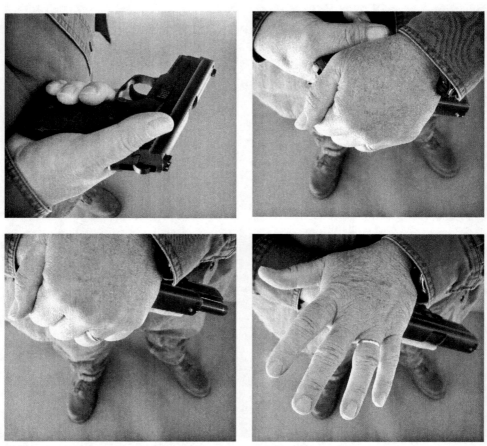

Grip the slide, pull it to the rear and let it go.

the slide itself as the slide is being pulled to the rear with enough force to cause the round to detonate at that point, causing injury to your weak hand and any other body part facing the ejection port. Therefore, with all autoloaders, it is

Chapter 17: Safe Gun Handling

recommended that the chambered round be removed from the chamber by pulling the slide rearward *keeping the hands and face clear of the ejection port.* The live round that was in the chamber is simply allowed to fall out on its own. It is best to unload over a soft surface so that the round is not damaged when it falls.

6. Keeping the muzzle pointed in a safe direction, again grasp the rear of the slide with your weak hand and pull it all the way back for a second time while simultaneously applying upward pressure to the slide stop lever with your strong-side thumb. The slide will lock to the rear and allow a visual inspection of the chamber, receiver and magazine well. The receiver is the area between the bolt face and the chamber as the slide is locked to the rear. *Get into the habit of inspecting the chamber and receiver both visually and physically using the little finger of your weak hand.*

7. During range exercises, I require students at the end of the unloading procedure (after the pistol has been inspected) to point the weapon downrange (safe direction) and dry fire. This allows the hammer to fall on an empty chamber and is the final check. On the range, I'd prefer to have an accidental discharge now rather than later. The dry fire step at the end also makes each student inspect his pistol very carefully. When unloading at home or some other place that is not a firing range, the dry fire step may be bypassed. With pistols that have a magazine safety, dry fire cannot be accomplished until an empty magazine has been inserted.

On most autoloaders, the slide-stop lever and the slide-release lever are one and the same. Therefore, the terms "slide-stop lever", "slide-release lever" and "slide-lock lever" can all be used interchangeably. Pushing the lever up as the slide is manually pulled rearward engages a notch and locks and holds the slide in the rearward position. Subsequently pushing the lever down releases the slide, allowing it to spring all the way forward.

As with any handgun, *the unloading and clearing process is not complete without a visual and physical inspection.* Look into and feel the chamber through the ejection port to make sure there is no round there. Also, look and feel down through the ejection port and through the magazine well to insure that the receiver and the entire magazine well are clear. It is not unusual for the top round in the magazine to come loose as the magazine is removed and lodge in the magazine well. If the slide is then allowed to go forward without a magazine well inspection, the loose round may chamber itself, thus loading the supposedly unloaded weapon.

Loading.

1. Turn into your gun, so that you are holding it close to and directly in front of your navel. Make sure that the muzzle continues to point in a safe direction.

2. With the slide locked to the rear, chamber vacant, magazine well empty, decocking lever down, the muzzle pointed in a safe direction and the trigger finger in register; insert a fully-charged magazine. Be sure to push the magazine into the magazine well as far as it will go with the heel of your strong hand. You should be able to hear a click as it locks into place. A magazine that is not locked in place is a common cause of stoppages.

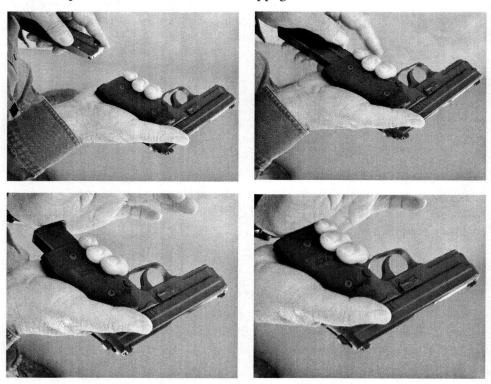

Insert the magazine using the heel of your strong hand.

3. Grasp the rear of the slide with your weak hand as before, and pull it all the way to the rear. Be sure to grasp the slide correctly as described above. Although the slide is locked to the rear, it will still move further rearward enough to cam down the slide stop lever. Once the slide stop is down, the slide will be free to move all the way forward. Therefore, at its rearmost position, release the slide and let it go all the way forward unassisted. As it goes forward,

Chapter 17: Safe Gun Handling

it will strip the top round off the magazine and chamber it.

Do not attempt to ride or assist the slide forward. This practice can cause a stoppage because the slide may be prevented from going all the way forward and locking into battery. With two-stage decocking autoloaders, at this point the decocking lever will already be down and the weapon will thus already be decocked, the hammer having followed the slide when the slide went forward into battery.

4. Enable the weapon (push the decocking lever up).

5. Turn to face downrange (safe direction) and holster the pistol. Be sure your finger remains in register and be sure the gun is firmly and completely holstered before your release your master grip on it.

6. Remove the magazine (as the gun remains holstered.)

7. Replace the round in the magazine that was chambered when the slide was pulled back and released. This topping off procedure insures that you now have a fully charged magazine.

8. With the magazine now fully charged, place it back into the pistol (as the pistol remains holstered) and push it up until it locks securely in place.

9. Tug on the magazine after it has been reinserted and try to pull it back out (without pressing the magazine-release button). If it comes right back out, it was not fully seated in the first place. If it does not come back out, it is fully

Push the magazine back into the magazine well, then try to pull it out.

153

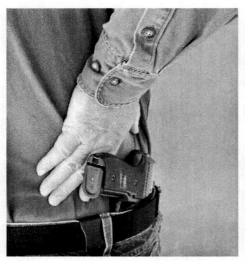 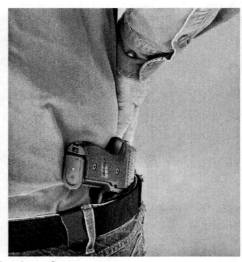

Sweep from back to front.

seated, as it should be. If gentle tugging does not suffice to dislodge it, you can be certain that it is properly locked in place and will not fall out without you knowing it.

10. Sweep the blade of your hand from back to front between the grip of the pistol and your shirt to insure that part of your shirt is not being pinched between the bottom of the magazine and the pistol's magazine well or that the gun did not drag part of your shirt into the holster with it.

Always sweep from the rear forward. If you sweep from the front to the back, you may inadvertently push the decocking lever down. Be sure to incorporate this "Push-Pull-Sweep" routine into your loading procedure, with all autoloading pistols.

The weapon is now ready to be carried and is in carry mode. When it becomes necessary to fire, simply draw the weapon, aim at the target and press the trigger.

Chamber check. When the pistol has been thus loaded, performing a chamber check is recommended. A chamber check will verify that there is a round in the chamber (as there should be) and that you are not walking around with an unloaded gun in your holster, unaware.

1. Facing a safe direction, draw the pistol. Do not turn into your gun when performing a chamber check. Continue to face downrange.

Chapter 17: Safe Gun Handling

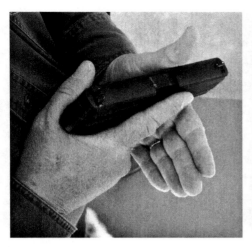

Grasp the frame between the thumb and index finger of weak hand.

Hook fingers over the top of the slide.

2. Move the pistol into the middle of your body so the butt is in contact with your midriff.

For the remainder of the procedure, you can then brace the pistol against you midriff as you complete the process. Be sure the muzzle continues to point downrange and your trigger finger is in register.

Pinch the strong hand to draw back the slide and clamp with the weak hand.

Physically check the chamber using the little finger.

3. Sterilize the pistol by pushing the decocking lever down.

4. Grasp the frame from underneath, immediately forward of the trigger guard, between the thumb and index finger of your weak hand.

5. Pull the entire gun backward until the butt makes firm contact with your midriff.

6. Rotate your strong hand counter clockwise until the thumb is under the tang of the frame and the fingers are hooked over the top of the slide.

7. Pinch with the strong hand, drawing the slide back a half inch, just far enough so that the chambered round is drawn back sufficiently for you to see it, feel it and confirm that it is there. Clamp the slide open by pinching it with your weak hand.

8. Check the round physically. This can be easily done with the little finger of the strong hand.

9. After the presence of the chambered round is thus confirmed, regain your master grip with your strong hand, then release your weak hand grasp. This allows the slide to spring forward into battery.

10. Enable the pistol by pushing the decocking lever up.

11. Reholster.

We also recommend that as an adjunct to the process, prior to reholstering, you

Release the slide and allow it to spring forward.

Verify that the slide is all the way forward with your weak hand.

Chapter 17: Safe Gun Handling

release the magazine and withdraw it from the magazine well far enough to check the lowest cartridge window, assuring yourself that the magazine is fully charged, as it should be.

There is another way of checking the chamber that is often seen but is not recommended. It is called a "pinch check" and it is accomplished by pinching the slide far enough back to expose the chamber mouth. In this case, the slide is pinched back by hooking the weak-hand thumb around the front of the trigger guard and the weak-hand index finger around the front of the slide just under the barrel. The slide can then be moved back by pinching the two fingers together. The pinch-check obviously will not work with autoloaders that have a full-length recoil spring guide as most autoloaders do. It sees its most common use with the Colt/Browning System autoloaders.

The problem is the weak-hand index finger often slips off the front of the slide during the pinching process. The thumb can then jerk back and hit the trigger with enough force to cause the weapon to discharge. These pinch-check-engendered unintentional discharges are common, even among ostensibly experienced shooters (who ought to know better), which is why *I strongly recommended against using this particular procedure for checking the chamber.*

Recommendations for storage. For storage around the home, where it is your intention to have the weapon available and able to be used on short notice yet safe enough to be left unattended, you may want to store it with the slide forward, hammer down on an empty chamber, fully-charged magazine inserted and the decocking lever up. This condition is called transport mode.

In this condition, pulling the trigger will cock and release the hammer but will not fire the weapon since there is no round chambered. The slide must be moved all the way to the rear and released to prepare the weapon to fire. This maneuver easily and quickly succumbs to adult strength but small children find it difficult. Of course, for the imaginative child, nothing is really impossible, but this procedure may serve as a reasonable deterrent.

To get the weapon in this condition:

1. Unload it
2. Allow the slide to go all the way forward on an empty chamber
3. Insert a fully charged magazine
4. Make sure the decocking lever is up

5. Put the pistol away in its quick-access lock box

In an emergency, quickly grab the pistol with your strong hand (master grip), grasp the rear of the slide with your weak hand, jerk the slide to the rear as far as it will go and immediately release it. The hammer will now be cocked on a live round and the weapon can be fired immediately by simply pulling the trigger. If you subsequently decide to move around, the weapon must first be decocked. The trigger finger should, of course, be in register as you move.

Long-term storage. For long-term inert storage in a safe or vault (storage mode), all the weapon's springs should be at rest in order to avoid spring fatigue and future failure. We would, therefore, want the slide forward and the hammer down. The magazine would be emptied and removed from the weapon.

Continuous motion autoloader

Only on continuous motion system autoloaders are the slide-release function (built into the squeeze-cocker located on the front of the grip) and the slide-lock function (built into a separate slide-lock button on the left rear of the trigger guard) separated. With all the other autoloader systems, the slide-release function and the slide-lock function are incorporated into the same lever.

Depressing the squeeze-cocker cocks the hammer (if the slide is forward) and automatically releases the slide if it has been locked to the rear. As indicated above, there is a separate slide-lock button on the left rear of the trigger guard that, when depressed as the slide is manually pulled to the rear, will lock the slide in the rear position. Unfortunately, this button is small, recessed, awkwardly located and is consequently difficult to operate gracefully. Many people, particularly women with long fingernails, find it impossible to use. An alternative method for locking the slide to the rear is to manually pull the slide to the rear after inserting an empty magazine. The slide will then lock to the rear automatically.

Even if you are able to get the slide-lock button to work, you will probably have to radically alter your grip in order to do so. *Be careful that you do not point the gun in an unsafe direction (e.g., at your own elbow) in the process.*

With continuous motion system autoloaders, the act of gripping the weapon actually depresses a "squeeze-cocker," incorporated into the front of the grip, which cocks the hammer. There is no manual safety. Relaxing the firing grip allows the squeeze-cocker to return to its rest position and safely decocks the

Chapter 17: Safe Gun Handling

weapon. It should be obvious that *when handling this weapon, special care must be taken not to depress the squeeze-cocker until and unless it is intended for the weapon to fire.* It is easy to inadvertently squeeze the grip and cock the weapon as it is being handled. During administrative handling, the squeeze-cocker must remain in its rest position. Administrative handling must be accomplished as the weapon's grip is pinched between the strong-side thumb and index finger. The rest of the fingers must remain extended or only slightly flexed so that no pressure is applied to the front of the grip. This is necessary in order to insure that the squeeze-cocker remains in its rest position and the hammer thus remains uncocked. Even in tactical situations, the operator must not fully acquire his normal shooting grip (thus depressing the squeeze-cocker) until after the weapon has cleared the holster and is safely pointed at the target.

Further, as with two-stage decocking autoloaders, the decocking process must take place as soon as the weapon begins to be lowered from the firing position. Otherwise, the weapon will still be cocked as you move with it or attempt to reholster it and an unintentional discharge into your foot or leg will be the likely result.

Loading, unloading and chamber check. These procedures are essentially the same as with the two-stage decocking autoloaders. Leaving the squeeze-cocker in the rest position is analogous to leaving the decocking lever in the "on" position. All the other cautions apply such as keeping the muzzle pointed in a safe direction, trigger finger in register, etc. When performing a chamber check, it is particularly easy to inadvertently depress the squeeze cocker. The maneuver must thus be practiced thoroughly.

Recommendations for storage. When storing the weapon at home, the advice rendered with regard to the two-stage decocking autoloaders is applicable also. However, when the gun is grasped in an emergency, the tendency is to immediately depress the squeeze-cocker. If the slide is then pulled to the rear and released (chambering a round) and the finger is already on the trigger, the gun will precipitously discharge. If that is what you wanted, fine; but such discharges are usually unexpected and unintentional. It is best to chamber a round, depress the squeeze-cocker and then press the trigger as *three separate and distinct maneuvers.*

One last caution with this system: The normal way to fire the weapon is to first depress the squeeze-cocker then press the trigger. However, it also works in the reverse order. That is, if there is already pressure on the trigger and the squeeze-cocker is in the rest position, depressing the squeeze-cocker will cause the hammer to fall and the weapon to fire. This is not a design flaw. The manufacturer wants to provide the customer with a gun that is going to fire without a lot of precise coordination and sequence-critical manipulations. Thus, *if you squeeze this gun with all your fingers simultaneously, it will go off!* However, responsible accuracy is attainable only when the gun is fired in the conventional way (squeeze first and then press the trigger) and that is the only way we recommend.

Trigger-cocking, single-stage decocking autoloading pistols

These guns have a spring-loaded single-position decocking lever but no manual safety. In other words, unlike in the two-stage decocking autoloaders, there is no safety function associated with the decocking lever. The decocking lever provides a convenient and efficient method for safely decocking the weapon. It neither disconnects the trigger nor blocks the firing pin. These weapons must, therefore, be handled as though the manual safety is always off. These guns can be easily and quickly decocked, however, rendering the weapon safe to carry. The decocking lever is depressed in order to decock the weapon. When released, it immediately springs back to its original position.

The loading, unloading and chamber check procedures are the same as with the two-stage decocking autoloaders, except that, with the single-stage decocking system, there is no way to sterilize the gun during administrative handling. When the slide is pulled back and released, chambering a round, the hammer will be cocked. The trigger is sensitive until the decocking lever is depressed, safely lowering the hammer. Therefore, *decocking must take place immediately after a round is chambered during the loading process or during a chamber check.* A brief mental lapse can easily cause you to delay decocking or forget it entirely. A disastrous unintentional discharge will be the likely result. Unlike the two-stage decocking autoloaders, these guns will necessarily be cocked during loading and chamber check.

Colt/Browning single-action autoloading pistols

On these guns, there is no decocking lever and there is no trigger-cocking provision. The only thing the trigger does is release the hammer from the full-cock position. The hammer is either cocked and locked (manual safety on) over a chambered live round (as the weapon is carried) or down on an empty chamber (as it is usually stored). "Cocked and locked" means that the hammer

Chapter 17: Safe Gun Handling

is cocked and the manual safety is in the "on" position. On some more recent versions of these weapons, there has been added a passive trigger/firing pin interlock. On these guns, pressing the trigger also unlocks the firing pin. The firing pin is otherwise always locked. However, this all happens automatically and the operator does not have any cognizant input.

The procedures for loading, unloading and handling Colt/Browning autoloaders are similar to those for the trigger-cocking autoloaders with the following exceptions:

Colt/Browning single-action system autoloaders are properly carried with the hammer fully cocked with a chambered live round and the manual safety on. With this system, the manual safety locks the hammer in the full-cock position and also locks the slide in the full-forward position (on most models), preventing it from moving to the rear. This is a feature unique to this system. It can be a valuable attribute because the operator is always assured that if the manual safety is on, the slide is fully in battery. All other autoloaders have a slide that is freely moveable even when in battery.

The manual safety operates in the opposite direction of the decocking lever found on the two-stage decocking autoloaders. It is properly operated (both directions) with the right thumb and when it is in the on (up) position it prevents the hammer from falling forward. When in the off (down) position, the weapon is enabled and will fire when pressure is applied to the trigger. With most pistols using this system, the manual safety will not go on if the hammer is down. On some, it will. Some pistols using this system also have a grip safety.

The pistol must be carried in a secure holster with the manual safety in the "on" position and the hammer in full cock. The manual safety must, of course, be pushed into the "off" position after the weapon has been withdrawn from the holster and is in the process of being brought on target. Your trigger finger should make contact with the trigger only after you has a sight picture and has made the decision to fire.

If the trigger is pulled when the safety is "on," the safety will prevent the hammer from falling. However, we have a similar situation to the one found on the Continuous Motion System autoloaders: If trigger pressure is maintained and the safety is then depressed to the "off" position, the hammer will immediately fall and the weapon will discharge! Therefore, it is usually a bad idea to attempt to operate the manual safety and trigger at the same time. *If you want the* weapon to fire, push the manual safety down first and then press the trigger.

Unloading and clearing. The unloading and clearing procedure is similar to those for the trigger-cocking autoloaders, but there are a few differences. The manual safety should remain "on" as the magazine is removed. After removing the magazine, push the manual safety "off." This is necessary to free the slide from battery and allow it to be pulled to the rear. The manual safety should remain on during the entire loading or unloading and clearing process on those models where it does not lock the slide. Remember that pushing the manual safety off enables the gun. Some defective autoloaders have been known to discharge as soon as the safety is released, even when there is no pressure on the trigger. This situation is usually engendered by a defective or broken hammer or sear. The sear is common to all trigger mechanisms. It is a trigger-activated catch that holds the hammer in the cocked position. Sears are small parts that can become brittle and occasionally break. To reiterate, *if the hammer and sear are broken, improperly modified or badly worn, the weapon may discharge the instant the safety is depressed to the off position, even if the trigger is not touched.* Accordingly, these parts need to be periodically examined by an armorer to insure they are serviceable.

Loading. A charged magazine is inserted and a round chambered as with the trigger-cocking autoloaders. The manual safety must be off on those models where it locks the slide forward. On those models where the manual safety does not lock the slide, keep the safety on. If the manual safety was off, *it is immediately pushed on as soon as a round is chambered.* The gun is now ready to carry, i.e. the gun is loaded, the hammer is cocked and the manual safety is on.

If desired, the chamber can be checked in the same manner as it is with the double-action autos, except that the safety must first be pushed off (on those models where it is necessary) in order to free the slide to move rearwards. *Be sure to reengage the safety as soon as the chamber check is completed.* Again, do not use the infamous pinch check, even though it is possible with most single-action autoloaders.

Recommendations for storage. In order to prepare the weapon for keeping at home:

1. Unload it.

2. Allow the slide to go all the way forward on an empty chamber.

Chapter 17: Safe Gun Handling

3. With the weapon pointed in a safe direction, press the trigger until the hammer falls (dry fire). Do not ride the hammer down manually. Allow it to drop. *If you never ride the hammer down, you can always be assured that the chamber is vacant any time the hammer is forward.*

4. With the hammer down, insert a fully charged magazine.

5. Put the weapon away in its quick-access lock box.

The weapon can then be quickly rendered ready to fire in the same manner as with the trigger-cocking autoloaders. When you do chamber a round, before moving with the weapon, remember to engage the manual safety. If you must move with the weapon, be sure your trigger finger is in register and *your right thumb is resting on top of the manual safety lever* (but the safety must remain on while you are moving). When it becomes necessary to fire, the safety is pushed off and the finger goes on the trigger after the weapon is brought to eye level, a firing position is assumed and the decision to fire is made. As with all autoloaders, storing the gun with the hammer down on an empty chamber, but with a charged magazine inserted (called transport mode), may offer a good compromise between safety and readiness for many situations.

Self-decocking autoloading pistols

The administrative procedures for self-decocking autoloaders are all the same as those for the trigger-cocking autoloaders. Remember that there is usually no manual safety and the gun will fire any time there is a round chambered and the trigger is pressed. On those self-decocking guns that also have a manual safety, it should be on during all administrative processes and then pushed into the "off" position prior to carrying.

Abandoned or unfamiliar pistols

It is not unusual for one to discover a firearm that has been carelessly left or abandoned. In most cases, a found weapon should be left exactly where it is and should not be touched. It may have been involved in a crime. The police should be called and the area quarantined until they arrive. Valuable and perishable physical evidence will thus be preserved.

However, there may be times when a found weapon must be handled for safety's sake. There may well be other occasions when, for a variety of reasons, you are required to handle unfamiliar firearms.

First of all, do not hesitate to ask the weapon's owner or some other knowledgeable person how the gun functions. Some people decline to do this because they fear the embarrassment associated with admitting there is something they don't know. However, where safety is a factor, embarrassment is a relatively minor consideration. You will be considerably more embarrassed if you commit a blunder with an unfamiliar weapon that results in a needless injury!

Your first objective is usually to unload and clear the weapon. It should then be safely secured until its ultimate disposition can be determined. Remember *that found or recovered weapons, even familiar ones, may be defective, broken, improperly modified or improperly maintained.* Be sure that you keep the muzzle pointed in a safe direction and your finger away from the trigger.

1. Point the weapon in a safe direction and keep your finger away from the trigger.

2. If the weapon has a manual safety, place it in the "on" position.

3. If the weapon has a removable magazine, remove it.

4. If the weapon has a moveable bolt or slide, move it to the rear or do whatever is necessary to expose the chamber(s) and remove any and all live rounds.

5. Remove all other live rounds from the weapon.

6. Inspect once more to be sure you haven't inadvertently chambered a round.

7. Deposit the weapon in a secure place.

8. If appropriate, notify the police.

With a double-action revolver that is cocked, the hammer must be lowered before the weapon can be unloaded. Refer to page 141 for the exact procedure.

User-level maintenance (cleaning)

As with all machines, your handgun needs to be looked after, so that it will continue to function satisfactorily and will always be ready when you need it. If something on your handgun breaks, you will, of course, have to get it to an armorer or gunsmith to be fixed. What you yourself need to do is:

1. *Inspect it regularly,* so you can spot rust, cracked or broken parts and other flaws before they lead to a malfunction or an accident.

2. *Keep it clean.* Handguns get dirty and they must be cleaned. The weapon must be periodically field stripped so that the individual parts can be inspected

Chapter 17: Safe Gun Handling

and cleaned, and the gun subsequently reassembled. "Detail disassembly" is not usually necessary and is not recommended unless you are an armorer or gunsmith.

"Dry" solvent is now available in aerosol cans. It is manufactured expressly for gun cleaning and is recommended. With the high-pressure nozzle, dirt and debris can literally be blasted free of the gun or sufficiently loosened so that it can be easily wiped off.

3. *Clean the bore, particularly the chamber, regularly.* Run a swab (treated with bore cleaner) through the bore several times. Then, run several clean patches through. It doesn't take long. A brass wire brush is seldom necessary. If the bore is not cleaned regularly, it can corrode and suffer from a build-up of copper and other fouling.

A dirty or corroded chamber is especially dangerous because rounds may not chamber completely. If a round is incompletely chambered, the handgun will probably not fire at all, or, in the case of a revolver, you may not be able to get it loaded. In a defensive firearm, this condition is obviously unacceptable. One quick way to keep chamber and bore continuously clean is via a device called a "Bore Snake." A Bore Snake is a fabric tube with a bore brush built right into it. They are inexpensive and commonly available at sporting goods stores. One simply drags the tube through the bore from the chamber end (each chamber too, with revolvers). Once usually suffices and the entire process takes only a few seconds and can be done in the field. Highly recommended!

4. *Keep it adequately lubricated.* There must be sufficient lubrication between moving metal parts that contact each other. If there isn't, your handgun will fail to function correctly, heat up excessively under rapid fire, and will wear out quickly. Ensure that all critical points are lubricated with either grease or oil every time the gun is cleaned. A *light* coat of oil on external metal parts will prevent rust. A light coat of oil on the inside of the bore will also prevent rust. Grease is best for internal lubrication of contact parts because it will stay where you put it. Oil runs out and will eventually evaporate.

5. *Don't use oven cleaner or other corrosive compounds.* Some have used oven cleaner to get their weapons "white glove" clean. However, oven cleaner is extremely corrosive. It will corrode nearly any material, but it positively dissolves aluminum and most polymers.

With regard to exact procedures, the literature that comes with the handgun will show you all the particulars. The point here is that *you can't continue to neglect your handgun and expect it to function forever.* If cleaning your weapon is not something you are inclined to do yourself, then have it done periodically by an armorer or gunsmith.

Make regular maintenance a habit and your pistol will always be ready. If you take care of it, it will take care of you.

Conclusion

The above procedures have been extensively tested and are widely taught. I am satisfied that faithful adherence to them will reduce risks to the minimum. However, if you have gleaned from the forgoing that firearms are hazardous and that a single lapse of judgment could cause a tragedy, you are absolutely correct! Guns are never safe. They must always be handled and stored with reasonable caution and proper procedures.

Chapter 18

Tactical Handgun Operation: Stance

There are four tactical procedures common to all defensive handguns: drawing (presenting), firing, reloading and reducing stoppages. No student of defensive shooting is truly prepared until he has a good grasp of all four. These will be presented in detail in the following chapters.

The goal when practicing with any defensive handgun is to be able to quickly and unerringly strike a twenty by thirty centimeter rectangle with a sufficient number of bullets to gain a decisive stopping effect on the target, at any likely defensive range and under a wide variety of environmental circumstances. *Rapid and consistent hitting is the main objective.*

There is a world of difference, for example, between a yachtsman and a mariner; between a soldier and a warrior; between a gun owner and a gunman. Anyone can launch bullets, but it takes a gunman to hit consistently. Consistent hitting requires the simultaneous execution of a number of reflexive subroutines that must have been previously and thoroughly burned in. You often hear, from the lips of the uninformed, the term "instinct shooting," as if people were somehow born with an innate ability to skillfully operate a firearm. The fact is that there is no such thing as instinct shooting. *All shooting skills and knowledge are learned.*

In fact, defensive handgun instructors are presented with a unique problem when teaching these skills. The good news is that handguns are relatively simple machines, far less complicated than other machines we operate routinely, like cars and microwave ovens. The bad news is that we have to teach our students to operate this particular machine under the worst conditions imaginable! That is, our students have to be able to operate this machine in a coordinated way when their brains are little more than swirling masses of electrons. Unfortunately, that depiction correctly characterizes most defensive scenarios. True defensive handgun shooting is unlike any other species of shooting. There are few forms of recreational use of the handgun that properly instill and exercise the skills necessary for one to be a good defensive shooter. A good defensive shooter is one that can be depended upon, even under extreme conditions, to fire his handgun quickly and with sufficient marksmanship to end the fight quickly and conclusively.

There are five reflexive subroutines that must be employed in order to get the handgun from the holster and bullets on target quickly. They are:

1. Stance
2. Draw
3. Sight alignment
4. Trigger control
5. Follow through

All five must be learned in the same way anything else is learned, via repetitive practice. The most effective method for using a handgun in most defensive shooting situations involves gripping the weapon with both hands and holding it strongly, directly in front of the face at eye level. There can be situations where you have no choice but to shoot one-handed or two-handed and below eye level, but they are the exception.

Stance. The stance is a positioning of the body that stabilizes and controls the weapon during firing. It is the platform from which you will shoot. A solid shooting platform is necessary for stability, controllability and consistent positioning of the weapon. The two-handed stance techniques that work best for most people are the Weaver and isosceles. Revolver users will be well served by either one. Autoloader users will find the Weaver technique is the only one that really works well.

In either case, stand up straight as you address the target and keep your body weight solidly on *both* feet. Bend your knees slightly to take the strain out of your legs and back and improve your balance. You should be able to pivot to engage any target within a 180-degree fan to your front without having to move your feet.

You should be semi-relaxed, not tense. Do not lean over forward or backward. Do not squat. Do not strain. Do not hunch your head down into your shoulders.

Shooting instructors used to believe that tense muscles in the legs, arms and back improved the stability of the shooting platform. We now know, however, that exactly the opposite is true. Straining and tensing the muscles will only slow your reflexes and make it difficult to keep the weapon's sights on the target. As in boxing and other fighting arts, it is the one who remains composed and

Chapter 18: Tactical Handgun Operation: Stance

calm that will be successful. *Extreme tension, mental or physical, is nearly always counter-productive.*

Your stance is of utmost importance, because, although it is possible to hit from nearly any position so long as the handgun's sights can be aligned, *your stance will consistently situate the weapon in the same position, enabling you to consistently hit the target whether you can see the sights clearly or not.* At night, when you often cannot even see the gun, much less the sights, you will still be able to hit, because, with a consistent stance, you know where your weapon is and where it is pointed. At night, you depend on your stance alone. If you do not know where your weapon is pointed, you will not be able to hit. Therefore, your draw and stance must be practiced to the point where you gun comes up in the same place every time.

To test your progress, establish your stance, look at a target and close your eyes. With your eyes closed, draw your pistol and point the weapon where you believe the target to be. Then open your eyes. The weapon should be pointed directly at the target. If it is not, you need more practice.

The isosceles stance. Here, you shoot straight off the center of your chest. Your arms and chest form an isosceles triangle. Your chest must be directly perpendicular to a line from your body midline to the target. The weapon is grasped with the strong hand and the strong hand is then reinforced with the weak hand. *If the isosceles stance is to be correctly assumed, it is critical that the hands be even with each other as they grasp the weapon.* If one hand extends beyond the other, the weapon will not be centered on the chest as the elbows lock. This is why the isosceles stance does not work well for most autoloader shooters. The shape of the grip of most autoloaders is such that an even-handed grasp does not support the weapon's grip properly. When the autoloader's grip is grasped correctly, the hands will not be even and the isosceles stance will therefore not work well.

To test to make sure the hands are even, after grasping the weapon with both hands, extend both index fingers. They should be exactly even.

The Isosceles stance.

If they are not, the grip is incorrect for the isosceles stance.

Thumbs should be exactly parallel and the weak-hand index finger firmly wedged under the trigger guard. *Do not wrap your weak-hand index finger around the front of the trigger guard* as you may have seen target shooters do. This is a bad practice, even when the front of the trigger guard is checkered or hooked to facilitate this particular maneuver. The problem is that, under recoil, the index finger will slip and change positions. You will then have to stop and reposition the finger or accept an inconsistent finger position from shot to shot. You are better off wedging the finger under the trigger guard, as is suggested here. That way it will stay put.

When the grip is correctly executed, the weapon is then pushed forward until both elbows lock. The weapon's muzzle will be centered on the body midline, and must be at eye level. If your chest is facing the target squarely, the weapon will be pointed directly at the center of the target. Some practitioners do not lock elbows when assuming the isosceles stance. This derivation works so long as both elbows are flexed to the same degree.

The Weaver stance. With the Weaver stance, you shoot directly down your strong arm. It is as if you were shooting a rifle, with your strong arm serving as the weapon's stock. With the weapon in your strong hand, face the target squarely. Then, drop your strong-side foot back until your chest rotates clockwise thirty-five to forty-five degrees. Turn your head to again face the target. Your foot position should be the same as if you were boxing with the target. Without rotating your chest, extend your strong arm toward the target until it nearly locks and point the weapon at the target. Leave it in that position as you wrap your weak hand around your strong hand and use your weak arm to pull your strong arm into your strong-side shoulder. As with the isosceles stance, the weak-hand index finger is firmly wedged directly under the trigger guard.

The strong-side elbow will be slightly bent. The weak-side elbow will be greatly bent and rotated so that it is pointed downward. When the weak-side elbow is pointed downward, the weak (supporting) arm will, with its downward pressure, balance the upward pressure on the strong hand that is produced by the weapon's recoil. If the weak-side elbow is allowed to point to the side, the balancing effect is lost. In addition, elbows pointed to the side are more likely to be hit by incoming rounds than are elbows pointed down.

It is important that the strong-side elbow not be locked. A locked elbow will deliver the weapon's recoil directly into the strong-side shoulder, torquing the

Chapter 18: Tactical Handgun Operation: Stance

entire upper body. This greatly increases the amount of time between accurate shots. A slightly bent elbow acts as a shock absorber and allows the upper body to remain correctly positioned. Conversely, if the elbows are locked in the isosceles stance, recoil is delivered equally to both shoulders and the upper body is pushed back slightly, but is not torqued in either direction.

The Weaver Stance

An exception must sometimes be made for small-statured people who are shooting a Glock or any other light-framed autoloader that is susceptible to stoppages caused by insufficient support of the frame. In these cases, it may be necessary to lock the strong-side elbow to attain sufficient support.

The muzzle should be at eye level in line with the axis of the strong arm and pointed at the target. Your dominant eye should be on line with the front and rear sights and the target, generating a usable sight picture.

The Interview stance. In the interview stance, your body is bladed so that your handgun is positioned to the rear and out of reach of a suspect who is being confronted. Your weak hand is extended up in front of your body and your strong hand is positioned so that it can index your handgun if necessary. Assuming this position, you ask, "Can I help you sir?" The interview stance immediately conveys the idea that you are aware of a threat and that you are ready to take appropriate action.

What we know today, as the "Weaver Stance" was first developed in the 1950s by Jack Weaver. As described above, the Weaver stance is very close to what Jack himself used and recommended, with the exception of the head position. Jack suggested "tilting the head down a little" in order to get it on line with the gun. I suggest not moving the head at all and bringing the gun up all the way to eye level. The other incongruity you may notice is that I suggest that the Weaver stance finds its optimum application with the modern generation of full-sized autoloading handguns. Jack preferred the double-action revolver and used his stance effectively with that gun. Finally, there are a number of additional alterations of the Weaver stance that are commonly taught today. With all due respect to Jack and other luminaries, I believe that what I have described and demonstrated in this instructional text is the best of the genre.

The Interview Stance

Chapter 19

Tactical Handgun Operation: Draw

The draw sequence starts with the deliberate conscious decision to brandish the gun and ends when the weapon is locked into the shooting stance pointed at the target, ready to fire. *Drawing does not always involve firing.* The decision to brandish the weapon and the decision to actually cause it to discharge require two separate judgments. The handgun is not necessarily fired every time it is drawn. Sometimes you will draw the gun and fire immediately. Other times you will draw but refrain from firing while holding your gun on the suspect — sometimes for long periods. When drawing the gun, you must always be prepared to fire but you may not actually have to fire if the offender's behavior suddenly changes. However, it is extremely important that, upon making the decision to brandish the weapon, you brandish it quickly so that you have the *option* of shooting at the earliest possible moment.

There are only two factors that determine the speed at which the gun is drawn. They are the physiological limits within which you function and the economy of motion that can be achieved.

Obviously, it is economy of motion that will allow you to achieve the fastest draw of which you are physically capable. In this example, we are using a strong side belt holster positioned directly adjacent to the strong-side kidney. This type of holster holds the handgun in a forward cant at waist level and on the strong side. However, regardless of the holster used, at no time during the draw should the weapon's muzzle point at any part of your body. Check this out during dry fire.

There are seven steps to the draw:

1. Index
2. Clear
3. Rock and lock
4. Hands merge (correct grip)
5. Up strong to eye level
6. Back to ready (guard) position

7. Reholster (only after a thorough scan has revealed no additional threats)

Notice that firing the gun is not included in the draw sequence. It is a separate act requiring a separate decision.

Index. To index a handgun, the strong hand makes contact with the front of the body then moves to the rear, brushing the coat out of the way in the process (if the weapon was concealed under the coat). Next the strong hand drops onto the butt of the holstered weapon and slides forward into a firm grasp. It is desirable to make initial contact with the weapon's grip deliberately low, because, for the best ultimate positioning of the shooting hand, it is necessary that the hand be allowed to slide upward into the final shooting grip (master grip). Rubber grips or sharp checkering or stippling on the grip are thus not recommended, because they cling to the hand and prevent it from sliding into position.

Index

Those with long fingernails will find safe and swift handgun handling techniques described herein impossible. When handling guns, administratively or tactically, long fingernails have to go! Those who would retain long fingernails are best advised to pass on gun ownership.

With holsters equipped with a thumb-break snap, the thumb must disengage the snap as the hand drops onto the weapon. It sometimes requires two separate movements of the hand. That is a weak point of this type of holster. A better choice is often the pull-through snap holster that features a draw-activated release. The gun is snapped in the holster but the draw itself automatically releases the snap. Most concealment holsters are open top. That is, they have no manually activated release. Conversely, all holsters intended to be carried in the open have some kind of manually activated retention strap (thumb-break snap) or other device.

Chapter 19: Tactical Handgun Operation: Draw

The firing grip must be established while the weapon is still holstered. Do not settle for a sloppy grip with the idea that you will correct it after the gun is drawn. That often results in a dropped gun. With autoloaders, *a sloppy wobbly grip is also a prime cause of stoppages, usually failures to eject.* If you are going to shoot an autoloader, you must learn to consistently acquire a correct grip and hold the weapon firmly as you draw and fire.

An important exception to this rule must be made for the continuous motion system autoloaders. The full shooting grip cannot safely be established until both hands are on the weapon and the muzzle is pointed at the target. This is necessary because fully gripping the weapon depresses the squeeze-cocker, cocking the weapon. There is no manual safety. Therefore, the weapon must be lifted from the holster by pinching the grip between the lower portions of the thumb and fingers. The little and ring fingers can lightly wrap around the front of the grip as the weapon clears the holster, but the index and middle fingers must remain off the squeeze-cocker. The squeeze-cocker is only pressed when both hands are together on the gun and the gun is in front of you and pointed downrange.

Shooting hand is as high as possible on the grip. Wrist is locked.

The web of the strong hand should slide firmly into the upper depression in the rear of the weapon's grip. With autoloaders there is a tang just below the hammer that forms a concave depression as it joins the weapon's backstrap. This will prevent the hand from sliding too high and into the slide path. Revolvers do not have such a tang but there is still a concave area on the backstrap just behind the hammer. Unfortunately, this small hump is often not sufficient to reliably stop the hand's forward movement. It is the concavity on the other side of the grip, just rear of the trigger guard that provides the grip index for revolvers. The second joint of the middle finger of the gun hand should locate itself in this arch. That indexes the grip and the rest of the hand will then fall into place.

In either case it is critical that the shooting hand be as high on the grip of the pistol as practicable and that the gun be grasped firmly. Ideally, as the gun fires it will recoil backward and slightly upward, but it should settle quickly back down on target, naturally preparing you for the next shot. You should not have to force it back down. The wrist should remain locked as the gun discharges and not break into an upward rotation. A low grip will cause the gun to rock radically upward and the wrist to unlock and angulate upward during firing making it difficult to shoot rapidly with accuracy. Therefore, rapid and accurate shooting is impossible without a high firm grip on the gun.

Alignment of the pistol's barrel and the bones of your forearm should be accomplished as the grip is being established. This is the preferred orientation of the gun with the hand. However, with high-capacity (double-column) autoloading handguns, this alignment is not practical for most people because it positions the trigger finger too far away from the trigger for proper manipulation. Accordingly, most people find it necessary to rotate the gun twenty degrees clockwise out of direct horizontal alignment with the forearm. This arrangement makes a linear point more difficult but it is unavoidable with these handguns. In fact, the grips on some double-column magazine autoloaders are so bulky that they approach the shape of a cylinder. Because they are nearly as wide as they are deep, it is difficult to tell by feel which direction the muzzle is pointed. Even when the weapon feels as if it is being properly gripped, it may not be pointed where you thinks it is. Therefore, these weapons are not recommended for people with small hands. Even people with average-sized hands sometimes have difficulty.

Vertical alignment of the wrist, however, is critical and absolutely required, particularly with autoloaders. If the wrist is angulated up or down, the frame of the pistol will not be properly supported and a stoppage may well result. Like a sloppy grip, *a vertically angulated wrist is an invitation to a malfunction.*

The Colt/Browning System autoloaders have a manual safety and it will be in the "on" position as the weapon is carried in the holster. During the index phase of the draw, the strong-side thumb must be positioned on top of the manual safety lever so that the safety can be depressed to "off" at the end of the rock-and-lock phase. The manual safety will be pushed to the "off" position when both hands come together on the pistol, that is, as the weapon is pushed up from rock and lock and into completion of the draw.

As the strong hand reaches the weapon, *the weak hand should simultaneously be placed flat on your stomach* so that the middle finger is directly over the navel. This correctly positions the weak hand to acquire its support position as the draw progresses and it also gets the weak hand out of harm's way in the event that you are forced to begin firing before the draw is completed.

Chapter 19: Tactical Handgun Operation: Draw

In addition, *you must practice moving to the side as soon as the draw is initiated.* We no longer stand in one place and draw the pistol. You must move and draw simultaneously, so that, by the time your pistol is at eye level and ready to fire, your body is no longer where it was when you started.

Clear (the holster). The strong-side wrist will be angulated downward as you acquire your grip on the stocks of the weapon, particularly if the gun is carried high on the waist and is canted forward. The angulation will usually increase as the weapon is drawn upwards in an effort to clear the holster. It is important that you not succumb to the temptation to bend your trunk forward or roll forward with the strong shoulder in order to relieve the wrist angulation. There are a few types of holsters where some forward roll of the strong side shoulder may be necessary but it should be minimized. *Exaggerated shoulder movement will slow the draw considerably.* Your trunk and head should remain motionless as your hands and arms do all the moving.

Finally, do not involve your weak hand in clearing the weapon from the holster. You must get used to clearing the gun with one hand only. The weak hand may be crucially occupied and not available. Also, when the weak hand becomes involved in grasping the gun or attempting to stabilize the holster, the muzzle of the gun will invariably cross it as the gun is drawn.

Gun clears the holster.

Rock and lock. As soon as the weapon's muzzle has cleared the top of the holster, you must rock and lock your forearm and wrist. The barrel and the axis of the strong-side forearm must become aligned as the weapon clears the holster. The axis of the barrel should be parallel with the ground at the end of this stage. This will position the gun so that it can be fired in a forward direction at the earliest possible moment in the draw sequence.

To accomplish this, at the moment the muzzle clears the top of the holster, you straighten your strong-side wrist as you rock your elbow downward. As stated above, the wrist must be vertically aligned with the forearm during firing. However, the wrist must first angulate in order to get a firm grip on the gun as the gun is in the holster. The idea with the rock and lock stage is to get the wrist locked vertically (and the gun pointed forward) as soon as possible during the draw routine so that reliable and effective firing can take place at the earliest possible moment.

Remember, *at this stage the trigger finger is still in register.* To review, the trigger finger has only two correct positions: in register or within the trigger guard and in contact with the trigger face. When in register, the trigger finger is outside of the trigger guard. It is straight and lies alongside the slide of an autoloader or the frame of a revolver. When necessary, the trigger finger quickly moves from register to inside the trigger guard making contact with the trigger face. Through repetitive practice, the trigger finger will learn the distance from register to contact with the trigger. After sufficient practice, there will be virtually no danger that, when positioning, the finger will hit the trigger too hard and cause an accidental discharge. It is, therefore, important that the register position be consistent, so that the finger always knows exactly where it is in relation to the trigger.

Hands merge. Hands merge when the supporting hand joins the gun hand at the point in the draw sequence just after the rock-and-lock stage has been completed. After joining together, the weak hand then supports the strong hand and the weapon's grip as the gun is lifted and extended into the firing position. *It is desirable to maximize hand contact with the grip of the weapon.* The flesh of both hands should make as much contact with the weapon's grip as possible.

Shot-to-shot control of a handgun is enhanced by maximizing grip contact, not by ardent squeezing. Severely squeezing the weapon's grip will only tighten muscles and slow you down. If you expect to hit quickly, you must be able to shoot from a semi-relaxed (but firm) grip and stance.

Hands must not separate during firing. If they do, you will lose control of the pistol. This could result in your support hand moving in front of the muzzle and being shot. During firing, your hands must stay together on the grips of the pistol. If your hands separate during practice firing, you must correct your grip and stance before going any further in your training.

In general, autoloaders have more supportable grip surface than do revolvers.

Chapter 19: Tactical Handgun Operation: Draw

With autoloaders, there is nearly always considerable area on the grip panel that is not in contact with the strong hand as the weapon is being grasped during the draw. *The supporting hand must fill in this unsupported area.* Remember that if you are using the isosceles stance, parallel hand positioning takes precedence over maximizing grip contact. For this reason, autoloader users are usually better served by the Weaver stance. In the Weaver stance, parallel hand positioning is not necessary or desirable.

At the point where the gun has cleared the holster and you have rocked and locked your wrist and forearm, the pistol's muzzle should be pointed straight forward and your elbow should be close to your body in the vicinity of the kidney. Your weak hand should still be flat against your midriff. If you are forced to shoot at this point, you can safely do so, since the gun will not be pointed at any part of your body and your weak hand will be against your navel and out of harm's way. The weak hand must sweep in from the side, parallel with the gun hand in order to join the strong hand. It is critical that the muzzle not cross the weak hand as the weak hand comes into its support position.

Hands merge.

With autoloaders, both thumbs must be up and each in contact with the weapon's grip, the weak-side thumb in tandem with the strong-side thumb. You should be able to see both thumbnails as the weapon is held at eye level. This is called the "full-contact" or "flying-thumb" grip. It is the only one we recommend for autoloaders. The strong-side thumb must not be so low that it crosses under the weak-side thumb. That diminishes hand-grip contact. Do not be concerned when the upper part of the weak-side thumb makes contact with the slide itself. Such light contact is necessary and normal. This contact will not hurt the thumbs nor interfere with the operation of the pistol, even if you are left-handed.

On most autoloaders, the ejection port is on the right side of the pistol. If left-handers grasp the weapon as suggested above, they usually find their right thumb directly adjacent to it. There is sometimes concern that the thumb will hamper case ejection as the weapon fires. Again, this is unlikely and you need not worry about it.

In any event, keep your thumbs high and tight into the grip. Do not let them fall forward where they will lose contact with the grip and interfere with the trigger or other controls. For example, do not let your thumb get under the slide-lock lever on your autoloader. Under recoil, the knuckle may push the lever up and lock the slide to the rear prematurely.

Thumbs up grip for autoloading pistols.

Revolver users should also maximize grip contact. However the thumbs should be bent down. That will get them away from possible interference with the cylinder release.

With either gun, the index finger of the supporting hand should be wedged under the trigger guard, not hooked around the front, where it will pull the front sight down and to the weak side. As previously discussed, not only does this faulty practice tend to pull the front sight down, it also makes it necessary to reposition the finger with each shot since it will not stay put under recoil. If you wedge the weak-hand index finger under the trigger guard, as is suggested, it will remain in position and no shot-to-shot readjustment will be necessary. Another incorrect position for the weak-side index finger is in the vicinity of the trigger itself. Only one index finger belongs on or near the trigger. An additional finger will just get in the way.

If you are using an autoloader, be sure that neither the weak-hand thumb nor any other part of either hand is positioned directly in the path of the slide. When the weapon fires and the slide moves violently backward, any body part that gets in the way will be injured and the gun itself will experience a stoppage. The outdated wrap-around grip technique is fatally flawed in this regard. This practice of wrapping the weak-hand thumb around the first knuckle of the strong-hand thumb as the weapon is grasped is obsolete anyway, even when used with revolvers. It was instituted in the days when it was believed that squeezing the grip enhanced controllability. We now know that such ardent

Chapter 19: Tactical Handgun Operation: Draw

Grip for the revolver.

squeezing, in any form, is profitless, indeed counter-productive.

Up strong to eye level. With both hands now joined on the weapon's grip, the entire unit is pushed out and brought up strong directly to eye level. Push the weapon straight to the target. Any deviation from a direct path will slow the draw. The most common deviation is the so-called "Zebco" draw in which the operator brings the weapon over his head then down to the target as if he were fly-fishing. It is easy to spot and should be corrected immediately. The other extreme is "bowling" or "scooping," that is, pushing the pistol way down then back up in a long arcing motion as if the operator were throwing a bowling ball.

As the weapon is brought to eye level, the strong-hand index finger remains in register until the decision to fire is made. On Colt/Browning System autoloaders, the manual safety is pushed "off" as soon as the hands have joined in the firing grip. Two-stage decocking autoloaders have a decocking lever but it will normally be in the "up" (enabled) position as the weapon is carried and will not have to be pushed up during the draw. Double-action revolvers do not have manual safeties.

The manual safety on Colt/Browning System autoloaders must be pushed "off" and "on" with the strong-hand thumb. Do not get used to pushing it off with the weak hand because the weak hand may not always be available. Left-handed operators of these guns need a left-handed manual safety. The strong-side thumb should operate the safety regardless of which hand is dominant.

Remember; bring the gun to your strong eye. *Do not try to bring your eye (and head) down to meet the gun.* Stand upright and let your arms move the gun. Your head should not be tilted or hunched into your shoulders. Your neck, shoulders and back should not need to strain to maintain your position. Also, if you're using the Weaver stance, don't overextend to the point where your chest rotates toward the target. You will be off balance and in a weak position. Your shoulders must remain directly over your hips.

You were initially looking at the target. Based on what you saw, you made the decision to draw. Then, as the weapon is drawn and brought up to eye level, the strong eye changes focus or accommodates from the target to the front sight. When the weapon is at eye level, *you should be looking at and be focused on the front sight, not the target.* In fact, if you are holding a suspect at gunpoint, your focus will change from suspect to front sight and vice versa many times, since your focus will change back to the target when the gun drops from eye level to the ready position.

Up strong

The total draw time, starting with the weapon in the holster and ending with it in both hands at eye level and ready to fire, should consume one second from an unconcealed strong-side holster. You are nominally allowed an additional two tenths of a second when drawing from a concealed holster. However, as a practical matter, times will vary depending upon the type of holster, method of concealment, etc. The important thing is that the weapon be drawn smoothly and brought into a usable firing position as quickly as practicable.

During this phase, the gun must continually be coming up onto the target. *The target must always be above the gun until the last moment of the draw movement*

Chapter 19: Tactical Handgun Operation: Draw

when the gun is actually on the target. Thus, if the target moves during the draw, you can easily follow it as the draw continues. It is when the gun overshoots the target (as in the Zebco draw) that the target has an opportunity to move without you being aware of it.

Remember, when it comes to a speedy draw, smooth is fast. Jerky is slow. Steps must be blended together smoothly so that there is no jerkiness or unproductive motions or over corrections.

Ready position, sometimes called the "guard position." The gun is not drawn for trivial reasons. That is, if one draws a gun in a public place, he must be prepared to shoot immediately and must have had good cause to brandish a gun to begin with. However, as a practical matter, the vast majority of times that a gun is brandished, its sudden presence suffices to defuse the situation, alter the offender's behavior and the actual immediate firing of the gun becomes unnecessary. Thus, when one draws a gun he must have the mental toughness to instantly end a human life, if necessary, but he must also be prepared to refrain from shooting if the situation suddenly improves. It could go either way! The point is, *once the gun is drawn and is on target at eye level, you must either shoot right then or quickly assume the ready position.*

Continuing to hold the gun at eye level is ill advised because your hands and the gun itself block your vision of everything beneath the level of the sights. This may make it possible for the person at whom you are pointing the gun to drop out of sight suddenly, making it necessary for you to drop the gun from eye level in order to look for him. That maneuver is time consuming, clumsy and often fatal. Therefore, don't hold him at gunpoint with your gun at eye level and your sights on his chest. Instead, when you draw, don't let your gun get any higher than his navel. With your front sight on his navel, you can still see his hands and most of his trunk. When you must fire, your first round should go into his navel. Subsequent rounds go up his body midline, but no higher than the neck. If you don't fire within two seconds of completing the draw, default to the ready position.

In order to assume the ready position, drop your gun from eye level until the muzzle is pointing downward at a forty-five degree angle. Do not alter elbow or wrist angles. Pivot the pistol down from the shoulders, leaving elbow and wrist angles unchanged. That way you can quickly bring the gun back up to eye level without having to do anything but pivot the arms upward. As the ready position is assumed, the trigger finger returns to the register position (all handguns). On the Colt/Browning system, the manual safety returns to the "on" position, or remains "off," at your option. The strong-side thumb remains on top of the manual safety lever, regardless of its position. If the autoloader has been fired, cocking the hammer via the action of the slide, it must be decocked.

Once in the ready position, the pistol should then be withdrawn straight back to the midriff. This changes wrist angles but it gets the gun close to the body, making a gun take-away exceedingly difficult for the suspect. The weak-side hand goes flat against the navel and the strong-side hand, grasping the pistol, goes directly on top of it. Elbows stay down. This is sometimes call "Position Sul (south)," because it keeps the pistol's muzzle close to the body and pointed down.

While in the ready position or in *sul*, *you should move laterally about every four seconds. You should also issue verbal challenges* if appropriate. Constant movement will make it difficult for the suspect(s) to plan an attack. Make it a habit to look left, right and behind every time your gun drops from eye level to the ready position.

Ready position.

Reholstering and reconcealing. Whether you have fired or not, reholstering should be done quickly and smoothly, but only after it is clear that the danger has passed and there is no longer any reason to have the gun out. *Look around first!* Scan the entire scene, particularly the area behind you, before deciding to reholster. Many people train in such a way that they are used to reholstering the moment the gun drops from eye level. That is a dangerous mistake. It is important that you go through the entire process, that is:

1. Go to the ready position or *sul* first.

2. Carefully look around by moving your entire head, not just your eyes. Remember, an attacker can sneak right up behind you if you fail to look all

Chapter 19: Tactical Handgun Operation: Draw

around.

3. Then if appropriate, reholster and reconceal.

Reholster the weapon using your gun hand only. Retract your weak hand in toward your body. Any holster that requires you to use two hands to draw or reholster is undesirable and is not recommended for defensive carry. Do not try to stabilize your holster with your supporting hand during reholstering. *You should not involve your weak hand in reholstering at all* because it may not always be available. In fact, do not involve your weak hand in any way in removing the weapon from the holster, replacing the weapon back in the holster, operating the decocking lever or depressing the magazine release. *Leave your weak hand free and available.*

The trigger finger must remain in the register position as the gun is reholstered. Under no circumstances can it be on the trigger. If it is, the top of the holster will force it into the trigger and may well cause the weapon to discharge at that point.

Carefully look around, then retract your weak hand to rest on your body.

The Farnam Method of Defensive Handgunning

Position the strong-side thumb on the back edge of the slide to prevent the gun from cocking when holstered.

Avoid looking at the holster during the reholstering process. Keep your attention focused in the direction from which danger is likely to come. The easiest way to find the opening of a belt holster with the weapon's muzzle is to bring the muzzle in from the rear, pointing the weapon down and catching the front edge of the opening on the top side of the muzzle. Then push the pistol down into the holster as far as it will go. Be careful not to allow the muzzle of your loaded weapon to point backward or forward as it is reholstered. The firing grip (master grip) should be maintained until the weapon is firmly back in the holster so the weapon can be quickly redrawn if necessary. Do not surrender the master grip until the weapon is completely seated in the holster.

An important exception to the above must again be made for the continuous motion system autoloaders. As soon as this gun is lowered from the fire position, the fingers must be relaxed and the squeeze-cocker allowed to return to its rest position (decocking the weapon). *It is especially important that the weapon be already decocked during the reholstering process.* This gun must be cocked only when it is in the firing position. At all other times, in order to avoid an unintentional discharge (especially during drawing and/or reholstering), it must be uncocked.

Chapter 19: Tactical Handgun Operation: Draw

Reholster without looking.

With manually-decocking autoloaders, *a dangerous mistake is to fail to decock the weapon before reholstering.* This mental lapse will likely cause the weapon to unintentionally discharge as it is being reholstered.

Autoloader users have one other concern: with inside-the-waistband (IWB) holsters and some tight external holsters, there is a danger that the friction between the holster and the slide will force the slide back as the gun is holstered. This can place the gun in half cock or even full cock as the user holsters it, and it can happen without him even being aware of it. Therefore, people using tight holsters and autoloading pistols need to *position the strong-side thumb on the back edge of the slide as the gun is holstered, forcefully holding the slide forward.* This may compromise the grip slightly, but it is important that the slide stay forward.

That is the entire draw routine. It must be practiced until all the steps are distinctly present but smoothly blended into a fluid motion. If you do it properly, the gun will never point at any of your body parts, no matter how fast you go (assuming a standing position). To reiterate, the actual firing of the gun is not

Reconceal quickly.

included in the draw routine because it requires a separate decision.

Close range. As mentioned before, there are some special situations that may require a divergence from the procedures described above. One such circumstance is shooting at extremely close range. In close-range shooting, it is permissible and may indeed be prudent, to allow the weapon to discharge mid-stroke, that is, before the front sight actually reaches eye level, but after the hands have joined, sometimes even before the hands have joined. In these cases, *you should begin to apply pressure to the trigger at the point in the draw where you know that if the weapon discharged at that point, the bullet would hit the target.* Continue the draw as normal while you increase pressure on the trigger. The weapon will discharge at a point in the draw where a hit is assured.

The forgoing is sometimes called the "retention draw." It is designed to help you to retain the pistol (keep it from being snatched away by an attacker) during the draw. *Retention is enhanced by keeping the weapon close to your body until both hands are on the weapon in the final grip position.* It is extremely hazardous to extend the gun away from your body when it is being held in only one hand.

Chapter 19: Tactical Handgun Operation: Draw

If your attacker is close and closing, you should try to rapidly move in a tight circle as you draw. As long as you move backward in a circle, he will have difficulty catching up with you. You may have to shoot while moving. If you move straight backward, he will quickly overtake you. If you allow him to get within arm's reach, he may be able to disarm you before you can shoot. If you stumble and fall as you attempt to move backwards, or if you get pushed down, *you must fall on your strong side.* Even when you are down, it is still possible to assume a usable shooting position and deliver accurate fire. Draw in your legs and extend your arms between your knees into a two-handed position.

Retention draw.

If your attacker is directly to your rear and you cannot turn far enough to engage him, you will have to move your feet as you turn. Take a step forward and to your strong side. Do not take a step backward. You have no idea where you are stepping and may stumble. If you step forward, you can at least see where your foot is going. Step forward with your strong-side foot as you turn around to the weak side and subsequently draw your pistol.

It is extremely important that you not lead with your strong side as you turn. If you do, you will be handing your gun to the attacker and you may be quickly disarmed. He will not be able to disarm you if you turn the other way. Don't just do a rotation in place. Move laterally as you turn.

Chapter 20

Tactical Handgun Operation: Sight Alignment

Now we will talk about actually firing the gun. The important point here is that all shooting must be surgically accurate and as quick as possible. Get used to shooting as quickly as you can and as slowly as you must. Accuracy is not optional.

Defensive handguns generally come from the factory with a front and a rear sight. The sights are mounted above the barrel, and an imaginary line connecting the two sights is coaxial with the barrel. The rear sight is usually a flat blade with a square notch in the middle. The front sight is usually a blade that is perpendicular to your eye. When the pistol is lifted to eye level and pointed downrange, look through the notch in the rear sight to the front sight. The blade of the front sight should just fill the rear sight notch (with equal amounts of light on each side), so that the top of the front sight is on line with the top of the wings of the rear sight. When thus aligned, assuming the sights are adjusted correctly, the bullet will strike whatever is covered by the top center of the front sight. Sight alignment refers to the

1. Front sight
2. Rear sight
3. The shooter's dominant eye

all being correctly aligned, irrespective of the target. Your dominant eye should focus on the front sight.

When your dominant eye, the weapon's front and rear sights and the center of the target are all exactly aligned and your dominant eye is focused on the front sight, you will have obtained a correct sight picture and hence, correct sight alignment. If your bullet is to strike the target, *correct sight alignment is mandatory.* In the vast majority of people, one

Correct sight alignment.

191

eye is stronger than the other. If you are contralateral, your dominant eye is on the opposite side of your body from your strong hand. If you are ipsilateral, your strong hand and dominant eye are on the same side. In either event, *you will have the greatest success shooting with your strong hand and your dominant eye, regardless of which is which.*

You must train your dominant eye to quickly pick up the front sight as soon as it reaches the peripheral zone and to automatically accommodate from the target to the front sight as your arms bring the weapon to eye level and lock into your stance. If you do not know which of your eyes is dominant, take this test:

1. Extend your strong arm and extend the thumb vertically.
2. With both eyes open, cover an object downrange (such as a large rock) with the thumbnail.
3. Look at and focus on the object.
4. You should see two ghostly thumbs; one will be in line with the object, and the other will be off to one side.
5. Without disturbing this alignment, close your right eye.
6. If you now see only one thumb directly in line with and obscuring the object, your left eye is dominant.
7. On the other hand, if you can still see the object and the thumb is off to one side, then it is your right eye that is dominant.

Use your dominant eye to sight, but you should shoot with both eyes open, if possible. Some people find it extremely difficult to shoot without closing the non-dominant eye. Nevertheless, you should try to avoid such eye closing. Closing the non-dominant eye severely reduces peripheral vision, making it difficult to see sources of danger or safety hazards (on the range) that may be off to one side or the other.

If the front sight is in sharp focus, as it ought to be, the rear sight and the target will be out of focus and blurred. This is as it should be. It is not possible to keep both sights and the target in focus simultaneously. Therefore, *concentrate on the front sight.* Remember to keep your front sight on the target and do not let it move. It must remain undisturbed, in the middle of the rear sight notch, and on the target right up to the instant of discharge. If the target is moving, you must track it with the front sight. That is, you must rotate at your waist and move your upper body and the weapon, so that the front sight stays on the

Chapter 20: Tactical Handgun Operation: Sight Alignment

target as the trigger is pressed. It is important that you do not stop when you think the weapon is going to discharge or move ahead of the target and wait for it to cross your sights. You must continue to track the target with the front sight as you press the trigger.

If your pistol's sights are adjusted correctly, *the bullet will strike at the top center of the front sight,* so don't cover the target with the front sight. Keep the front sight just below where you want to hit and hold it steady as you press the trigger.

The stance will get your weapon generally on target, but the sight picture will provide verification that it is exactly on target. Sighting is ninety percent stance and ten percent aligning sights in front of the dominant eye. *Your stance aims. Your eye verifies.*

The sight picture must be established before the weapon is allowed to discharge, and it must be reestablished immediately after discharge. As a practical matter, nobody can obtain and maintain a perfect and motionless sight picture. The sight picture will always float around in the area of the center of the target. This floating is normal and will usually not be severe enough to cause a miss. *What will cause a miss is an enthusiastic over correction,* by means of a convulsive muscle spasm in the arm and hand, otherwise known as a trigger jerk.

Chapter 21

Tactical Handgun Operation: Trigger Control

Manipulating the trigger. If the circumstances are such that firing the gun is indicated and justified and you have a correct sight picture, then you should begin firing without delay. Only precision shooting will do. Misses resulting in the attacker not being stopped (and probably unintentional hits in addition) will result from your trying to shoot faster than you can hit. Experience has shown that *it will likely take more than one solid hit to reliably stop a determined attacker* so you must plan on hitting multiple times. Remember, your target is the body midline, navel to neck. All bullets must hit that area. *A slow hit is better than a quick miss.*

The secret of correct trigger manipulation is to slowly press the trigger straight back as the sight picture is maintained. When the weapon discharges, it will come as a surprise. In fact, it *must* come as a surprise. Trying to predict the exact moment of discharge is impossible without jerking the trigger and such muzzle-jarring trigger jerks virtually guarantee a miss. *A surprise break is thus mandatory.* A solid hit is assured if you have a correct sight picture and maintain correct sight alignment at the moment the gun discharges. The entire sighting process may appear to take too much time and at first it probably will. However, in time you will learn to do it quickly. *Force yourself to shoot no faster than you can hit.*

Trigger press. The trigger finger is gently placed in contact with the trigger and the slack is taken up. Triggers on defensive guns should have some slack. The trigger must then be pressed *straight back,* smoothly and steadily and all in one motion. Don't start with your finger out of contact and try to get a running start on the trigger. Crashing into the trigger with the trigger finger is a guaranteed miss. Make gentle contact first; then press the trigger through smoothly. In fact, there are only two places your finger should be when you have a gun in your hand, in register or in contact with the trigger. *One place your finger should never be is within the trigger guard, hovering above the trigger.* Smooth, steady pressure continues to be applied until the weapon discharges. The sight picture is maintained during the entire process and reestablished immediately after discharge. Jerking or flinching at the expected moment of discharge is a problem common to all shooters and has caused more misses than all other reasons combined.

Many people flinch, not only with their hands and arms, but with their legs also. They actually push up off the ground with their toes and push their entire body forward at the expected moment of discharge. The entire body moves and, of course, disturbs the sight picture. This can usually be cured by keeping both feet (especially the heels) solidly on the ground with the body weight distributed equally on both. Be sure to keep ground contact with both the heels and toes. Do not lean or thrust over forward.

Again, do not try to jerk the trigger when you think the muzzle is on target or pull the trigger through in jerky steps. *Smoothness is the key.* Once pressure is started, do not let up. Do not try to anticipate the exact moment of discharge. If you do, you will lose the sight picture, because your concentration will shift from the front sight to the trigger. If you expect to hit the target, the weapon must be allowed to discharge when it is ready -- not when you want it to. It must be that way. Just relax and keep the weapon steady with the front sight on the target. Slowly apply smooth and steady pressure to the trigger. To reiterate, the exact moment of discharge will and must be a surprise.

The first shot will set the tone for the rest of the shots. If the first shot is a hit, the follow-up shots will all be hits too. However, if you miss with the first round, it usually requires several additional misses before you recompose yourself and finally get your first hit. Such a time lag during gunfights is often fatal. *You must hit with the first shot!*

The violent motion of the handgun upon discharge will, of course, disarrange the sight picture momentarily. However, it must be reestablished immediately in preparation for the next shot. A proper shooting stance and firing grip will attenuate the unsettling effects of recoil and reduce to a minimum the time necessary to restore the sight picture.

The speed at which you press the trigger will always be a compromise between urgency and accuracy. The main determining factor will be the difficulty of the target. If you press the trigger too fast, you will miss. If you press the trigger too slowly, you will consume more time than is necessary and thus give your opponent more of an opportunity to kill you. The sure sign of the true gunman is that *he will press the trigger at just the right speed to achieve the minimum accuracy necessitated by the difficulty of the target.* He does not go too fast or too slow, always just right. It can be likened to a blind person approaching the edge of a cliff. If he goes forward too fast he will arrive at the edge before

Chapter 21: Tactical Handgun Operation: Trigger Control

he realizes it and will fall over. If he stays way back and approaches slowly, he won't fall over, but he will not get close to the edge either. The idea is to get right up to the edge, but stop short of it. Learning how to control the trigger is like gaining your sight!

We strongly recommend practicing with full-charge ammunition in your defensive pistol rather than with underpowered reloads. Target shooters who use a lot of reloads tend to be surprised at the blast and recoil of service rounds on those rare occasions when they actually shoot them. Such surprises are undesirable during lethal confrontations.

Continuous trigger contact. Once your finger has contacted the trigger, *it should not lose contact until all required shots have been fired.* As soon as the gun drops from the sighting plane to the ready or *sul* position, the trigger finger returns to the register position. In order that follow-up shots be rapid and accurate, after the sight picture has been reestablished, the finger allows the trigger to move forward (after the first shot) just far enough to reengage the sear (catch the link or reset the trigger), then rearward pressure is again started on the trigger for the next shot. In other words, the finger never loses contact with the trigger as the gun is firing, regardless of how many shots are ultimately discharged. If the finger does lose contact as the gun is firing, it will come out ahead of the trigger then slam back into it for the next shot. Accurate fire is impossible if the trigger is manipulated in that manner.

Remember to reacquire the sight picture first and *then* reset the trigger. *You must hold the trigger all the way back during recoil.* Once the sight picture has been reestablished (and additional shooting is required), reset the trigger and immediately start pressing it back again. Repeat the cycle until additional shooting appears unnecessary.

As a general rule, when shooting defensively, you are advised to continue to shoot at the offending individual until he either (1) falls to the ground or (2) runs away. If the felon has failed to do either of these two things, firing should continue.

A common error seen during rapid fire is loosening the grip and then compulsively regrasping between shots. This is sometimes called milking the grip. Milking is a common cause of missed shots. Once established, the grip should remain firm, neither loosening nor tightening.

Sight settings. Some target shooters set their sights to hit the middle of the bull's-eye circle when they hold the top edge of the front sight on the bottom edge of the circle. This arrangement is commonly referred to as bull's eye sights or the six-o-clock hold. For defensive shooting, battle sights are preferred. Battle sights are sights that are set so that the point of aim and the point of impact are the same. That means that the bullet will strike whatever is in the middle of the top edge of the front sight. For most domestic defensive handgun shooting, your handgun should have battle sights set for twenty-five meters. They will be dead-on from point blank to twenty-five meters and close out to fifty meters.

There are three things to remember with all handguns, but particularly with autoloaders:

1. Locked wrist on the strong hand. To reiterate, if your wrist is not locked, the frame of the autoloading pistol may not have sufficient support for the pistol to cycle properly. The result is usually a failure to eject or some other stoppage. Needless to say, such stoppages are inconvenient when they occur in the middle of a gun battle. The term locked refers to the straight, vertical alignment of the hand, forearm and the pistol barrel. Horizontal alignment is also desirable, but, as stated above, it is not achievable for many people with small hands.

2. A high, firm grip with the pistol deep into the strong hand. The gun must automatically and quickly settle back onto the target after it discharges in order for you to prepare for a quick and accurate follow-up shot. It will not settle properly and quickly if the grip is too low on the pistol's stocks.

3. Continuous physical trigger contact. Your trigger finger must never lose contact with the trigger as the gun is firing. When you press the trigger through for the first shot, it should be pressed all the way to the rear. When the gun discharges and settles back on the target, allow the trigger to move forward just far enough to reengage the sear, or catch the link. You can usually feel the click when that point is reached. Without allowing the trigger to move any further forward, begin to press the trigger back again for your next shot. Repeat this cycle until you choose to stop shooting. Then return the trigger finger to the register position. With practice, continuous trigger contact will become reflexive.

Revolvers are not really an exception, as we still want to see continuous trigger contact. However, the trigger must be allowed to return to its full, forward position after each shot because that is the way the trigger mechanism is designed. Revolvers (and some self-decocking autoloaders) are thus inherently

Chapter 21: Tactical Handgun Operation: Trigger Control

slower from shot to shot than are most autoloaders.

What every student of defensive pistol shooting must avoid is allowing the trigger finger to move too far forward after the shot and thus losing physical contact with the trigger. When this happens, the trigger finger will start its rearward movement for the next shot from somewhere in space, thus getting a running start on the trigger and subsequently slamming into it. The resulting shot will consistently miss the intended target because trigger slamming, yanking, jerking, etc. always moves the entire pistol just before discharge.

To summarize, when the pistol is drawn and brought up to eye level and the decision has been made to fire:

1. Hit the brakes! Don't try to fire before the sight picture has been confirmed.
2. Confirm that the sights are on target and that the sight picture is correct.
3. Carefully establish finger contact with the trigger.
4. Start rearward pressure while holding the pistol steady or tracking the target if the target is moving.
5. Keep the front sight on target.
6. Wait for the gun to discharge.
7. After the gun discharges, hold the trigger all the way to the rear and immediately recover and reestablish a correct sight picture on the target.
8. Hold the gun steady as you let the trigger up until you catch the link. Let it up no further (maintain continuous trigger contact).
9. Assuming additional shooting is necessary, immediately start rearward pressure on the trigger again.
10. . Repeat the cycle as many times as necessary.

Trigger technique for specific guns

The Colt/Browning system autoloader. These weapons are properly carried with the hammer cocked, live round in the chamber, manual safety on. The first and all other shots are fired from a cocked hammer. Typically the trigger only moves 1.5mm (.06 inches) against a resistance of 2.3kg (5 lbs) to release the hammer and discharge the weapon. *The center of the pad of the trigger finger should lie on the center of the trigger.* The triggers on Colt/Browning System autoloaders should be narrow but may be grooved so long as the grooves are not sharp.

During firing, the correct grip must be maintained. Thus, the strong-side thumb must push the manual safety off (down) during the draw (immediately after the hands merge) and *must remain on top of the safety, maintaining continuous downward pressure as the weapon is fired.* If the strong-side thumb gets under the manual safety during firing, the weapon's recoil may force the thumb upward so that it unintentionally forces the manual safety back on (up) thereby making the weapon temporarily unfirable. The best place for the manual safety lever is sandwiched between thumbs.

Trigger finger placement for the Colt/Browning System.

Fingers and thumbs must be kept away from the slide-release lever. If a finger or thumb is positioned under the slide release, the weapon's recoil may force it to push the slide release upward, locking the slide to the rear while there are still rounds in the magazine. Conversely, if finger pressure is applied to the top of the slide-release lever, the slide may not lock to the rear when it is supposed to, after the last round is fired. The slide, of course, should lock to the rear when the last round is fired. This is to remind you that the weapon is empty. Obviously, the slide should not lock to the rear when there are still cartridges in the magazine.

In defensive shooting, the trigger finger must be able to make contact with the trigger as the target is tracked. You must be able to touch the trigger in anticipation of having to shoot, then, at the last moment, decide not to shoot. When holding a Colt/Browning system autoloader on a suspect, your trigger finger is properly in register and the manual safety is on or off, at your option. Either way, with the strong-side thumb resting on top of it. If you must fire, the safety is pushed off (if necessary); sight picture is established; contact is established with the trigger and the trigger is pressed. If you choose to have the manual safety on when both hands are holding the pistol, you may have to

Chapter 21: Tactical Handgun Operation: Trigger Control

push it off, then back on several times during the confrontation, all the time keeping your finger in register. Simply leaving the manual safety off any time the pistol is being held in both hands is a simpler solution.

Some heavily involved target shooters suggest that when the Colt/Browning system autoloader is being held in the firing position, the trigger finger should be held slightly out of contact with the trigger, poised just in front of it. They contend that the shooter can then simply bump or slap the trigger gently when he wants the weapon to discharge. Like so many other techniques developed by naive contest shooters, this procedure is counterproductive in defensive shooting. The problem is that this technique requires a super-light trigger (less than 1 kg). A bump forceful enough to release a legitimate 2.3kg defensive trigger will invariably bump the front sight right off the target.

Double-action revolver. Here, as is the case with all trigger-cocking pistols, *the center of the trigger should lay in the first joint of the trigger finger, not on the pad.* You need that much finger on the trigger in order to have sufficient strength to pull it through smoothly. When the weapon discharges, the trigger must be allowed to return all the way forward to its original rest position. The sight picture must then be immediately reestablished and trigger pressure may then be started once again for the next shot.

Trigger finger placement for revolvers.

If the weapon is intended for defensive use, the double-action revolver trigger itself should be smooth (no grooves) and narrow. Wide sharply grooved target triggers and triggers equipped with trigger shoes are a liability in defensive shooting. When shooting in the trigger-cocking mode, the trigger finger must actually *slide slightly* across the face of the trigger during the trigger pull in order to keep the muzzle stationary. A grooved trigger tends to adhere to the finger as soon as contact is made. When the trigger finger is thus not permitted to smoothly slide across the trigger face, the trigger finger will force the entire weapon to move during the trigger pull and the sight picture will be disturbed.

Manually-decocking autoloader. In this case, trigger movement for the first shot will be similar to that of a double-action revolver. As with a double-action revolver, the first joint of the trigger finger lays in the center of the trigger. Hence, the weapon should have a smooth narrow trigger similar to that on a defensive double-action revolver.

Trigger finger placment for manually-decocking autoloaders.

With manually-decocking autoloaders, the second and all subsequent shots (until the weapon is decocked) are fired from a cocked hammer and a trigger position near the rear of the trigger guard. Therefore, manually-decocking autoloaders have two distinctly different trigger pulls -- one for the first shot and another for all subsequent shots.

It is inadvisable to try to shift finger position after the first shot. Such finger shifting is time-consuming, distracting and clumsy. Instead, continue to use the first joint position but reduce the pressure used for the second and subsequent shots. As mentioned before, the trigger will be in a position near the rear of the trigger guard and will only require 1.5mm (.06 inches) of movement against 1.8kg (4 lbs) of resistance to release the hammer and discharge the weapon.

Fingers should also be kept clear of the slide release lever, the same as with the Colt/Browning System autoloader, for the same reason.

Chapter 22

Tactical Handgun Operation: Follow Through and Decocking

The final part of firing a gun is follow through. *Sight picture and stance must be reestablished immediately after discharge.* Do not turn into jelly the instant the hammer falls. Since you do not know the exact moment the hammer will be released anyway, hold your position steady before, during and after the hammer falls. Maintain your stance and sight picture for at least three seconds after the last discharge and be prepared to shoot again should it become necessary. When you are satisfied that it is safe to reholster, lower the weapon from eye level and move your head left and right looking to see if there is anything that escaped your notice. It does not suffice to merely shift your eyes. You must move your entire head, taking care to look all around, including directly behind you. This may also be a good time to reload.

As you lower the weapon from eye level, the trigger finger automatically comes off the trigger and returns to register. Do not put your finger on the right extension of the slide stop pin, as you might inadvertently push it in, causing the weapon to instantly disassemble itself! If the pistol has a decocking lever, it must be used when you go to the ready position or holster.

The continuous motion system autoloader is decocked by relaxing the grip sufficiently to allow the squeeze-cocker to return to the rest position; however the grip should not become so loose that it has to be re-indexed before the weapon can be fired again. Decocking must be accomplished as the weapon is lowered from eye level. If it suddenly becomes necessary to fire again, the firing grip is reacquired (depressing the squeeze-cocker) as the weapon comes back up to eye level.

With manually-decocking autoloaders, the weapon is decocked by manipulating the decocking lever with the strong thumb only. *Neither the trigger nor the hammer is ever touched during decocking.* With the trigger finger in register, the strong thumb pushes the decocking lever down and then immediately pushes it back up. Of course, it springs back up by itself in the single-stage decocking autoloaders. The lever should not stay in the down position for more than an instant because pushing the lever down not only decocks the weapon but sterilizes it as well. Since holding a sterile weapon in one's hand in the middle of a threatening situation is not a prudent thing to do, the decocking lever is in the down position only long enough to decock the weapon. It is then immediately pushed back up, re-enabling the gun.

Left handers using SIG pistols and others that have the decocking lever on only one side of the pistol must decock using the left index finger (trigger finger).

Manual decocking

After the first shot with a manually-decocking autoloader, you are always holding a gun with its hammer cocked (until the last round is fired and the slide locks to the rear). If you desire to stop shooting and reholster your gun prior to the last round being fired, you are presented with a problem: the gun cannot be safely carried or holstered with the hammer cocked. The hammer must be safely lowered. The decocking lever is there to permit you to quickly, safely and conveniently lower the hammer without the danger of firing the gun accidentally. There are four sets of circumstances when any manually decocking autoloader should be decocked:

Decocking lever in "on" position.

Decocking lever in "off" position.

1. Prior to holstering.
2. When holding a suspect at gunpoint.
3. Prior to moving with the gun in hand.
4. Any other time your trigger finger loses contact with the trigger.

Holding a cocked pistol on a suspect for extended periods is an invitation to tragedy, because there is not sufficient trigger movement or spring resistance to assure total control over the gun. Any sudden or loud sound that is sufficient

Chapter 22: Tactical Handgun Operation: Follow Through and Decocking

to engender an involuntary spasm in your hand may cause the gun to discharge unintentionally with tragic results. In addition, users of these guns have learned how to move their trigger fingers quickly from register to trigger contact, but only when the trigger is in the forward position as it would be when the weapon is decocked.

If you try to fire suddenly with a cocked weapon when your finger is in register, the trigger will not be where your finger has trained itself to expect it. What often happens is that your finger falls through the empty space within the trigger guard and ultimately slams into the trigger (in its unfamiliar rearward position), often with sufficient force to cause an accidental discharge.

Single-stage decocking lever.

Therefore, *with any manually decocking autoloader, when your trigger finger loses contact with the trigger, you should immediately return the trigger (via manual decocking) to its forward position, where your finger expects to find it.* If you suddenly have to shoot again when your finger is in register and the hammer is still cocked, you will probably fire long before the sights ever reach the target, for the exact reason depicted above.

You often hear instructors describe the "crunch, crash, bang syndrome" when talking about manually-decocking autoloaders. They are describing a common occurrence when new shooters are introduced to these handguns. The first shot requires what seems like an agonizingly-long trigger pull. That is the crunch. New shooters often put too much muscle on the trigger, pulling the muzzle down or heeling the shot off to the left. For the next shot, the trigger is now in its rear position and requires much less movement and pressure. Inexperienced shooters will now put as much pressure on the trigger as they did for the first shot. This is the crash. The gun will discharge prematurely, mightily surprising the shooter. The shot predictably goes way wide because the sights were not yet on target. After thus squandering the first two shots, the astute shooter finally settles down and gets a hit with his third shot. That is the bang.

The point is, every time your trigger finger leaves contact with the trigger and returns to the register position, the gun should be immediately decocked (and immediately re-enabled in the case of the two-stage decocking autoloaders). This is a necessity because the trigger must be repositioned to where your trigger finger expects to find it. There is really no viable alternative. As long as you keep firing and your finger is thus in continuous contact with the trigger, the trigger's location within the trigger guard is irrelevant. However, when trigger contact is lost, as it will be when your trigger finger returns to register, decocking is necessary. The alternative is to inherit a high probability of missing with the next shot and maybe even wounding yourself.

An exception to this rule is made during the reloading and stoppage reduction procedures. In these cases, we want your trigger finger in register during the entire process but the weapon is not decocked prior to the resumption of firing. This is necessary because we want you to be able to resume firing as quickly as possible.

Once more, it is imperative that on all manually-decocking autoloaders, the decocking process be accomplished via the decocking lever without manually manipulating the trigger or the hammer. Trying to lower the hammer by holding the hammer back as you press the trigger and then slowly lowering the hammer all the way down is a procedure that will surely cause an accidental discharge sooner or later. A person may get away with it for a time but at some point the hammer will slip during the manual lowering process and the gun will go off causing extreme embarrassment, property damage and maybe even personal injury. Don't do it! *Use the decocking lever as you have been taught.*

There is another problem with improper decocking: Recently, a detective in a western city police department drew his autoloader from a shoulder holster during an armed confrontation. He accidentally lost control of the gun as it was released from the holster and it dropped to the ground, hitting the pavement on the hammer spur. It discharged upon hitting the pavement and the bullet narrowly missed the startled officer. A subsequent examination of the pistol by an armorer revealed that it was in perfect working order. Normally, this particular autoloader and virtually all other modern autoloading pistols are "drop safe."

This is the result of several internal design features. *However, with several models, the drop safety feature may not work if the gun is decocked improperly.* In this case, the detective had decocked his pistol by lowering the hammer with his thumb while holding the trigger back (a practice with hazards all its own, as noted above). This allowed the hammer to go all the way forward instead of going into its normal rest position, which it would have, had the gun been decocked correctly. In the incorrect all-the-way-forward position, the pistol is not drop safe as the surprised detective found out. The manufacturer (SIG) has since

Chapter 22: Tactical Handgun Operation: Follow Through and Decocking

corrected this design issue, but many of the old production pistols are still in circulation. *Therefore, decock your autoloader when it needs to be decocked and decock it correctly.*

Chapter 23

Tactical Handgun Operation: Reloading

During gunfights, ammunition is consumed rapidly and the reserve contained in the handgun itself is limited. Sooner or later reloading will become necessary. Therefore expeditious and efficient reloading is an important component of effective defensive shooting. It should, like drawing, firing and follow through, be practiced until it is reduced to a conditioned response that can be accomplished fumble-free every time.

First of all, you are well advised to *reload when you want to, not when you have to.* Try not to get surprised by an empty gun. Choose the time you want to reload. Do not let the situation choose it for you. As a general rule, *you should reload as soon after the initial exchange of fire as practicable,* no matter how many rounds you fired or think you have fired. Your ability to accurately recall the number of rounds you just fired is notoriously deficient. It is best not to trust your memory. In fact, if you can remembering firing at all, get your weapon reloaded the first chance you get, even if it means dropping some live rounds or a partially charged magazine on the ground. Experience has shown that you will have actually fired two to three times as many rounds as you can recall firing.

Don't reholster an empty weapon. You will probably not discover the weapon is empty until you need it. Then it will be too late.

When possible, reloading should be accomplished from a covered and concealed position rather than out in the open.

Double-action revolvers. Reloading a double-action revolver should take no more than six seconds if you are using speed loaders.

1. Bring the weapon down from eye level and into your midriff (position sul).

2. Release the cylinder with your right thumb and simultaneously push it out of the frame as far as it will go with the two middle fingers of your left hand.

3. Wrap your left thumb around the cylinder, pull the cylinder out as far as it will go and hold it there with your thumb and two middle fingers.

4. Turn your left wrist clockwise until the muzzle is pointed upward. The

cylinder continues to be held open.

5. Forcefully strike the ejector rod with the palm of the right hand, expelling the fired cases downward and free of the weapon.

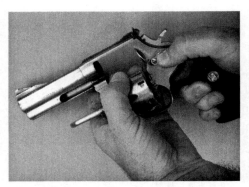 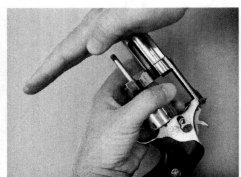

Release the cylinder, hold it between your thumb and fingers, point the muzzle up and strike the ejector rod.

If you are left handed, you will probably be able to release the cylinder with your left index finger. Push the cylinder out using your right thumb and wrap the middle two fingers of your right hand around the cylinder. Turn your right wrist until the muzzle is pointed upward and continue to hold the cylinder open. Forcefully strike the ejector rod with the palm of your left hand.

Come straight down with your palm on the ejector rod. You may bend it if you strike it at an angle. Allow the empty cases to fall directly onto the ground. Do not try to catch them. Short-barreled revolvers have short ejector rods and some of the fired cases may hang up and not fall completely free. These recalcitrant cases must be plucked out by hand.

"Pumping" the ejector rod with the thumb often fails to completely clear the spent cases from the cylinder and is not recommended.

Be sure you are holding the revolver muzzle up when you strike the ejector rod. That way the expended cases and all the particles of unburned powder and other debris they contain will fall down and away from the weapon. If the revolver is muzzle down or even horizontal as the cases are ejected, particles of unburned powder can fall under the extractor star and eventually build up to the point where they prevent the cylinder from locking into position within the frame. Also, an expended case can fall under the extractor star and go back into the chamber. The revolver will then be out of action because the extractor star cannot return to its normal position, and it will prevent the cylinder from

Chapter 23: Tactical Handgun Operation: Reloading

rotating back into the frame.

6. Turn your wrist counter-clockwise until the muzzle is again pointed down.

7. Hold the weapon close to the body as you cup the cylinder in your left hand. Be sure the cylinder continues to be held out as far as it will go.

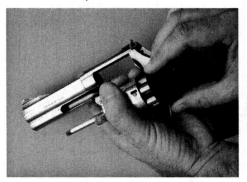 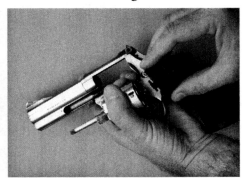

Reloading using a speed loader.

If you are left handed, you will hold the gun with your right hand and use your left hand to handle a speed loader or loose rounds.

The entire speed loader is grasped (strong hand) by the drum itself while it is still in the carrier. Do not try to grasp it by the knob at the top. Withdraw the speed loader from the carrier and push it directly into the cylinder by the drum, turning it slightly to allow the bullets to find and drift into the mouths of their respective chambers.

If you're using Safariland speed loaders, keep pushing on the drum until you hear a click which indicates that all the rounds have been released. They release automatically and only when they are well inside the chambers. The loader is designed in this way so the rounds cannot be released prematurely.

If you're using HKS speed loaders, push the drum until the rounds are as far in as they will go. Then, turn the knob and release the cartridges to fall in the chambers the rest of the way. Don't grab the HKS speed loader by the knob or you'll release the rounds prematurely.

When the cartridges are released, quickly pull the speed loader backwards and immediately twist your wrist and release it, *allowing it to fly free of the gun and fall to the ground.* This is necessary to allow all the rounds the opportunity to clear the speedloader and fall all the way into their respective chambers. If you merely let go of the speedloader as soon as the rounds are released and then shear it off as you push the cylinder back into the frame, any cartridge that did not go all the way into its chamber can get caught with its front end in the chamber and its rear end still in the loader. When the cylinder is then immediately and forcefully pushed back into the frame, it will seize and will not go all the way in. It then becomes necessary to push the cylinder back out in order to get rid of the (now bent) cartridge.

With either brand of loader, it is best to grasp the unit by the drum with the index finger lodged between two rounds. As the cylinder is held open by the left two middle fingers and the left thumb, the thumb should come to rest on a cylinder flute. Cylinder flutes are always cut between the chambers. Since your left thumb is then between two chambers and your right index finger is between two rounds, it is a simple matter to just touch the two fingers together. *Two rounds will be thus aligned with two chambers and the rest of the rounds will automatically line up.*

Be sure to rotate the weapon all the way over so that the bore axis is perpendicular with the ground. That way gravity will cause the live rounds to fall into the chambers with dispatch.

With the Bianchi rubber Speed-Strip brand of loader, rounds are loaded two at a time. First, load the two outermost chambers with the two outer rounds on the strip (either end). Then, flip the strip end for end, and load the next two chambers with the other two outer rounds. Load the last two chambers with the two middle rounds. Once all cylinders are loaded, allow the empty strip to fall to the ground.

Reloading a revolver with loose rounds from either a dump pouch or a pocket is the least satisfactory of all methods. It is tedious, slow and there is a good chance some live rounds intended for the revolver will be accidentally dropped and end up on the ground. However, if it becomes necessary to reload this way, get all the loose rounds into your strong hand then load each chamber as it reaches the outer position (as you rotate the cylinder with your thumb) until they are all loaded. *Rotate the cylinder in the opposite direction that it rotates during firing.* With Smith & Wesson and Ruger revolvers, push with the left thumb rotating the cylinder clockwise as each chamber is successively loaded. With Colt revolvers, pull with the thumb rotating the cylinder counter-clockwise.

While reloading, hold the revolver close to the body. If loose live rounds are accidentally dropped at this point, they usually fall into the left hand and can

Chapter 23: Tactical Handgun Operation: Reloading

be quickly recovered. Otherwise, they will fall to the ground and be lost. If you do accidentally drop live rounds and they land on the ground, do not stoop to pick them up unless they are the only ones you have. It is better to have only a partially loaded weapon than to grovel around on the ground looking for lost rounds.

8. When the chambers are reloaded, push the cylinder back into the frame quickly as you reassume your normal shooting stance.

The revolver is now reloaded and firing can be resumed as soon as the weak hand is replaced in its normal support position and the firing stance and sight picture are reacquired.

We must now depart slightly from what you learned about the administrative process of loading the revolver. In tactical reloading, it is not necessary to index the cylinder after it is pushed back into and locked into the frame. Such indexing is time consuming and unnecessary. If the cylinder closes so that the firing pin is between chambers, pulling the trigger will simply rotate the next chamber into position and discharge the round. The cylinder thus indexes itself during firing.

In some special situations, the sound of brass or an empty speedloader hitting the floor may betray the fact that you are reloading and reveal your position. In these cases, you may want to pocket the brass or set it and the empty speed loader gently on the floor. Such silent reloading obviously takes longer but is sometimes necessary. Under normal circumstances it is best to get the gun reloaded as quickly and efficiently as possible.

Safariland speedloaders will wear out within three to five hundred operations. When worn out, rounds will fall out of the loader before they are released. Worn loaders cannot be repaired. They must be discarded and replaced. HKS speedloaders last longer.

To test a speedloader for excessive wear, charge it with live rounds then shake it violently. No amount of shaking should be sufficient to cause any of the rounds to fall out. If rounds do fall out, the loader is faulty and should be thrown away.

If you carry rounds loose in a pouch and the pouch holds more than six rounds, put as many in it as it will hold since some will probably be dropped during the reloading process anyway.

Autoloaders. In order to reload an autoloader, you simply exchange a depleted magazine for a full one, ensure the slide is in battery and there is a live round in the chamber. Changing magazines in an autoloader is a four-second job. Expended magazines are normally jettisoned and not salvaged.

With any autoloader, the fresh magazine must be in your weak hand and ready to insert into the pistol *before* the empty magazine is ejected and allowed to drop to the ground. There may be some rounds left in the expended magazine and you do not want to drop it until you are sure you have another one, and it is ready to go. In addition, those weapons equipped with a magazine safety will not fire when there is no magazine in the weapon even if there is a live round chambered. *It is advisable to reduce the time that there is no magazine in the weapon to the absolute minimum.*

Unlike revolvers, autoloaders are reloaded as the weapon continues to be held at eye level and in front of you. That way, you do not have to look down and divert your attention from the source of danger. Also (unlike revolvers), the reloading process does not require the pistol to leave your strong hand. The master grip is maintained throughout the entire process.

Autoloading pistols can be in one of three possible conditions when you make the decision to reload:

1. Slide is in battery with a live round chambered.
2. Slide is locked back with an empty chamber and magazine.
3. Slide is in battery with an empty chamber and magazine.

The trouble is that when the gun is being held at eye level, it is not readily apparent which of these three possibilities is actually the case. *At eye level, it is difficult to tell whether the slide is in battery or locked to the rear.* Further, the slide is supposed to lock to the rear after the last round is fired but it doesn't always. On any autoloader it is possible for the slide to go forward into battery (on an empty chamber) when the last round is fired, instead of locking to the rear as it is supposed to.

Because of the forgoing, *the slide is always jerked to the rear and released after magazines have been exchanged regardless of the position of the slide or the suspected condition of the chamber.* That way, you can always be assured that a live round is chambered and that the slide is all the way forward and in battery. If there was already a round chambered, it will simply be ejected as the new round is chambered in its place. The loss of one round is a small price to pay for the assurance that the gun will fire.

Chapter 23: Tactical Handgun Operation: Reloading

There will be times when magazines stick and refuse to fall free of the magazine well when the release is depressed. When this happens, you will already have a fresh magazine in your weak hand, so grab the base of the sticky magazine between your weak-side thumb and index finger (thumb in back, index finger in front) while continuing to hold the new magazine, flick your wrist, flinging the old magazine free of the pistol, then the fresh magazine can be inserted normally. If the magazine has seized in the magazine well and cannot be dragged out by hand, hook the forward extension of the recalcitrant magazine base over the top edge of your belt and push the pistol forward and down as you hold the magazine release button in. This maneuver will usually get even sticky ones out. A rigid, double-layered, wide, high-quality gun belt is required to make this work. It is good practice to wear one when carrying a pistol. Be careful not to point the gun at your leg or foot as you do this.

It is best to perform the entire reloading operation with the barrel remaining parallel with the ground and grip remaining vertical. This will allow the magazine to fall directly out of the magazine well. Unfortunately, some people are not able to reach the magazine release button with their right thumb unless they tilt the grip of the pistol inward. If you are one of the people who find this maneuver compulsory, it is acceptable. It should be avoided, however, by people whose hands are large enough to make it unnecessary.

Magazine bumper pads are a useful but not a mandatory accessory. The extra bulk assures the magazine will seat when it is pushed up. However, pads should not be excessively bulky. They should be securely screwed to the base of the magazine, not merely glued. Many manufacturers now make magazines with integral magazine pads.

Most domestic gun battles are over in a few seconds, so we usually do not worry about dropping expended magazines on the ground. We can always pick them up later or simply buy new ones. However, in military situations new magazines may be hard to come by, and we cannot afford to drop many, as they may be both unrecoverable and irreplaceable. Therefore, as an alternative to ejecting the empty magazine and allowing it to fall to the ground, you can perform a "military reload" by salvaging the expended magazine. This is accomplished by performing a standard reload, as described above. Then, if you have time, the expended magazine may be picked up with your weak hand and placed in a pocket. If you inadvertently place an empty magazine into the carrier, you may try to insert it into the pistol later, thinking it is fully charged.

If it is desired that expended magazines not be dropped during a military reload, one can remove the expended magazine from the magazine well while holding the new one in the same hand. After the new one is inserted, the old one can be placed in a pocket and the slide cycled. This variant requires that two magazines be held in one hand at the same time. Big hands may carry it off, but small hands probably won't. The only alternative for small-handed people is to remove and secure the expended magazine first and then go for a new one. This leaves the pistol without a magazine for several seconds, and you must assume you have a fresh magazine available at the beginning of the procedure.

Reloading procedure. Upon making the decision to reload,

1. Drop the weapon slightly out of the sighting plane so you can look over it as you reload. Keep the weapon up. Don't lower it and then bend over to look at it. Keep looking around as the reloading procedure progresses. Don't become so involved that you lose track of what is going on.

2. Place your trigger finger in register.

3. Leave the weapon in your strong hand as you grasp a fresh magazine (from the magazine carrier) with your weak hand.

Grasp a fresh magazine with your weak hand, release the spent magazine and insert the new one.

Be sure that the spare magazine is properly oriented in its carrier so that it can be correctly grasped without one or more grip readjustments. The forward edge of the fresh magazine's base extension should be at the base of your weak-hand palm, while the pad of the weak-hand index finger comes to rest on the nose of the top round in the magazine. *The weak-hand index finger will then serve as a guide to get the magazine properly started into the magazine well mouth.* While

Chapter 23: Tactical Handgun Operation: Reloading

in the carrier, the spare magazine should be base up with the cartridges facing forward.

Strike the magazine with the heel of the weak hand, then jerk the slide.

4. With the fresh magazine firmly in hand and lifted clear of the carrier, depress the magazine release button with your thumb, and allow the empty magazine to fall free of the pistol and onto the ground.

5. Push the fresh magazine straight into the magazine well and strike the bottom of it with the heel of the weak hand to insure that it seats and locks into place.

Sometimes it is helpful to start the rear surface of the magazine against the rear edge of the magazine well. Then, rock the magazine forward and up. This procedure is helpful with single-column magazines. Double-column magazines can generally be pushed straight in.

Reach over the top of the slide, jerk it back and let it go.

217

6. Once the magazines have been exchanged, jerk the slide to the rear and let it go. Then return your weak hand to its normal support position and if necessary, resume firing.

In order to pull the slide, reach over the slide to the rear of the ejection port with the weak hand, taking care not to obstruct the ejection port. Cup the rear of the slide between the fingers and the base of the palm and jerk it forcefully rearward. When the slide reaches its rearmost position, let it go completely and allow it to spring forward unassisted. Then, drop your weak hand and, making a small circle, come right back into the normal support position. Don't ride the slide forward.

Do not "sling-shot" the slide by pinching it between the thumb and index finger. This is a weak grasp and it may slip. It also causes the muzzle to be deflected far off the target.

With manually-decocking autoloaders that have a slide-mounted decocking lever, take particular care not to inadvertently push the decocking lever to the down position as the slide is pulled to the rear. If the lever is in the "on" position, the pistol will not fire.

Double-column autoloaders. Many autoloading pistols have double-column (staggered-column) magazines. There are actually two parallel rows of cartridges staggered in the magazine. The magazine body tapers near the top to expose only one round for feeding. This arrangement yields a greater magazine capacity than would be possible with a single-column scheme; however, as noted before, the weapon's grip inherits considerable bulk. A tapered, double-column magazine is easier to insert into the pistol than is a single-column magazine, because the tapering causes the magazine to drift to center as it is shoved upward and enters the magazine well mouth.

Single-column autoloaders. Some autoloading pistols have a single-column magazine that does not taper toward the top. Most everything said about reloading double-column weapons applies here also. The exception being that, since the magazine does not taper, it can be rocked in from the rear of the magazine well mouth instead of being shoved straight up, as mentioned previously. The fresh magazine is grasped in the same fashion as a double-column magazine, but it is held out in front of the pistol, then tilted backward and brought rearward until the rear surface of the magazine makes contact with the rear edge of the magazine well mouth. The magazine is then rotated forward until it starts moving upward and into the magazine well.

Chapter 23: Tactical Handgun Operation: Reloading

Continuous motion system autoloaders. In these pistols the slide release is built into the squeeze-cocker. If the pistol has been shot dry and the slide is locked to the rear, relax the firing grip to allow the squeeze-cocker to return to the rest position. After replacing the empty magazine with a fresh one, simply reassuming your normal firing grip will cause the slide to go forward automatically as the squeeze-cocker is re-depressed. If you decide to pull the slide to the rear, it will release and go forward also, as it would with any other autoloader.

Depressing the squeeze-cocker may be faster and it is necessary to grip the weapon in preparation to fire anyway. However, it is a good idea just to get in the habit of jerking and releasing the slide with these pistols. The squeeze-cocker will release the slide if it is locked to the rear, but it will do nothing if the slide is in battery on an empty chamber.

Base-latch magazine release. Some autoloaders have the magazine release in the form of a latch at the rear of the magazine well mouth. It is placed there for the sake of ambidexterity. In this case, the empty magazine must be released with the weak hand after the weak hand already contains a fresh magazine. As noted above, handling two magazines in the same hand simultaneously is something not everyone is going to be able to do well. However, here is how it is done:

Simply position the fresh magazine between the index and middle fingers of the weak hand leaving the thumb and index finger free. With the fresh magazine thus positioned, the second knuckle of the weak-hand index finger is hooked over the front extension of the base plate of the depleted magazine while it is still in the pistol. The weak-hand thumb will then be in a position to pull (or push, depending on the particular latch system) the magazine release latch forward, thereby releasing the magazine. Once released, the depleted magazine can be forcefully dragged out with the weak-hand index finger. It should, of course, fall free of its own accord but yanking it free speeds the process. After it is clear of the weapon, it is released and allowed to fall to the ground as the fresh magazine is inserted and driven all the way up (until it locks in place) by the heel of the weak hand. The alternative to the foregoing is to simply release and discard the old magazine first and then acquire a fresh one and insert it into the magazine well.

If you shoot your autoloader dry, the slide should lock to the rear as the last round is fired. In this situation, the empty magazine is exchanged for a fresh one in the normal fashion (as described above) and the slide is pulled and released to chamber a fresh round. Depressing the slide release will also cause the slide to thus move forward. Pulling the slide all the way to the rear, then releasing it is the preferred method of getting the slide forward, because it develops increased slide energy for positive feeding and involves a gross body movement rather than a fine finger movement (which is required to depress the slide release lever). In addition, the location and shape of the slide-release lever varies greatly with brands of pistol. Learning the location on a particular pistol will only be helpful with that pistol. By contrast, pulling the slide to the rear and releasing it will chamber a round on any autoloading pistol. The slide release lever itself should be used only in unusual situations, such as when the weak hand is disabled.

With nearly any autoloader, changing of magazines is greatly facilitated by a mild beveling of the sharp edges on the magazine well mouth. This is an easy modification and it is highly recommended.

Chapter 24

Tactical Handgun Operation: Stoppages

A "stoppage" has occurred any time there is an unscheduled interruption in the weapon's normal cycle of operation. The first symptom is that you attempt to fire your weapon and have every expectation that the weapon will fire, but it fails to fire.

A "jam" has occurred when the slide is seized with the frame and the two are bound together so tightly that the slide cannot be moved by hand without great effort. Fortunately jams are uncommon. Sometimes the term jam is incorrectly used to describe a simple stoppage, such as failure to feed or a failure to eject. *All jams are stoppages but all stoppages are not necessarily jams.* Happily, the vast majority of stoppages are not jams.

Contrary to popular myth, even when they do occur, the vast majority of stoppages are easily and quickly reducible through the application of "immediate action."

Manifestations of stoppages are:

- Failure to feed
- Failure to chamber
- Failure to fire
- Failure to extract
- Failure to eject

Causes are:

- Defective, worn or broken parts (defective magazine, broken/worn springs, broken extractor, broken ejector, broken firing pin, broken barrel, slide or frame)
- Sterile ammunition
- Dirty or defective ammunition
- Gun maintained poorly or improperly lubricated
- Failure to operate the weapon properly (improper grip or stance, improper

trigger manipulation)

- Chamber or barrel blockage

Stoppages are rare in good quality weapons that are conscientiously maintained and loaded with good quality ammunition. However, they do happen sometimes, no matter how virtuous the shooter or the weapon. *When a stoppage does occur, the immediate goal is to get the weapon functioning again in the shortest possible amount of time.* "Immediate action" is the term used to describe the reflexive subroutine called into play to reduce stoppages. The purpose of immediate action is not to discover the cause of the stoppage. The cause is irrelevant. Immediate action is a broad-spectrum procedure designed to quickly reduce the stoppage, regardless of the cause. Therefore, *there is no diagnostic stage to immediate action.* You simply do it and do it quickly.

The steps of immediate action are applied in correct sequence until the stoppage is reduced. Attempt to fire after the completion of each stage so as not to waste time executing unnecessary operations.

Double-action revolvers

The most common stoppage encountered in the revolver is running out of ammunition. The second most common is the frozen gun. A frozen revolver is one in which the cylinder has seized and will not rotate. During rapid fire, it is possible for you to fail to allow the trigger to go all the way forward before starting to pull it back again for the next shot. The mechanism will try to rotate the cylinder before the bolt has unlocked it and the weapon will thus freeze. *Pulling the trigger all the harder will not free it.* Improperly seated primers, bullets of incorrect length, bullets seated to an improper depth or bullets that jump beyond the front of the cylinder because they are improperly crimped can also cause the cylinder to seize.

Immediate action for the double-action revolver:

1. As you rapidly move laterally, keeping the weapon in a position to fire, release the trigger completely and immediately pull it again. This usually frees the mechanism and rotates the next round under the hammer.

2. If the weapon still does not fire, repeat this step. That is, release the trigger and attempt to fire one more time.

3. After attempting unsuccessfully to fire twice, reholster. Draw your back-up

Chapter 24: Tactical Handgun Operation: Stoppages

gun and continue to fire (sometimes called the "New York reload").

4. If you do not have a back-up gun, seek cover (if possible). Reload the weapon in your covered position (regardless of how many rounds have been fired), reestablish a shooting position and continue to fire.

If one round is sterile, chances are all the rounds in the weapon are if they all came from the same box. It is also possible that you could have shot the weapon dry and did not realize it.

Autoloaders

Feeding, extraction and ejection are processes common to all autoloaders and are the weak link in the cycle of operation. The slide must strip a round off the top of the magazine and force it forward into the feed ramp, past the chamber lip and ultimately into the chamber. After firing, the empty case must be extracted and ejected. If the round or empty case is retarded for any reason during the process, a stoppage is the usual result.

The "drawbar" is the part, usually a yoke, which draws the hammer back as the trigger is pressed. On many trigger-cocking autoloaders, the drawbar is an inherently weak part. It needs to be inspected regularly.

Immediate action for autoloaders:

1. As you rapidly move laterally, dropping the weapon slightly out of the sighting plane, return the trigger finger to the register position.

2. Release the supporting hand and use it to strike the bottom of the magazine "(tap)."

3. Continue to keep the weapon in the firing position as you grasp the rear of the slide (to the rear of the ejection port) with the weak hand.

4. Forcefully yank the slide to the rear as far as it will go, then immediately release it and let it go forward by itself "(rack)."

5. Drop your weak hand and, making a small circle, come right back into your normal firing grip and immediately attempt to fire "(bang)," if it is still appropriate to do so.

If the slide is stuck and you cannot move it, re-grip the slide with your weak hand, release your firing grip and withdraw your strong hand. Then punch forward with your strong hand and strike the grip of the weapon with the webbing between your strong-hand thumb and index finger. If this does not dislodge the slide, better go for your back-up gun.

Strike the bottom of the magazine, then yank the slide to the rear.

Let the slide go forward, return the weak hand and fire if necessary.

6. If the weapon still does not fire, reholster the weapon, draw your back-up weapon and continue to fire, moving laterally all the time or shooting from cover.

7. If you do not have a back-up weapon, seek cover or keep moving laterally.

8. Grasp the rear of the slide with your weak hand and force it to the rear as you simultaneously apply upward pressure with the right thumb on the slide release lever. The slide will lock in the rear position.

Chapter 24: Tactical Handgun Operation: Stoppages

You must lock the slide to the rear before attempting to remove the magazine because if the magazine is stuck, locking the slide to the rear often takes enough pressure off to enable it to be dragged out. If you attempt to manually drag the magazine out without first locking the slide to the rear, you may not get it to budge.

9. With the slide locked to the rear, release the magazine and forcefully drag it free of the pistol. Place it in a pocket.

10. With the slide locked to the rear and the magazine removed, grab the slide with your weak hand, taking care not to obstruct the ejection port, and run it back and forward violently several times, allowing stuck rounds or cases to break free and fall out of the pistol through the empty magazine well.

Don't just pull the slide to the rear and let it go. Vigorously move it in both directions several times.

11. Let go of the slide and allow it to go all the way forward.

12. Insert a fresh magazine, or insert the one just removed from the pistol if there are still rounds in it, and it is the only one you have.

13. Grab the slide with your weak hand. Yank it to the rear as far as it will go, then release it (chambering a live round).

14. Return your weak hand to its normal support position and resume firing, if it is still appropriate to do so.

With autoloaders, the recoil, main and firing pin springs should be inspected at least every three thousand rounds. After three thousand rounds, the recoil spring should be replaced. It will probably continue to function in the weapon long after three thousand rounds. For that matter, even when broken, it will probably continue to function in the weapon. However, on a defensive gun, it is not proper to take chances. Springs are not expensive. It is foolish to carry a gun full of worn or defective parts.

The firing pin spring should also be replaced when it becomes weak. A worn, fatigued or broken firing pin spring can, because of its weakness, allow the firing pin stop on Colt/Browning autoloaders to fall out of its slot during firing. When this happens, the firing pin stop will catch on the rear of the hammer as the slide moves forward, causing a stoppage -- a stoppage that is difficult to reduce quickly.

The extractor must also be checked regularly for signs of wear and cracks in the claw. A pistol with a broken extractor claw is out of action until the part can be replaced.

Sights, particularly adjustable rear sights, must be checked for looseness and drifting. Adjustable sights rarely stay in adjustment and often break. *For this reason, no adjustable rear pistol sight is recommended. Fixed rear sights are superior.*

Both the slide and frame should be examined for cracks and signs of excessive wear. The barrel bushing should also be checked for cracks and wear. Other parts that should be periodically inspected include the barrel, firing pin, slide stop, magazines, magazine springs and the recoil spring guide.

Magazine springs can fatigue when magazines are left fully charged for long periods. Unneeded magazines should therefore be stored empty. Magazines that are kept charged must be loaded into the weapon and fired at least once per year in order to make sure they still work. Unserviceable magazine springs should be immediately replaced.

Chapter 25

Ammunition Recommendations

To be effective, pistol bullets must be capable of substantially disrupting the circulatory system of a human being. Unfortunately, the abruptly paralyzing "neural shock" effect imparted by hyper-velocity rifle bullets is rare with pistol bullets. Likewise, critical components of a person's nervous system, such as the spinal cord and the brain, can be physically struck and destroyed by pistol bullets, but this is also rare. The brain is heavily protected by the skull and facial sinuses (neither of which are commonly penetrated by pistol bullets) and the spinal cord is too small to be considered a legitimate target for a pistol shooter in defensive circumstances.

For any defensive pistol shooter, the heart and major arteries in the vicinity of the heart are, by far, the most lucrative object of attack. Collectively, the body midline, between the navel and neck, make a target that is big enough and accessible enough to be successfully attacked with pistol bullets. It is easy to locate and is not protected by substantial bones, as the sternum and ribs provide scant resistance to penetration by pistol bullets. To hit this target area consistently requires a degree of precision, but it is well within the capability of adequately trained pistol shooters.

An attack on a person's circulatory system will have the effect of precipitously lowering his blood pressure. The first of his organs to be affected is the brain. With inadequate blood pressure, a person will first become foggy, then become thoroughly disoriented and finally faint and lose consciousness all together. The process can take from a few seconds to as long as a minute, depending upon the rate of blood-pressure loss. Thus, a catastrophic ruination and literal shredding of the aforementioned target area through rapid multiple bullet impacts is the best strategy because it lowers an attacker's blood pressure faster than anything else one could do.

Thus, when under life-threatening attack by a criminal and you are defending yourself with a pistol, the best thing you can do is zipper him up the body midline, move and repeat the drill until the threat has abated and additional shooting appears to be unnecessary.

For maximum effect, bullet penetration after impact must be limited but adequate. In addition, bullets must not fragment and break into pieces. Ideal performance of a pistol bullet is when it stays in one piece and transversely penetrates a human chest, subsequently coming to rest just under the skin on the opposite side having fully expanded. Remember, not every person you'll be compelled to shoot will be facing you. You may be required to shoot someone from the side or even from the back. In the former case, your bullet will have to first transversely penetrate the arm, exit, then enter the chest and still travel thirty centimeters through soft tissue to get through the target area. In the latter case, your bullet may have to first smash through the spinal column and then still travel through soft tissue before getting to the center of the chest.

Hardball (FMJ) pistol ammunition is extremely common but, in any caliber, is a poor choice for most defensive work. It feeds well through nearly any pistol, but it tends to penetrate through-and-through, emerging from the opposite side of a human chest cavity, unexpanded, with enough residual velocity to pose a real danger to innocent people downrange. In addition, as noted above, hardball does not expand significantly in human soft tissue. Therefore, the amount of tissue destruction of which it is capable is low compared with that produced by controlled-expansion pistol bullets normally associated with high-performance ammunition.

Finally, hardball ammunition is not normally loaded to high velocities. In fact, 9mm hardball ammunition is notoriously wimpy. Hardball is commonly used for practice during training sessions, because it is relatively inexpensive but should be carried only when nothing better is available.

Unjacketed lead-bullet ammunition is also available and is usually less expensive even than hardball. This kind of ammunition is typically loaded to low velocities and is intended for practice only. It is surely not recommended for any serious application. In addition, extensive use of ammunition with unjacketed, lead bullets will often smear the inside of a pistol barrel with lead residue and greasy bullet lubrication. This makes cleaning the pistol's bore an arduous task and often turns the whole pistol into a greasy gummy mess!

Cor-Bon, Winchester, Remington, Federal, PMC, Speer and others all manufacture high-performance pistol ammunition that is intended for personal defensive applications. It is substantially more expensive than hardball and is typically loaded to high velocities and features a controlled-expansion bullet, usually with a hollow nose. Federal uses its signature Hydra-Shok™ bullet. Winchester the SXT®. Remington the Golden Saber™. Speer the Gold Dot®. PMC the Starfire™. Cor-Bon Pow'RBall™ and DPX bullets are the best

Chapter 25: Ammunition Recommendations

From Left: Cor-Bon Pow'RBall 9mm, Federal Personal Defense 9mm, Eldorado Starfire 38Spl, Federal Personal Defense 38Spl, Winchester SXT 40S&W, Remington Golden Saber 40S&W, Speer Gold Dot 357 SIG, Cor-Bon Pow'RBall 357 SIG, Speer Gold Dot 45ACP.

of the lot.

All the bullets mentioned above perform well when driven at high velocities. All normally expand in soft, human tissue causing substantial tissue destruction with limited penetration. Therefore, the factors to keep in mind when selecting pistol ammunition are:

- **Functional reliability** in all pistols in which the ammunition is to be carried and used.
- Limited, but **adequate penetration** of the human torso.
- **Manageable recoil**.
- **Adequate performance** after the bullet has penetrated heavy clothing or intervening barriers, such as auto glass or plywood.
- **Price**.
- **Legality** of use and possession where you live and work.

Functional reliability is the most important of all selection criteria. Ammunition which experiences more than a rare and occasional feeding or other functional failure in the pistol you're carrying for defensive purposes should be dropped from consideration. Only after firing several hundred rounds of a particular brand of ammunition through my pistol (without any failures) would I feel comfortable carrying that brand. Happily, most name brand high-performance pistol ammunition functions well in most reputable defensive pistols. However, surprises still happen! *Only through exhaustive and* *continuous testing of your personal protective equipment can you be confident that it won't let you down.*

The characteristics of autoloading pistol ammunition that most contribute to reliable feeding and chambering are:

- Long gently tapering bullet profile
- Short tapered case

The nine-millimeter (9mm, or 9x19) is the most reliably functioning serious pistol cartridge available. The 45 ACP and 40 S&W are also reliable. Cartridges with long non-tapered cases and short squatty bullet profiles are the least reliably functioning. The forgoing pretty well describes the ten-millimeter and explains why it consistently fails to function reliably in nearly any pistol chambered for it.

Two new cartridges have recently been introduced, one of which has become extremely popular in a short period of time, the 357 SIG and the 400 Cor-Bon. The 357 SIG is a 40 S&W necked down to 9mm caliber. The 400 Cor-Bon is a 45 ACP case necked down to forty caliber. Both cartridges are exceedingly powerful, and both obviously use a bottleneck cartridge. The 357 SIG has garnered a significant following, and both Glock and SIG make factory pistols chambered for this round. The 400 Cor-Bon cartridge has not yet caught on, and only modified existing pistols are chambered for it.

Another new cartridge is the 45 GAP (Glock Automatic Pistol). Glock is the only manufacturer currently making a pistol chamber for this round, which is a 45 ACP with a rebated rim and a slightly shorter case.

The 32 NAA (North American Arms) is another newcomer. It is a 380 Auto case bottlenecked down to 32 caliber.

Penetration. Pistol bullets must be able to transversely penetrate a human torso, even after penetrating heavy clothing, yet not exit the body. We don't always get perfect performance, but this is the goal. Cor-Bon Pow'RBall provides the best performance in this regard.

Recoil. Recoil is a significant issue. I consider a good workout with a pistol to be four hundred rounds in an afternoon of shooting. If your hands and arms are so pummeled after only two hundred rounds that you can't go on, you probably need to look at a different caliber, a different gun or different ammunition. Shooting will always involve recoil, but it should not be painful or you will never be able to get enough practice. In addition, severe recoil

Chapter 25: Ammunition Recommendations

increases the time between shots because it expands recovery time. If it takes a long time to recover from each shot, you will not be able to shoot fast enough to be effective. Ideally, you should be able to fire accurately, recover and fire accurately again within a half second. If severe recoil is preventing you from achieving this goal, it's time for a change.

Performance. For a hollowpoint bullet to expand properly, the hollow cavity must fill with fluid. After penetrating heavy clothing, many hollowpoint bullets plug up with clothing material and, thus plugged, subsequently fail to expand after penetrating the body. The only way to overcome this inherent problem with hollowpoint bullets is with high impact velocities. Accordingly, heavy bullets, which are always driven at relatively low velocities, are extremely susceptible to plugging. Cor-Bon Pow'RBall solves the plugging problem completely, as the ball does not slough off until several centimeters of penetration into tissue.

Price. I don't consider price to be a particularly serious barrier if a particular brand of ammunition is demonstrably superior. I will have and use that ammunition regardless.

Legality. Some jurisdictions now ban the private possession of any kind of hollowpoint ammunition. Unfortunately, softpoint bullets do not normally expand at pistol velocities, so they are not an adequate alternative. Happily, Cor-Bon Pow'RBall solves this problem too. It is not a hollowpoint from

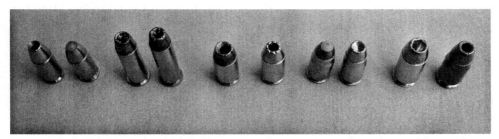

9mm Federal, 9mm Pow'RBall, 38 Starfire, 357 Starfire, 40 Golden Saber, 40 SXT, 357 SIG Pow'RBall, 357 SIG Gold Dot, 45ACP Gold Dot, 400 Cor-Bon.

outward appearances, but functions as one after penetration.

Pistol ammunition featuring pre-fragmented bullets is produced by several manufacturers. It is not recommended.

For revolvers chambered for 38 Special and pistols chambered for 9mm and 357 SIG, the best choice is a high-performance bullet weighing 100 to 125 grains. Lighter bullets tend to penetrate inadequately. Heavier bullets generate formidable recoil and tend to be too slow to expand reliably in soft tissue. In small-frame 38 Special revolvers, even a 125 grain bullet is unpleasant to shoot because of severe recoil. Small revolvers do best with bullets in the 115 grain range.

A revolver chambered for the 357 Magnum cartridge will also chamber and fire 38 Special cartridges. The same is true for 44 Magnum and 44 Special cartridges. This is claimed by many to be a great advantage of the 357 Magnum revolver since 38 Special ammunition is less expensive than 357 Magnum ammunition. However, there are some problems with this practice. Shooting a lot of 38 Special practice ammunition in a 357 Magnum revolver will deposit lead, soot and bullet lubricant on the inside of the chambers everywhere ahead of the mouth of the 38 Special case. The subsequent chambering of the longer 357 Magnum rounds is nearly impossible until the contamination is removed.

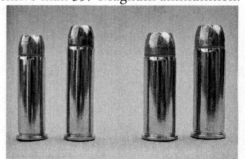

38 Special, 357 Magnum, 44 Special and 44 Magnum cartridges.

This condition can be more than just a nuisance. If you have been shooting 38 Special practice ammunition in your 357 Magnum revolver and it is time to leave the range, you will have to clean the weapon then and there or be forced to load it with the underpowered practice ammunition for the trip home, since you will not be able to get your 357 Magnum rounds in it. Another problem is that the hot gases associated with bullet launch eventually cause spalling on the walls of the chamber. The chamber will gradually be ringed with tiny spall marks where the bullet comes off the 38 Special case. When the longer 357 Magnums are then fired in the same chambers, the brass will expand into the spall ring, making rapid case extraction difficult and eventually impossible.

What all this means is that shooting a lot of 38 Specials in a 357 Magnum

Chapter 25: Ammunition Recommendations

revolver will eventually ruin the weapon for 357 Magnum rounds.

As a solution to the problem you can do one of two things:

- Simply dedicate the weapon to 38 Special and do not bother with 357 Magnum rounds at all.
- Shoot only 357 Magnum rounds in it, both for practice and for duty.

Practice 357 Magnum ammunition is common and is available from most commercial ammunition remanufacturers. It is only slightly more expensive than 38 Special practice ammunition.

The bullets on some revolver reloads are not properly crimped and when chambered, can jump forward under the recoil of other rounds being fired. Sometimes they jump forward far enough to protrude beyond the front face of the cylinder. This condition will obviously seize the cylinder as it attempts to rotate, producing a frozen gun. Therefore, it is prudent to examine and test a particular brand of reloaded ammunition before acquiring large quantities of it.

For pistols chambered for 380 Auto (sometimes called the 9 mm "Kurz" or "Corto"), a 90 grain bullet is as heavy as you're going to be able to go. This represents the minimum caliber that most people should consider for realistic self-defense. You need to appreciate that multiple hits will probably be required for any kind of terminal effect with this caliber and adequate penetration is unlikely. Use it with that understanding.

In pistols chambered for 40 S&W and 400 Cor-Bon, high-performance bullets of 135 grain to 150 grain represent the best choice. Bullets outside that range have all the same problems that they do in 9mm.

In pistols chambered for 45 ACP, high-performance bullets of 185 grain to 200 grain represent the best choices for the same reasons. There are several 230 grain high-performance loadings available in 45 ACP that have performed well in the field, but recoil is, of course, substantial.

Definitions

Bullet. A bullet is a single, tube-launched projectile. After launch (firing) from a firearm, a bullet is propelled downrange by virtue of its own inertia, influenced thereafter only be gravity and air friction. It will remain airborne until it strikes an object or the ground. Bullets are made chiefly from dense but soft metals, such as lead. During their flight through the air, pistol bullets travel at speeds ranging from seven hundred feet per second to fourteen hundred feet per second, much slower than most rifle bullets.

FMJ. Full metal jacket bullets consist of a lead core surrounded by a jacket made usually of gilding metal. The bullet's base may be open (exposed lead) or completely encapsulated. Most FMJ bullets have a conical nose and a flat rear. Some have a truncated nose. FMJ bullets rarely expand after impact with human tissue. Rather, they commonly pass all the way through, exiting on the opposite side. Ammunition with FMJ bullets is normally considered to be suitable only for practice. FMJ ammunition is not recommended for defensive purposes, unless that is all that is available. FMJ ammunition is also known by the term "hardball."

JHP. Jacketed hollowpoint ammunition is usually the best choice for defensive handgun shooting. JHP bullets have a lead core and a gilding metal jacket, but there is exposed lead at the nose and a hollow cavity therein which protrudes deep into the core. JHP bullets are designed to change shape after impact, expanding their frontal area as they spin through tissue. The twin benefits are an incapacitating wound and a reduced likelihood of the bullet exiting the body and continuing downrange. JHP bullets usually expand to some degree after impact, but the expansion is not always complete, and it is rarely symmetrical. However, on balance JHP ammunition is still better than most other bullet choices available for defensive handgun shooting.

Hollowpoint bullets sometimes "plug up" with clothing as the bullet passes through. Once "plugged," JHP bullets don't expand reliably. In general, the higher the velocity at which the bullet is driven, the less of an issue plugging becomes. However, high velocity pistol bullets are necessarily light and often render inadequate penetration after impact.

JSP. Jacketed soft point bullets have a lead core, gilding metal jacket and conical nose. The metal jacket does not extend all the way over the nose. Therefore, there is exposed lead at the nose itself. JSP bullets are ostensibly designed to expand much as do JHP bullets, but JSP expansion in human tissue at normal pistol velocities is erratic. Often they do not expand at all and then perform much like FMJ bullets. Like FMJ, JSP bullets are not recommended for defensive shooting unless that is all that is available.

Wadcutter. Wadcutter bullets, as the name suggests, are simply lead cylinders, flat on both ends. Sometimes there is a slight projection on the leading end

Chapter 25: Ammunition Recommendations

to facilitate feeding. When fired at paper targets, they cut a sharp, round hole. The pretty holes are pleasing to target shooters but are of little interest to the rest of us. For defensive shooting, there are better choices. Wadcutter ammunition is thus suitable only for practice.

EFMJ™. Expanding Full Metal Jacket bullets, produced exclusively by Federal, look like FMJ, but have elastomer putty in the nose, under the cap. Upon impact, the elastomer changes shape and ruptures the jacket, expanding the frontal area of the bullet. EFMJ has proven itself to be excellent defensive ammunition, as the bullets expand reliably and consistently.

Pow'RBall™. Made exclusively by Cor-Bon, Pow'RBall bullets feature a conventional hollowpoint bullet, but with a hard plastic sphere in the hollow cavity. Upon impact, the bullet penetrates several inches, and then the plastic sphere sloughs off and falls away. The bullet then expands violently. Pow'RBall thus does not have the plugging problem that plagues conventional JHP bullets. Penetration is adequate also, because several inches are achieved before expansion is initiated. Pow'RBall thus represents a genuine improvement over most other serious pistol bullets. It is recommended highly.

Caliber. Caliber is the inside diameter (groove diameter) of the barrel of a gun, expressed in English or metric units of measurements. The caliber, along with other characteristic logos, is used to specifically identify a particular cartridge and distinguish it from all other cartridges. This is important, because *every firearm is manufactured to accept only one type of cartridge.* Similar-looking cartridges, which may even have the same bullet diameter, are usually not interchangeable. Attempting to load a cartridge into a gun for which it is not chambered is extremely dangerous. *A gun should be loaded only with the exact cartridge for which it is chambered.* The caliber is almost always stamped on the outside of the barrel, so it can be easily seen.

During the manufacturing process a rifle barrel blank is first drilled or "bored." Rifling grooves are then cut (sometimes cold formed or produced by electrical discharge machining techniques) in the barrel. It is then the groove diameter that is the diameter of the bullet intended for the barrel. The remaining part of the original bore diameter, called "lands," engrave into the bearing surface of the bullet as it is propagated down the barrel.

Cartridge. A cartridge is a cylindrical metal (or plastic in the case of shotgun cartridges) casing that contains a primer, powdered propellant and a bullet or multiple projectiles. The entire package is self-contained, stable and designed to stay together even though stored for long periods or handled roughly. The primer is what is struck by the firing pin in order to initiate ignition. Once ignited, the powdered propellant burns. The burning propellant generates large volumes of gas, and it is the gas pressure thus generated which propels the bullet from the mouth of the cartridge, down the barrel and ultimately out of the muzzle and toward the target at high speed. Powdered propellant in cartridges burns explosively when solidly confined such as would be the case in the chamber of a firearm. If ignited in the open, powdered propellant burns at a much slower rate.

Pistol, shotgun, and rifle cartridges should be handled with reasonable care but are generally very stable and sturdy and have a shelf life of at least several decades, so long as they are kept cool and dry. Other commonly used terms that are interchangeable: round, shell or ammunition. All modern defensive firearms use brass or brass-plastic cartridges.

Although most cartridges have a long shelf life, those maintained for serious purposes need to be rotated frequently, so that ammunition carried in a serious gun is never more than two years old.

Cartridge cases are also made of aluminum and steel, neither of which is as satisfactory as brass. Aluminum-cased ammunition is relatively inexpensive and is thus used for practice by many shooters. It is not as reliable as brass-cased ammunition and is thus not recommended for any serious purpose. *Steel-cased ammunition is not recommended for any purpose at all,* as it is hard on the gun and causes parts to break, particularly extractors.

Centerfire. Centerfire means that the cartridge's primer compound, used to ignite the main charge of powdered propellant contained within the long axis of the cartridge, is encapsulated in a metallic dish (called the primer) that is pressed into a cavity in the center of the base of the cartridge. Most rifle and pistol cartridges are centerfire.

Hangfire. When a firearm's hammer or striker falls on a chambered cartridge, the cartridge should, and usually does, discharge at once. When there is a delay between the hammer falling and the cartridge discharging, a hangfire has occurred. Such delays are usually less than a second, but dwells of up to minute have been recorded. In modern ammunition, hangfires are extremely rare.

Headspace. Headspace is actually a noun that describes the horizontal movement leeway of the cartridge once it has been fully chambered. When used as a verb, to headspace means to move the cartridge forward in the

Chapter 25: Ammunition Recommendations

chamber until its forward movement is stopped. In most autoloading pistol cartridges, forward movement is stopped by the cartridge neck colliding with an internal shoulder machined into the forward portion of the chamber. Most revolver cartridges use an external rim at the rear of the case to achieve proper headspace. Necessary manufacturing tolerances in both pistols and cartridges insure there will be some headspace in all firearms. Excessive headspace will cause unreliable ignition and poor accuracy. Insufficient headspace will lead to unreliable functioning. Thus, headspace in defensive handguns should be neither too tight nor too loose.

Misfire. A misfire is an outright failure of a cartridge to discharge. When a firearm's hammer or striker falls on a chambered cartridge and the cartridge fails to discharge, a misfire has occurred. As noted above, a second blow of the hammer will often cause a misfired cartridge to discharge normally. In other cases, misfired cartridges cannot be made to fire at all. Misfired cartridges that are permanently impotent are called duds.

Rimfire. Rimfire means that the cartridge's primer compound is located in the rim at the base of the cartridge case. With rimfire cartridges, this is necessary, because the case itself is so small that a standard primer will not fit in the middle of the base, as it will with the larger, centerfire cartridges. Rimfire cartridges are small, unsubstantial and intended for recreation, not serious defensive shooting. Thus, rimfire rifles and pistols are all small, and all find their most suitable employment in recreational shooting and the taking of small game. Rifles (and pistols) in rimfire calibers can be deadly, but are too underpowered to be reliably effective in the self-defense role. All recommended defensive rifles and pistols are centerfire.

Comparison of Serious Handgun Cartridges

	Feeding Reliability	Availability	Terminal Performance	Controllability	Gun Size/Weight
380 Auto	Good	Fair	Fair	Excellent	Excellent
9 mm	Superior	Excellent	Good	Superior	Excellent
38 Special	N/A	Excellent	Good	Excellent	Excellent
38 Super	Fair	Poor	Good	Excellent	Fair
357 Magnum	N/A	Good	Excellent	Poor	Fair
40 S&W	Excellent	Good	Excellent	Good	Good
10 mm	Poor	Poor	Superior	Fair	Fair
45 ACP	Excellent	Excellent	Excellent	Fair	Fair
357 SIG	Excellent	Fair	Excellent	Excellent	Good
400 Cor-Bon	Good	Poor	Superior	Good	Fair

"Superior" terminal performance on the part of the 10mm auto is only realized in its full-performance loadings, which are, unfortunately, difficult to find. Most ammunition currently manufactured for the 10mm has been reduced to 40S&W ballistics. These "wimp-10" loadings (as they are called) were first introduced by the FBI, because agents complained about the recoil of the full-performance loads and have since become standard.

Chapter 25: Ammunition Recommendations

Maximum Range of Small Arms

By "maximum range," we mean the maximum distance a specific projectile is capable of remaining airborne over level ground, regardless of the angle of launch. The downrange danger area extends to the maximum range of the most powerful weapon allowed on that particular range, unless the bullets are otherwise constrained.

Caliber	Yards	Meters	Miles
RIFLE:			
22 Rimfire (LR)	1450	1326	0.82
5.56mm (223 Rem)	3000	2769	1.70
7.62mm (308 Win)	4000	3692	2.72
PISTOL:			
380 Auto	1400	1292	0.80
9 mm	1900	1737	1.08
38 Special	1800	1646	1.02
357 Magnum	2350	2149	1.34
357 SIG	2550	2354	1.45
40 S&W	2000	1846	1.13
400 Cor-Bon	2600	2400	1.48
45 ACP	1640	1500	0.93
SHOTGUN:			
12 Ga 00 Buck	748	684	0.40
12 Ga Slug	2000	1846	1.13
12 Ga #4 Birdshot	300	277	0.17
12 Ga #7.5 Birdshot	225	208	0.13

Chapter 26

Dry Fire and Maintenance

Dry firing or dry practice with a firearm (i.e. drawing, tactically manipulating, loading or reloading with dummy ammunition and dry firing an unloaded firearm) is a valuable activity that can bolster one's skill and confirm correct habits. In general, it is recommended as part of your firearms training methodology. However, there are a number of inherent hazards in this practice of which you must be aware.

1. There is the danger that an unloaded gun used for dry-fire practice is actually loaded or becomes loaded during the practice session.

2. There is the danger that a gun that has been unloaded for practice is not loaded again when it needs to be.

3. There is the problem that dry firing the gun may actually damage the gun.

4. There is the problem that someone suddenly coming upon a person who is dry practicing with his or her gun may become frightened or think they are being assaulted.

Most modern handguns are not at all damaged through dry firing. Even extensive dry firing of current revolvers and autoloaders will not damage them in the least. Many rim-fire weapons and some center-fire rifles and shotguns are damaged by dry firing and the practice should not include these guns. If you are not sure of the advisability of dry practicing with a particular gun, consult the manufacturer or a competent gunsmith.

Other issues I believe are adequately addressed in the list of guidelines below. If you adhere to these guidelines, you should be able to dry practice safely under most circumstances.

1. Select an isolated place, such as a room with no one else in it, that you can control and prevent the entry or passage of others.

Dry practice is best done alone. Don't try to do it with others in the area or along with others, except on a regular firing range. Dry practice only in the area you have designated and only during the time you have set aside for it. Go through the entire safety procedure outlined below *before* starting your dry fire session.

Don't spontaneously sneak in a dry shot at an unplanned time. People who do have unpleasant surprises!

2. Limit your practice session to thirty minutes or less. Many short practice sessions are better than a few long ones.

3. See to it that you are not interrupted or distracted at any time during the session. Keep others away. Lock the door(s) and unplug the phone. Put your pager and cell phone away or turn them off. Turn off the television and the radio. Advise others to stay clear of the area and leave you alone during the practice session. You must concentrate on what you're doing if the dry practice is going to be beneficial.

4. Bring only one firearm at a time into the practice area and carefully unload it. Take all live ammunition out of the area. Do not have any live ammunition anywhere in the room with you when you are practicing.

5. Post a suitable target on a vertical surface that will stop a bullet from the weapon with which you are going to practice. Most interior walls in residences will not stop handgun bullets. On the other hand, the door of a gun safe makes an excellent place to hang a target during dry practice.

6. Prior to starting your drills, thoroughly inspect the firearm one more time to insure that it is unloaded. Check it often during the session.

7. When you are finished, *be finished!* Stop the session and don't do any more practicing from that point forward. Don't take one last shot as you are leaving the room. Remove the target and put it away.

8. Secure the gun.

9. Leave the room.

10. Resume your normal routine.

Firearm maintenance

Firearm maintenance is performed at three levels:

1. User

2. Armorer

3. Factory

User-level maintenance includes only field stripping of major components,

Chapter 26: Dry Fire and Maintenance

cleaning, lubricating, tightening of screws and adjustment of sights. This is what gun owners themselves do to keep their guns safe and reliable.

Detailed disassembly, internal adjustments, parts replacement and fitting of parts are properly reserved for armorer-level maintenance and should be performed only by certified armorers.

Factory-level maintenance includes all work beyond the training and ability of the field armorer and is properly performed in machine shops and only by experienced gunsmiths.

Chapter 27

Epilogue

The Second Amendment: *A well regulated militia, being necessary to the security of a free state, the right of the people to keep and bear arms, shall not be infringed.*

In the debate over the private possession of firearms, there has been much talk about accommodating police and sporting interests, but no talk about preserving the Militia, upon which the security of a free state depends. Therefore, you need to understand there is no constitutionally sound way to ban the private ownership of firearms in the United States of America. They can be banned only by discarding the constitution. *The Second Amendment to the United States Constitution has nothing to do with recreation.*

In a free society, the Militia is composed of every able-bodied citizen who is capable of owning and bearing military arms, in voluntary associations, independent of government. This Militia is not to be confused with the National Guard or other government-controlled military organizations. Indeed, when the Constitution was written, there was no National Guard.

The Militia has two purposes:

1. **To assemble voluntarily** at the government's behest for the purpose of repulsing a foreign invader.

2. To serve as the **peoples' ultimate insurance** policy against tyranny.

That is, by virtue of their individually armed presence, to dissuade would-be dictators and other tyrants from imposing enslavement upon the people.

In fact, and contrary to the rubbish promulgated by the agenda-driven popular news media, the last time the US Supreme Court said anything definitive about the Second Amendment was in 1939. In that decision, the Supreme Court not only reaffirmed the right of Americans to privately own military weapons, but also strongly suggested that citizens have an *obligation* to own them. The Court cited numerous early state laws where citizens were encouraged and sometimes even required to privately own and maintain military firearms and other military equipment.

Today, leftist politicians tell us we don't need individual rights and liberties any more. We need to voluntarily give them up in exchange for "protection" and "safety" they insist will be provided by a police-state-oriented, benevolent government. With the contemptibly dishonest pretext, "We're doing it for your own good," they would sweep away all our rights. What the leftists really want is protection from us, the People. They want no effective opposition when they establish their police state.

It is privately owned military firearms that, more than anything else, keep the power of would-be dictators and overly enthusiastic government employees in check. Ultimately, it is not the fear of the law or of public opinion that bridles the excesses of autocrats, *it is the fear of the armed citizen.*

Accordingly, the curtailing, registration and finally the seizure of all privately-owned firearms, particularly those capable of competing on equal terms with those of the government, is something every tyrant dreams of. Unfortunately, this nightmare is today becoming a reality. I would hate to think that I, after shedding my blood in the service of this country, would have to witness the establishment in The United States of America of a socialist police state.

Don't ever let leftists tell you the issue here is your right to go deer hunting. The issue is the fact that, in this country, the government serves only at the pleasure of the people, not the other way around. "The right of the People to keep and bear arms" is one of the elements of checks and balances that guarantees this basic American principle. Our courageous forefathers fought a Revolutionary War because they refused to be forcefully disarmed by a totalitarian government. Today we enjoy the rights they purchased with their blood.

We the People are tired of being told by leftist politicians that we are too stupid to own firearms. I don't notice any governmental agency suggesting *they* give up *their* guns.

In this country, the People are sovereign. **For us to be sovereign, we have to be armed.** We must all protect the Second Amendment. It makes all the others work. The fight will never be over. "Who dares prevails. Who lives on hope will die fasting."

DTI Defensive Handgun Proficiency Test

Shooter setup:

Interview stance. The pistol is firmly seated in the holster and the holster retaining device (if present) is snapped. The strong hand is not touching or hovering over the pistol. The pistol must be concealed or in a duty rig if carried openly.

Weapon setup:

Autoloader: One live round in the chamber. Four live rounds and one dummy round (mixed at random) in the magazine. The dummy round is not to be the first or the last round in the magazine, but rather the second, third or forth. The exact location of the dummy is unknown to the shooter. The test requires a total of seven rounds.

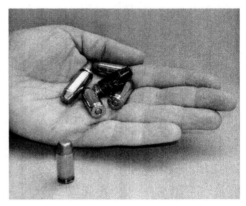

Ammo for proficiency test.

The magazine to be used for reloading is in its carrier and is fully charged with live rounds (no dummies).

Revolver: All chambers loaded with live ammunition (six shot or five shot). The shooter loads to capacity and fires all rounds, then reloads and fires two more. No dummy rounds are required with the revolver.

The speed loader used for reloading is fully charged with live rounds and is in its carrier.

Target setup:

20 x 30cm (approx) rectangle or oval, either steel or paper, placed at eight meters from the shooter.

Safety equipment setup:

All present must be wearing adequate eye protection, hearing protection and a baseball cap with the bill pulled low over safety glasses.

An electronic shot timer is necessary to run this test.

Standard:

The student achieves a passing score if he hits with all shots within the required amount of time, does not commit any safety errors and does not commit any procedural errors. Students qualify only at one hundred percent hits. A single miss or a single procedural or safety error means a failed attempt.

Safety errors:

- Shooter's weak-side hand or arm gets in front of the muzzle during the draw, reloading, stoppage reduction or reholstering.
- Shooter's trigger finger enters the trigger guard before the signal to fire, during reloading or stoppage reduction or when moving.

Procedural errors:

- Failure to move laterally during draw.
- Failure to move during stoppage reduction or reloading.
- Failure to scan prior to the start signal.
- Incorrect stoppage reduction procedure.
- Incorrect reloading procedure (e.g. old magazine dropped from the magazine well before new one has cleared the carrier).
- Incorrect slide manipulation (e.g. hand too far forward, "slingshotting" the slide).

Move laterally while drawing.

Notes:

As with any "standard," these criteria are selected based on our experience with many students of defensive shooting, of all levels of experience, training and competence. If this test or these standards are adopted or used for any purpose, they may have to be modified to accommodate variations in equipment, range facilities, expected levels of performance, etc. We believe the standards enumerated below are reasonable when competent students are

DTI Defensive Handgun Proficiency Test

equipped with open-top holsters, open-top ammunition carriers and full-power service ammunition. If other equipment, ammunition or conditions are the norm, as noted above, the times might have to be altered to achieve a reasonable standard.

Test (autoloader):

The student reports to the line and assumes the interview stance, facing downrange. At the command, "Start moving," the student starts moving laterally (staying behind the line) at random, within a three-meter area. Between the command to start moving and the start signal, the student must scan all the way behind him at least once. On start signal, shooter moves and draws simultaneously. Movement must be lateral and involve a displacement of at least one meter. The student then continues to hold on target (trigger finger in register) until he hears the start signal from the electronic timer.

Firing at rotator target.

Upon hearing the signal, the student must move laterally again before shooting. He fires continuously at the target. The shooter must be in continuous movement during his stoppage reduction and reload.

When the stoppage is encountered (dummy round), the shooter immediately reduces the stoppage (tap, rack, bang) and immediately resumes firing. While doing so, he must be moving and his trigger finger must be off the trigger and in register. When the last round is fired, the student immediately reloads and fires two more rounds. While reloading, the student must be moving with his trigger finger in register.

Test (revolver):

When testing with revolvers, everything is the same, except the shooter fires six (five) shots, then reloads (all chambers) and fires two more. The student must move during the draw and during the reload. Qualifying times with five-shot revolvers are the same as with six-shot revolvers, because the difficulty of accurately shooting the small guns is compensated for by the fact that the shooter is required to shoot seven rather than eight.

Cumulative qualifying times:

Autoloader: Student Level: 22.00 sec, Instructor Level: 15.00 sec

Revolver: Student Level: 22.00 sec, Instructor Level: 16.00 sec

Resources

This section lists recommended products and where to get them. It is up-to-date when the book is printed, but things change. If an item cannot be found, see the DTI Publications web page (www.dtipubs.com) and look for a *Resources* page.

Cold Steel Knives:

Cold Steel
3036-A Seaborg Ave
Ventura CA 93003
Phone 805-650-8481
Toll Free 800-255-4716
http://www.coldsteel.com/

Cor-Bon Pow'RBall and DPX ammunition:

CorBon/Glaser
1311 Industry Road
Sturgis SD 57785
Phone 605-347-4544
Fax 605-347-5055
Toll Free 800-626-7266
http://www.corbon.com/

Ayoob Dejammer:

Police Bookshelf
P. O. Box 122
Concord NH 03302-0122
Phone 603-224-6814
Fax 603-226-3554
Toll Free 800-624-9049
http://www.ayoob.com/

Desert Snake Skin Camo:

Les Leturno
Custom Firearm Finishes
PO Bx 773534
Eagle River, AK 99577
Phone 907-694-4440
http://www.customfirearmfinishes.com/

The Emergency Bandage:

Performance Systems, Medical Division
3050 Post Oak Blvd, Suite 1710
Houston TX 77056
Phone 713-723-6000
http://www.firstcareproducts.com/

Fox Pepper Spray:

Fox Labs International
20752 Miles Street South
Clinton Township MI 48036-1948
Phone 1-800-FOX-LABS (369-5227)
Michigan 586-783-5100
Fax 586-783-5151
Email sales@foxlabs.net
http://www.foxlabs.com/

Safe Direction Ballistic Containment System and Reactive Steel Targets:

The Ravelin Group
Phone 630-834-4423
http://www.RavelinGroup.com/

Index

Symbols

357 Magnum 232
357 SIG 230
380 Auto 233
38 Special 232
400 Cor-Bon 230
40 S&W 233
45 ACP 233
45 GAP 230

A

Ability 52
Accidental discharges 86
AD 95
Administrative procedures 86
Aerosol sprays 30
Aggravated 77
Ammunition 227
Ammunition Comparison 238
Ammunition Range 239
Arrest 73
Assault 77
Autoloader 213, 223
   Continuous motion 219
   Double-column 218
   Single-column 218
Autoloaders, all other 109
   Advantages 109
   Disadvantages 109
Avoidance 54

B

Bail 81
Barrel 116
Baton 32
Battery 77, 116
Blowback system 134
   Gas-retarded 133
Body armor 40
Bond 81

Bondsmen 81
Bore Snake 165
Brandishing firearms 61
Buckshot 37
Bullet 233

C

Caliber 235
Carry mode 100
Cars 20
Cartridge 235
Catch the link 197
Centerfire 236
Chamber 116
Chamber check 156
Chambering 112
Charged 122
Choice 42
Citizen 73
Citizen's arrest 82
Clear 117
Clear (the holster) 177
Clips 123
Close confrontations 24
Close range 188
Cold Steel 35
Colt/Browning autoloader 104, 160
  Loading 162
  Storage 162
  Trigger technique 199
  Unloading and clearing 161
Concealment 61
Confronting criminals 59
Consent search 76
Continuous motion autoloader 104, 158
  Chamber check 159
  Loading 159
  Storage 159
  Unloading 159
Continuous trigger contact 197
Cor-Bon Pow'RBall 228, 230, 231, 232
Coroner's jury 80
Cover 14
Cycle of operation 111

Index

D

De-escalation of force 57
Deadly weapon 79
Decock 117
Decocking 141
Decocking lever 118
Dejammer 33
Detention, temporary 82
Disconnector 118
Disengagement 54
Double-action only 113
Double-action revolver 103, 107, 139, 201, 209, 222
  Advantages 107
  Decocking 141
  Disadvantages 107
  Loading 144
  Trigger technique 201
  Unloading and clearing 142
Draw 173
Drop-lock system 131
Drop safety 126
Dry fire 241

E

EFMJ 235
Ejection 113
Ejection port 119
Ejector 119
Emergency Bandage 66
Enabled 119
Engagement mode 100
ERD 31
Escalation of force 58
Escape 54
Excessive force 58
Extendable baton 32
Extraction 113
Extractor 119

F

Feeding 112
Felony 78
Firearm safety 85
Firing 112
Firing pin 119

First Aid 65
Flexible baton 33
Flying-thumb grip 179
FMJ 228, 234
Follow through 203
Force, necessary 55
Four D's of Defensive Shooting 19
Full-contact grip 179
Functional reliability 229

G

Gas-retarded blowback system 133
Grand jury 79
Grip 175
  Flying-thumb 179
  Full-contact 179
  Thumbs-up 179
Grip safety 126
Guns 36

H

Half cock 119
Hammer 121
Handgun 38
Handgun system comparison 110
Hands merge 178
Hangfire 236
Hardball 228
Hate crime 71
Headspace 236
Hollow point 234
Homicide 79

I

Immediate action
  Autoloader 223
  Revolver 222
Index 174
Interacting with law enforcement officers 67
Interview stance 171
Isosceles stance 169

J

Jam 221

Index

Jeopardy 52
JHP 234
JSP 234

K

Kevlar 40
Keys to Survival 3
Knives 34
  Push 35

L

Law 83
Legality 231
Loaded 122
Locking 112

M

Magazine 122
Magazine release, base-latch 219
Magazine safety 123
Magazine well 122
Maintenance 164, 242
Manifest intent 52
Manipulating the trigger 195
Manual decocking 204
Manually-decocking autoloader 202
  Trigger technique 202
Manual safety 125
Master grip 128
Mechanical systems 131
Mechanical systems comparison 135
Militia 245
Misdemeanor 78
Misfire 237
Modes 99
Movement 18, 177, 184, 189
Moving targets 21
Multiple targets 21
Muzzle 128

N

Necessary force 55
Non-deadly force 57

O

Objectively reasonable force 55
OC 30
Operator systems 103
Opportunity 52

P

Penetration 230
Pepper spray 30
Performance 231
Personal defense weapons 30
Personal tactics 11
Persuader 33
Pistol-caliber carbine 38
Post-Violence Trauma Syndrome 7
Pow'RBall 235
Preclusion 53
Price 231
Probable cause 55
Proficiency test 247
Protected speech 70

R

Ready, depressed 96
Ready position 189
Reasonable force 55
Recoil 230
Register position 96, 138, 185
Reholstering 184
Reloading 209
  Autoloader 213
  Double-action revolver 209
Reloading procedure 216
Resisting arrest 74
Retaliatory force 58
Retention draw 188
Rifle 37
Rights, reading 75
Rights and powers 67
Rimfire 237
Rock and lock 177
Roll out technique 14
Rotary-barrel system 134
Rotator target 249

Index

S

Safe Direction 88
Safe gun handling 137
Safe Storage 90
Safety 137
Safety Rules 87
Search, consent 76
Second Amendment 245
Self-decocking autoloader 108, 163
  Advantages 108
  Disadvantages 108
Self-Defense 51
Serious bodily injury 77
Shotgun 36
Sight alignment 191
Sight picture 191, 193
Sight settings 197
Single-action revolver 103
Slide 128
Slide-release lever 129
Soft body armor 40
Speech, protected 70
Speed loaders 209
  Bianchi Speed-Strip 212
  HKS 211
  Safariland 211, 213
Stance 168
  Interview 171
  Isosceles 169
  Weaver 170, 179
Stealth Existence 45
Sterile 129
Stoppage 221
Storage mode 99
Survival 3
Suspect 75
Switchblade 35

T

Tachy-Psyche Effect 4
Tactical engineering 19
Tactical errors 22
Tactical procedures 85
Thumbs-up grip 179
Tilt-barrel system 132

Tort 81
Transport mode 99
Trigger-cocking 129
Trigger-cocking autoloader 145, 160
   Chamber check 156
   Decocking 145
   Loading 152
   Storage 157, 158
   Unloading and clearing 148
Trigger-cocking autoloaders 104, 105
Trigger control 195
Trigger finger 138
Trigger lock 91
Trigger press 195
Trigger reset 197
Trigger Shoe 93
Trigger technique
   Colt/Browning autoloader 199
   Double-action revolver 201
   Manually-decocking autoloader 202

U

Unfamiliar pistols 163
Unintentional hits 89
Universal cover mode 96
Unlocking 113
Unnecessary force 58
Up strong 181

V

Verbal challenge 62
Victim selection 59
Violence 51
Voided 122

W

Wadcutter 234
Weapon 79
Weaver stance 170, 172, 179
Wounding shots 22

Y

Yawara stick 33

Books available from DTI Publications Inc

The Farnam Method of Defensive Shotgun and Rifle Shooting (Second Edition) by John S. Farnam, 2010

The Farnam Method of Defensive Handgunning (Second Edition) by John S. Farnam, 2005

Teaching Women To Shoot: A Law Enforcement Instructor's Guide by Vicki Farnam and Diane Nicholl, 2002

Guns & Warriors: DTI Quips, Volume One by John S. Farnam, 2006

Women Learning To Shoot: A Guide for Law Enforcement Officers by Diane Nicholl and Vicki Farnam, 2006

DTI Publications, Inc
3571 Far West Blvd
PMB #94
Austin TX 78731

Find us on the web at: www.dtipubs.com